A WATERED GARDEN

A Brief History of the Protestant Reformed Churches in America

"*Thou shalt be like a watered garden...*"

Isaiah 58:11

Gertrude Hoeksema

Illustrated by
Jeff Steenholdt

Reformed Free
Publishing Association
P.O. Box 2006
Grand Rapids, MI 49501

Library of Congress Catalog Card Number: 92-64328
ISBN 0-916206-43-2

PRINTED IN THE UNITED STATES OF AMERICA

Preface

In 1985 it was suggested to the late Professor H.C. Hoeksema that a new history of the Protestant Reformed Churches ought to be written. The only existing formal account, *The Protestant Reformed Churches in America,* by Rev. Herman Hoeksema, had been good for its time and necessary to explain and justify the existence of the Protestant Reformed Churches. But besides being very polemic in its approach, it had covered only the first eleven years of the existence of the Protestant Reformed Churches which were already more than sixty years old. It was further suggested to Prof. Hoeksema that because of his intimate knowledge of and deep involvement with much of this history, he ought to be the author of such an updated book. Prof. Hoeksema gave this suggestion thought and consideration, and in 1987 constructed a detailed outline of some twenty-five pages together with an extensive listing of source materials. He intended to begin the actual writing in his spare time while serving as pastor in Tasmania, Australia, in 1989. But the spare time never materialized, and his work there was suddenly cut short by the discovery of rapidly developing cancer. In the few remaining weeks of his life he urged his wife Gertrude to complete the project and dictated instructions to her regarding its character, structure, emphasis, and completion. So in a very real sense this is his unfinished work but written by Gertrude Hoeksema in her words and style, so that the finished product is the result of their cooperative effort.

Important to the understanding of any book is an appreciation of the perspective of its author. The perspective and theme of this book are organic in character.

The organic idea of the church, its salvation, and its development is strong in Scripture. The Bible presents the church as being a living spiritual organism. An organism, in distinction from a mechanism, develops from and along the lines of a common principle, as does a plant from a seed. Christ is the spiritual principle of the church, by type and

i

promise in the Old Testament. This explains the abundance of Scriptural figures which point to this truth. In the Old Testament there is the figure of the temple as a unified whole, as well as Isaiah's figure of a garden from which the theme of this book is taken; and in the New Testament the relation of Christ to the church is presented under the figures of the head and the body, Colossians 1:15-20, the vine and the branches, John 15:1-5, and the chief cornerstone upon which living stones are laid, I Peter 2:4-9.

The Protestant Reformed Churches are a manifestation of this organic church of the Scriptures. The church of God is essentially one in all ages, whether Old Testament, New Testament, or today, and finds its unity in its salvation by Christ. Thus the history of salvation is the history of the church. To the extent that a specific church or a particular denomination is faithful and obedient to the revelation of that salvation in the Scriptures, to that extent it belongs to the history of the church as a whole.

The purpose of this book is to define the place of the Protestant Reformed Churches in this larger organic whole of the church of all ages, and to do so in a twofold manner. First, the roots of the Protestant Reformed Churches are traced to the Reformation of the sixteenth century in order to show that the Protestant Reformed Churches are the continuation of the church of the Reformation, especially from the viewpoint of its emphasis on sovereign, particular grace. Thus, as faithful to the revelation of that grace in Scripture, the Protestant Reformed Churches are one with the church of all ages in its obedience to the revealed will of God in the salvation of His people. Second, the development of the Protestant Reformed Churches over almost seventy years of history since their formation is outlined. Detailed is the defense in times of controversy of the faith once delivered to the saints, whether in the events surrounding 1924, which led to the separate existence of the Protestant Reformed Churches, or in the upheaval of 1953, which led to the purification of the church in a controversy in which basically the same issues were disputes as in 1924. Also outlined is the *development* of that faith in the Protestant Reformed Churches, both in their doctrines and teachings, especially concerning sovereign grace and the covenant, and in the practical organic life of the church and the covenant schools established by Protestant Reformed people.

The result for the reader will be educational and stimulating reading. The author, being herself Protestant Reformed, obviously has a Reformed bias, just as any historian will exhibit some bias in viewpoint. Yet the book is objective and fair in its presentation of the facts of history, in its proof and documentation, in its conclusions, and in its revelations of the faults and foibles of those who grace its pages. Particular benefit will accrue to those both within and outside the Protestant Reformed Churches, who are unfamiliar with much of the historical picture painted herein. Especially the younger generations of Reformed people will gain a sense of who they are and from whence they came so that they may pass on to future generations an appreciation of the Reformed heritage entrusted to God's people in the Protestant Reformed Churches.

M.H.

Acknowledgements

I thank all those who contributed to this book by giving me their help.

1. The pastors in the denomination who furnished historical information concerning their congregations.

2. The clerks of the consistories who sent photos of their church buildings and often more information about their congregations.

3. The personnel of our schools who sent me the histories of their schools.

4. Those who furnished me with court records.

5. Our missionaries who gave me resumes of their work on the various mission fields.

6. Professor H. Hanko, who gave me guidance and criticism, and help when I needed it.

7. My children, who made suggestions and encouraged me.

G.H.

iv

Contents

Section One: ROOTS
Chapter 1
Reformed Plantings

Scattered across the face of North America from Pennsylvania and New Jersey on the east coast to California and Washington on the west coast, and from Alberta, Canada, in the north to Texas in the south are twenty-six congregations, some large, some small, known as the Protestant Reformed Churches in America. Who are they? What was their origin? Why, amid the myriad of denominations, do they lead a separate existence?

The answer to these questions is expressed, at least partially, in their name: they are the Protestant Reformed Churches. By this name the members of these churches mean to express that they have their roots in the great Protestant Reformation of the sixteenth and seventeenth centuries. They also take as their basis the unity of the Reformed standards which were born in that Reformation: the Heidelberg Catechism, the Confession of Faith (Belgic Confession), and the Canons of Dordrecht. In addition, the Protestant Reformed Churches take seriously their calling to *defend* and *develop* the Reformed truth which is based on these creeds.

This means that the churches, as a denomination, have firm roots which dig deeply into church history. Therefore, in order to understand the Protestant Reformed denomination and its doctrines, one must go back in history to dig up and discover its roots and to find out where those roots have been planted.

During the period of ancient church history (311-590), the preachers and scholars studied and developed the truths which Jesus had taught in His days on earth. Then came the middle ages (590-1517), with its heresies and the rise and rule

1

of the Romish Church. Near the beginning of the sixteenth century the Lord raised up a Martin Luther and a John Calvin to call His true church back to the pure truths of the Scriptures. These men called God's people to *re-form* their doctrines and their lives according to the true principles of God's Word; and the churches organized during the period of the Protestant Reformation were called *Reformed churches*.

The reformers also urged the members of the Reformed churches to recognize the need to express their beliefs in Reformed creeds, creeds which were born in the battles for the truth. The days of these reformations were troubled days and times of intense struggle, but the elements of perseverance and even joy to preserve God's pure revelation were always present.

In quick succession, in the years 1561 and 1563, two of the major Reformed confessions were born: the Confession of Faith (or the Belgic Confession) and the Heidelberg Catechism. In God's providence, the Reformed faith spread rather quickly throughout the whole European continent, also north to the lowlands of Belgium and the Netherlands, where the sturdy Dutch folk studied the doctrines formulated during the Reformation and based on the Scriptures. They eagerly embraced these doctrines as the pure interpretations of the truths of God's Word. For some three centuries the members of the Reformed churches lived according to these truths and taught their children the doctrines of the Reformed faith.

However, through the years, as generations changed — also in The Netherlands — they slipped from the high spiritual plateau of the days of fighting for the pure interpretation of God's Word and fell into a lethargy which often follows the enthusiasm of such battles. Gradually the truth tended to become humdrum, and many cardinal doctrines, such as predestination, total depravity, and even the divinity of Christ, were denied by Reformed leaders; and rationalism took their places.

In the lowlands of The Netherlands, by the decade of the 1830s, the time was ripe for another call to come back to the purity of God's Word. This reformation took place in 1834, and was called the *Afscheiding* — the departure, or separation (from heresy). It was a relatively small movement, led not by great scholars of leaders, but by small and humble clergy of the farming communities. These reformers called the people back to the truths of God's sovereign salvation — without the help of man — and to the Scriptural doctrines of sin and grace. The *Afscheiding* called the people back to obedience to the Scriptures and the creeds but did not go on to develop the beauty of those doctrines of grace any further.

They should have. They should have followed all three of the cardinal elements of all church reformation, based on the Scriptures and embraced by the Reformed churches.

The first element assumes that there has already been a deformation, a departure from the biblical and historical Christian faith. It is a *call* to return to the historic Christian faith, the faith of the Scriptures. Ever since the Fall, God has been calling His people to leave their evil ways and return to the truth. Through the pen of Jeremiah to God's church on earth, Jehovah said, "Thus saith the Lord, Stand ye in the ways and see, and ask for the old paths, where is the good way, and walk therein, and ye shall find rest for your souls," Jeremiah 6:16.

The second element is a *condemnation* by the church of the existing errors in the controversy. An example in the Scriptures of God's condemnation of those who have left the pure paths of the Scriptures is spoken through the mouth of Stephen the martyr: "Ye stiffnecked and uncircumcised in heart and ears, ye do always resist the Holy Ghost: as your fathers did, so do ye," Acts 7:51.

The third element in the reformation of the church on earth is the *positive* and on-going *development* of the truth, particularly in rejecting the errors in the dispute and teaching the full-orbed truth. David understood when he asked the Lord, "Let not mine enemies triumph over me .... Let them be ashamed which transgress without cause. Show me thy ways, O Lord; teach me thy paths. Lead me in thy truth, and teach me," Psalm 25:2b - 5a.

Fifty-two years later the State Church (the *Hervormde Kerk*) in The Netherlands was again riddled with evil: the doctrines of the Scriptures were again so polluted that many Reformed church members denied the death and resurrection of the Savior. The sacraments were improperly celebrated, and there was a total lack of Christian discipline.

How was it possible that in a reformation in which great numbers of believers had embraced these doctrines of the Scriptures and the Reformed faith with such enthusiasm, they forsook those same truths in so short a time? The main reason was that the *Afscheiding,* the Secession of 1834, had by no means been a complete reformation. It was a regional and limited movement of the humble and the poor — not of the theological leaders of that era. Besides, a spirit of tolerance began to prevail in the State Church, and those who did not agree with the Reformed truths were left undisturbed to speak and live as they wished.

In the providence of God, as the years went by, some members of the State Church repented and went back to the searching of the Scriptures; and they came to understand and believe the truths of the Reformed faith. It was at this time that Abraham Kuyper became active in the battle for the Reformed faith. He could understand the thinking and the mind-set of those who rejected the Reformed faith, for spiritually he had been there. In his youth he had enjoyed a liberal education and had not been converted to the Reformed faith until early in his ministry. Now it was time for another reformation in The Netherlands, and the Lord would use Abraham Kuyper to call His people back to the truths of the Scriptures.

This reformation did not merely go back to the old truths, but through the genius of Dr. Kuyper, these doctrines were defined and developed; for a cardinal principle in the history of God's church is that it always develops. God's church in the world is never stagnant, but He develops and enriches the doctrines of His church, often through the struggle with the lethargy of His people, or through heresies which require the earnest searching of the Scriptures, and a new and deeper insight into the doctrines of His Word — a *re-formation*.

The State Church in The Netherlands in the 1880s was very large. Some two million members were involved in the reformation of the *Doleantie*. This name is difficult to translate: it comes from the Latin verb *doleo — ere*, which means "to mourn." Therefore the *Doleantie* are the *grieving churches*. In this separation, which took place in 1886, about one hundred thousand members left the pseudo-Reformed doctrines of the State Church. Historical records show that it was not a peaceful shaking of hands and parting of ways, but, as in all the struggles of reformation which touch the core of one's life, the separation was filled with disputes, bitterness, name-calling, loss of church properties, and separations across family boundaries. Yet, because this reformation did not involve two distinct groups of opposing churches, it was a reformation from *within* the *church*.

Through the prolific writings of Dr. Abraham Kuyper in *De Heraut* (*The Herald*) at this time, the members of the Reformed churches were instructed in the principles of Reformed doctrine. During the years of his leadership, Dr. Kuyper also developed and introduced the proper Scriptural structure of church government, along with the rules and the various offices in Reformed church government.

After he had left the active ministry and was already an emeritus minister, Dr. Kuyper took a look at the political scene in The Netherlands, and became deeply involved with the Anti-Revolutionary Party. However, in his efforts to try to apply the principles of the Reformed faith to every sphere of life, also in the secular government of his nation, he addressed the frictions due to the class of *belief* and *unbelief* between the godly and the godless. They had no common basis. Yet he wanted to find some common ground for believers and unbelievers to function together.

With the lasting influence of his early, liberal education as a background for this wish of a common ground with the ungodly, and because of his interest and involvement in politics at the time of the *Doleantie*, Abraham Kuyper persisted in finding a common ground for believers and unbelievers to cooperate in all spheres of life. He "attempted to apply the principles of the Reformed faith to every sphere of life."[1] What he overlooked was that although the struggles of God's people on earth touch every area of life, they are *spiritual* struggles, battles which unbelievers cannot share. Yet he tried to show that, in a measure, there is a ground for a common grace where believers and unbelievers can meet and work in harmony. Little did Dr. Kuyper know when he developed this concept of common grace that it would have far-reaching effects in the Reformed church world of the twentieth century, leading to major disputes and more reformations.

After the reformation of the *Doleantie* in 1886, there were two groups of Reformed churches in The Netherlands: the churches of the *Afscheiding* and the churches of the *Doleantie*. Although the reformations of the two groups were not similar in all respects, both groups embraced the same Scriptural beliefs, as outlined in their Reformed confessions. It was a natural conclusion that these two groups of God's people, who shared the same confessions and the same beliefs and the same national background, would merge into one denomination. In 1892 this union took place. The new denomination took the name of the *Gereformeerde Kerken van Nederland* (the Reformed Churches of The Netherlands), or the *GKN* for short.

Nevertheless, the two groups never really merged organically. Each group insisted on its own theological identity: the A-wing, which represented the *Afscheiding* of 1834, insisted on the preaching of the theological emphases of *their* denomination. And the B-wing, the wing of the *Doleantie* of 1886, emphasized especially the following: supralapsarianism, eternal justification, immediate regeneration, and presupposed regeneration.

Congregations, especially in the larger cities, were orga-

---

1.   Cf. Herman Hoeksema, *The Protestant Reformed Churches in America,* Grand Rapids, 1936, p. 278.

nized into A and B congregations; and members of an A congregation would not think of inviting a B pastor into their pulpit, nor would they attend a B church. And the same rules held for the B congregations over against the A congregations.

As the unrest between the two groups escalated, at times into theological battles, the leaders called representatives of both factions to Utrecht in 1905. At this session they drew up the Conclusions of Utrecht, an attempted compromise to bring peace to the GKN. The result was that the true peace they had anticipated was not achieved. The best they could do was establish an uneasy truce between the two Reformed groups. For about three decades the GKN lived with this truce, until the period near the end of World War II, when problems again began to surface. After the war the A and B wings parted ways. The A-wing, under the leadership of Doctors K. Schilder and S. Greijdanus, left the GKN and became the Liberated Churches.

* * * * * * *

This brief history, far from the midwest area of the United States, and more than a century back in time, furnishes not only an important background for the various Reformed churches in America, but the events in this history were the indirect — and some not so indirect — causes for the history and the struggles and the schisms of the Reformed denominations in the United States: for the early immigrants in the nineteenth century, many of whom settled in western Michigan or eastern Iowa, were members of the *Afscheiding,* the sons and daughters of the Secession of 1834. In the states, until the year 1857, they belonged to the already established Reformed Churches in America. But in the year 1857 many members seceded and re-organized as the Christian Reformed denomination.

The last decade of the nineteenth century, after the reformation of the *Doleantie* in 1886, saw another large influx of immigrants: the members of this reformation poured into America, again mainly into the midwest.

The inevitable result was that the differences and problems of the A and B-wings of the reformation which had taken place in The Netherlands were transplanted into the Christian Reformed denomination in America. Although the Christian Reformed Synod of 1908 adopted the Conclusions of Utrecht to make peace between the two groups, in greater or smaller measures their differences continued.

The reader may wonder why this background and overview of several decades of life in a foreign country and the details of the makeup of the immigrant groups, with their ecclesiastical backgrounds, is necessary to an account of a church history of a denomination in America. The answer lies in a Dutch proverb: "In 't verleden ligt het heden, in het nu wat worden zal." Translated, it tells you that "in the past lies the present, and in the present what will be in the future."

Put in other words, this background shows the *roots* of the Reformed faith. The struggling reformers and their churches, from the sixteenth century on, were the farmers who planted the roots of the truth of God's sovereignty in their garden of Reformed plantings.

Chapter 2
Transplantings in the West Michigan and Midwest Areas

In the decades before World War I, life was comparatively simple. Many of the immigrants of Dutch heritage had settled down to a comfortable life in their new "Little Netherlands" in various areas of the midwest United States. Many had kept their language, customs, and even their dress, in their new country. They also kept their customs of worship. Already before the war, some outspoken leaders in Reformed circles criticized this Dutch isolationism, and they pleaded and prodded for Americanization.

In the Reformed churches of their old homeland at this time, a new movement, the rise of the *Jongeren*, had gained impetus. These *Jongeren* were a group of younger people in the Reformed churches who were dissatisfied with their own churches and the way in which the Reformed faith was preached. These young people rebelled against the emphasis on the antithesis between the church and the unbelieving world around them, between those children of God who were regenerated and the non-regenerate. They complained that there was too much cold dogma and not enough gospel; but the gospel these *Jongeren* wanted was one which erased the straight line between sin and grace, between the sphere of the church and the sphere of the world. The *Jongeren* wanted no separation between the two. They wanted to work in society and to broaden the scope of the church into social areas of the world around them. They were willing to soft-pedal, or even forfeit, some of the main Calvinistic, Reformed truths such as predestination and total depravity in order to broaden the sphere of the church.

As the philosophy of the *Jongeren* began to be transplanted in America, a spirit of unrest came over the people
living in their Reformed communities. If the *Jongeren* had
asked the immigrants to make *cultural* changes, adjustments
from their Dutch isolationism to the culture of their adopted
country, they would not have complained. After all, America
was their home and the home of their children. They wanted
to become Americans. But this was not the kind of change the
Jongeren preached. These *Jongeren* wanted them to leave
their *spiritual* isolation, the separation of which the Scriptures speak, and which had occurred in the Reformation of
the sixteenth century. The *Jongeren* wanted them to mute the
doctrines of the Reformed faith and join with unbelievers in
various spheres of life.

Although many of the members of the Reformed and
Christian Reformed Churches turned deaf ears to the propaganda of these *Jongeren,* the false teachers had left their mark
on the lives of the members of the churches. As a result of
their thinking, and because war loomed on the horizon,
many leaders, also leaders in the Reformed churches, began
to urge the people to follow the popular philosophy which
taught that to be a good patriot — that is, to work for the
cause of freedom — was to be a good Christian. If these
leaders did not equate the two, they at least found a strong
connection between democracy and Christianity, between
the American way and the way they worshiped in their
churches.

In the pre-war years of 1912 to 1915, Herman Hoeksema,
a Hollander who had immigrated in 1904, settled in the
Chicago area. Later he moved to Grand Rapids, Michigan,
and enrolled as a seminarian at Calvin Theological School in
Grand Rapids, Michigan. In his last year of seminary, as was
the custom for senior seminary students, he was assigned to
fill pulpit vacancies for the churches in the West Michigan
area. Through all of his theological training, he had been
eager to learn the language of his new country. While most

of the students preferred the comfortable Dutch language which was still spoken in their homes and in their small communities, Herman Hoeksema worked with the language of his adopted country. He asked the faculty to give him the English-language preaching assignments. Maple Avenue Christian Reformed Church in Holland, Michigan, was one of the few congregations at that time which sent in requests to the seminary for preaching in the English language.

Before the days of the convenience of cars, the students took the inter-urbans, electrically-powered transportation between the towns and cities, when they were scheduled to preach in a neighboring town. When Student Hoeksema went to preach at Maple Avenue Church, he left on Saturday afternoon and came back on Monday morning. It was a three-day excursion. He went often to preach to this congregation, and the people seemed to enjoy his sermons. However, Student Hoeksema noted that most of the members sent their children to the public schools instead of the Christian schools already established by the families in the Christian Reformed Churches. The inconsistency of the confession of this congregation — that they were spiritually separate from the evils of the world around them, and at the same time were sending their children, in the years in which they were most impressionable, to receive their basic training in the sphere of total unbelief and evil — alarmed Student Hoeksema. And one Sunday in his prayer, he prayed that the parents in this congregation might not deliver their children to the gates of hell.

From then on, Maple Avenue Church did not want Herman Hoeksema in its pulpit. The members made propaganda against him among the members of other congregations in the area; and as a result, when the seminary received requests from these stirred-up congregations, they specified "not Hoeksema." Student Hoeksema was president of the student body and was popular with his colleagues. The student body answered that if they boycotted Hoeksema, they would get no one.

In spite of these troubles during his student days in the Holland, Michigan area, when Herman Hoeksema graduated from the seminary, he received a call to Fourteenth Street Christian Reformed Church, the parent church of the Maple Avenue congregation. He did not really want to accept this call, but after having a heart-to-heart talk with the members of the Fourteenth Street congregation, where he stated his theological position, he concluded by saying, "Now if you still want me to come, shake hands with me after the meeting." They did, and he accepted the call. He knew it was God's will.

Soon rumblings of World War I were heard, and when the United States entered the war, everyone turned patriotic and helped in the war efforts. Everywhere people were hoisting flags, also in the churches. On Sunday morning, February 10, 1918, a flag appeared in the auditorium of the Fourteenth Street Church. Pastor Hoeksema said nothing that morning, but after the service, he asked his consistory to see that it was taken down before the evening service. The flag disappeared.

This little episode became public, of course, and led to a literary exchange in the daily newspaper, the *Holland Daily Sentinel,* in six rather lengthy articles in successive issues, between Pastor Hoeksema and the Rev. P.P. Cheff, pastor of Hope Reformed Church in Holland. Rev. Cheff and others challenged Hoeksema's beliefs and motives: He must be unpatriotic, or worse — pro-German!

Pastor Hoeksema took it as a challenge, an amusing one, if it were not so serious. In his first answer to the Rev. Cheff's complaint, he wrote: "Amusing I would call this controversy in time of peace, for amusing it is to note how gentlemen that ought to know better, question the old truth, embodied in the laws of our own dear country. I refer, of course, to the truth of the separation of church and state ...."

In the following issues he explained:

1. My personal attitude toward our country and
the war.
2. My views on things pertaining to government.
3. My view of the church of Jesus Christ."

Summing up one of his newspaper polemics on the
relationship between church and state, he wrote:

> Now what are the practical implications of this
> view? This, that we as Calvinistic people always
> obey our government, and that for God's sake.
> And the Rev. Cheff makes a sad mistake if he
> separates this true obedience for God's sake from
> the true feeling of loyalty. The love of country, Mr.
> Cheff, is not a higher principle nor is it the source
> of nobler feelings than the love of God, is it? And
> if I state that I obey for God's sake, I do not at all
> mean to say that this obedience is a cold, objective
> duty, imposed from without, but at the same time
> a truly living principle, inspiring me to be always
> loyal, as long as the Word of God allows.

After several more exchanges in the *Holland Sentinel,*
the final issue of this debate told that the pastor "Comes to
the Conclusion of His Argument." He wrote:

> And the impression is given by them (the patriots)
> that I would object to raising a flag in the church
> building. Now those that have understood it in
> that sense have not taken great pains to read my
> statement, for even as it appeared in the *Sentinel*
> it could never create that impression .... I plainly
> stated that the church as such is universal in
> character, and that as such the church raises no
> flag, and as such it sings no national anthems .... Is
> that building universal?
>   But let me help you out of the dilemma. The
> church is not a building but the church is the
> people of God as a whole ..... I would have no
> objection personally if a flag were raised in the

church building when our chorus gives one of its
excellent concerts.

And yet, I maintain that the church as such
never raises a flag. The church and state are
separate.

This little storm in the Reformed church world was just
one evidence of the changes in the thinking of some of the
leaders in the churches of the Reformation during the upheavals of war times, and also in the immediate post-war era.
There was a spirit of broadening, of re-examining the old
ways, of an open-mindedness to new thoughts, new interpretations, new ways of life. Perhaps the atmosphere which
often pervades a country at war was somewhat responsible
for these changes.

Then the war was over. The scars were healing, and life
was different. Gone were the patriotic parades, the fiery
speeches, the flaring tempers of those who had accused
fellow Americans of being pro-German. The memorial
services had been held, the doughboys came home, the
privations were over. In theory, the citizens of the United
States could return to the normal kinds of lifestyles they had
enjoyed before they entered the war.

But wars always leave scars. Besides the devastation,
deprivations, and grief, this war affected the way in which
people lived: their customs, habits, and even their thinking.
There was a broadening in cultural spheres, a love of democracy and the American way of life, even to an extent of a
dissatisfaction with the Reformed truth which they claimed
was being presented as cold dogma (this may or may not
have been a valid complaint). And finally, there was the wish
to broaden the boundaries of the Reformed scene, to examine
other interpretations of the Scriptures, and to live a little
closer to other ecclesiastical or non-ecclesiastical groups.
Many people of Reformed faith reasoned that if one cooper-
ates for victory and peace, one will be able to cooperate in

other spheres of life as well. The spirit of the *Jongeren* in the Netherlands had come full circle in many of the confessionally Reformed churches in America.

However, none of these tendencies had as yet been accepted as new dogma for Reformed people in the immediate post-war era. Just as the whole post-war spirit of unrest which hovered over them, so the clouds of new ideas and of uncertain doctrines and ways of life hovered in the ecclesiastical skies. These clouds pressed upon them; and the various people in the Reformed communities underneath these clouds criticized, tolerated, or spread these beliefs, depending on who was viewing these clouds of new ideas.

In the Christian Reformed Church, those leaders who welcomed the new ideas of synthesis over against a strict antithesis were the publishers and contributors to a magazine which was born about this time, titled *Religion and Culture.* These men, under the umbrella of the common grace taught by Dr. Abraham Kuyper of The Netherlands, found it the ideal method for spreading their broadening views of Calvinism. Herman Hoeksema, in his book on the history of this era, wrote: "These men were wont to speak of the urgent need of a 'restatement' of the truth;... they frequently appealed to the alleged development of a 'new mentality,' that required new methods of approach, new forms, and new truths. They embraced the slogan 'Jerusalem and Athens,' the synthesis of godliness and worldly philosophy."[2]

Already before the war, in the year 1914, when Herman Hoeksema was still a student at Calvin Theological School, Dr. Ralph Janssen, an able scholar and an interesting teacher, was appointed to the chair of Old Testament Exegetical Theology at the school. The students liked him and enjoyed his teaching. It was vibrant and interesting. But gradually

2.   *Ibid.,* p. 16.

complaints began to surface both from four of his colleagues and many of his students. These rumors spread through the college and seminary, and then on to the Christian Reformed churches of the area. The crux of the complaints both from four of Janssen's fellow professors and from his students was that the professor taught the truths of the Old Testament from the viewpoint of higher criticism.

Higher criticism has as its premise that *man*, a human being, can pass judgment on the origin and authenticity of the Holy Scriptures. Because God inspired men — human instruments — to write the Scriptures, the higher critics concentrate on the "human element" as they call it, and view the Scriptures as being of human origin. Embracing the hypothesis, the higher critics find possibilities of error in the Scriptures. They find evidences and overtones of earthly viewpoints adjusted to the customs of the times when the human person penned the words of the Scriptures. In other words, higher critics posed the possibility — and probability — that the human writers might slant or adjust the inspired Scriptures according to the circumstances and understanding of the times in which they lived.

With the above premise that the Scriptures are of human origin — at least in part — the higher critics teach that these Scriptures, which are human and time-bound writings, are subject to the critical analysis of the writings of any other authors.

It was in this atmosphere of the criticism of Holy Scripture that the students of the post-World War I era studied. The fact that these students consulted sources and used documentary evidence was not wrong in itself. However, when the scholars pitted documentary evidence and information from the earliest manuscripts against the Scriptures, or worse still, made their own interpretations of God's Word, they put themselves in the position of criticizing the authenticity of God's Word.

The basic premise for higher criticism is unbelief. Dr.

Janssen and his fellow scholars said that anyone can interpret the Scriptures — even an unbeliever; and Dr. Janssen found that the *possibility* and the *basis* of this higher criticism lay in the doctrine of common grace. Under the umbrella of common grace, the theory that unbelievers can also do good in God's sight, Dr. Janssen saw the way of *validating* and *legitimatizing* the intellectual criticism of the Scriptures. Therefore, when he accepted and taught the principles of higher criticism, he based them on common grace.

The legitimacy of higher criticism, he taught, was a direct *consequence* and a *practical application* of common grace. One was the necessary result of the other; and the premise was common grace. On that basis Dr. Janssen concluded that the use of higher criticism was legitimate.

Herman Hoeksema, with his spiritual sensitivity and intellectual insight, understood that Dr. Janssen was teaching his unbelieving theories of criticism under the umbrella of common grace, and that his theory of common grace justified his views. He also understood that Dr. Janssen denied the infallibility of God's Word.

These were harsh accusations to be leveled against a professor of theology; and the members of the Reformed faith were disturbed. Rumors and counter-rumors traveled fast in their closely knit communities. In these early days of the twentieth century, an exchange and distribution of pamphlets was common; and a brief exchange of pamphlets, *for* and *against* the teachings of Dr. Janssen, went on in the denomination. Herman Hoeksema, who had already seen the notes of some of the students, was convinced that Professor Janssen's position was not Scriptural, but higher-critical. As editor of the denomination's official magazine, *The Banner,* Hoeksema published his findings and criticized them as being unbiblical.

In 1921 the curatorium, or board of trustees of Calvin College and Seminary, found it necessary to appoint a committee of seven men to conduct an orderly investigation of the teachings of Dr. Janssen. The Rev. Hoeksema, now living in Grand Rapids, as pastor of the Eastern Avenue Christian Reformed Church, whose call he accepted in 1920, after serving five years in the Fourteenth Street Church, was a member of the curatorium and was appointed to the committee.

Dr. Janssen preferred not to cooperate with the committee who was responsible for investigating his notes and his teachings. Therefore the investigating committee went to the students for information. The student notes were not merely notes of individual students, but notes which had been systematically compiled by a group of students.

For weeks these seven committee members pored over piles of notes. Then problems arose. The committee could not agree. They were divided — four and three. The majority of four came to the Synod of the Christian Reformed Church in 1922 with a report that the allegations against Dr. Janssen were true and substantiated. The minority of three upheld Dr. Janssen. The result was that, after much probing, the synod condemned the unscriptural teachings of Dr. Janssen, and he was relieved of his office as professor. Shortly afterward he left the denomination.

Meanwhile, the supporters of Dr. Janssen, who liked him as a person and who embraced his beliefs of higher criticism, vowed to get vengeance for Dr. Janssen. They did not have to wait very long before they took their revenge.

Along with the supporters of Dr. Janssen, the four professors, his former colleagues who had criticized him and who did not want to go so far as Dr. Janssen had gone, still held to the underlying principle — the theory of common grace. These men, who had asked for Herman Hoeksema's support and cooperation in exposing Dr. Janssen's heresy, now turned against Hoeksema. The four professors had welcomed Hoeksema's help in the battle for the pure interpretation of the Scriptures, and had stood with him during the investigation; but when they did some re-thinking of the

issues, they did not want to believe that *common grace* was the
real issue in the Janssen case. Not all of them knew just what
to do with this common grace, and not all wanted to go so far
as Janssen had, but the four professors wanted to have a
grace for the godly and ungodly alike — a grace, in certain
spheres, for all. The secular press (*Holland Sentinel,* November 22, 1923) also recognized the issue and the victim.
Titled "Battle of the Books Going on in Church Circles," the
article said:

> Two controversial books recently published
> are arousing a great deal of interest in church
> circles in Holland because of their contents and
> because of their authorship. "The Leader," pub-
> lication of the Reformed Church, devotes an edi-
> torial to the books this week under the caption,
> "Christian Reformed Problems."
>   The books are *The Synodical Conclusions,* by
> Dr. Ralph Janssen, and *Sin and Grace* by Rev. H.
> Hoeksema and Rev. H. Danhof. Dr. Janssen was
> formerly a resident of Holland township and Rev.
> Hoeksema was for some years pastor of the 14th
> St. Christian Ref'd Church. Another minister,
> Rev. B.K. VanBaalen, well known in Holland and
> who has relatives in this city, is writing another
> book, it is announced, that is said to be an attack
> on *Sin and Grace.* The title of the VanBaalen book
> will be *New Departure and Error.*
>   The present battle of the books has grown
> directly or indirectly out of the now famous
> "Janssen Case" that is still exercising the attention
> of the Christian Reformed Church and that is
> likely to be one of the major questions at the next
> general synod of that denomination. The attack
> and counter attack are for the most part in regard
> to the doctrine of common grace, which doctrine
> is said to be rejected completely by the authors of
> *Sin and Grace,* and which is affirmed by the other
> parties in the controversy.
>   And the personality of Dr. Ralph Janssen, who

was deposed as a professor of the Christian Reformed Theological Seminary in Grand Rapids, is also an element, directly or indirectly, in the battle. Dr. J.E. Kuisenga, writer of the "Leader" editorial, closes his article with this estimate of the former Grand Rapids professor: "Meanwhile Prof. Janssen stands a lonely, heroic, tragic figure."

Although no one in the days of the early twenties realized the importance and the impact of the so-called "Janssen Case," this widely publicized dispute acted as a catalyst for a major controversy which erupted at the Synod of the Christian Reformed Church in the year 1924.

It was also a grievous disturbance for the garden of Reformed plantings, which — having been replanted in this land across the seas — was being threatened by the weeds of higher criticism of the Scriptures.

Section Two: RE-ROOTINGS
Chapter 3
A Storm of Protest

Although Dr. Janssen had left the Christian Reformed denomination, many of his views, particularly his interpretation of common grace, remained. At the time of his exit, the denomination was divided into three camps:

1.   those who gave whole-hearted support to Dr. Janssen and his views;

2.   those who condemned Dr. Janssen's views but wanted to keep common grace;

3.   those who wanted none of his teachings.

Just what was this burning issue of common grace? Before this question can be answered, the idea of the attribute of God's grace, *in Himself,* must be defined. God's grace is His pleasantness and attractiveness, His divine goodness. But God does not keep that grace to Himself. He gives it to His children who are sinners. He gives it to those whom He has *chosen to be His children* as an unmerited and undeserved favor, for He loves them. He shows His love by giving them the promises of the payment for their sins through Jesus' sacrifice on the cross. He also promises them perfect, everlasting life in glory. Because He has this grace only for His chosen ones, it is a sovereign and a particular grace. It is the only grace which God possesses.

Herman Hoeksema puts it this way: "When God is graciously inclined toward men, He blesses them; and the contents of that blessing is His grace; even as, when He is displeased and unfavorably inclined to men, He curses, and the result is misery and death."[3]

---

3.   Herman Hoeksema, *Reformed Dogmatics,* Grand Rapids, R.F.P.A., 1973, p. 110.

21

When Pastor Hoeksema preached that God has no common grace for the wicked, those who hate God, he was preaching his convictions, based on the Scriptural truth of particular grace. In fact, in his preaching he showed, through the Scriptures, what God's thoughts about the ungodly are. He showed that the psalmist Asaph was at one time in a dilemma concerning God's grace. Was God gracious to the evil citizens who were prospering with material goods on this earth? In Psalm 73:3-12, Asaph related his experiences with evil men. He witnessed that they had more than they needed or even wanted on this earth, while Asaph served the Lord ... and suffered. He asked the Most High God whether these earthly goods were some kind of blessing to these unbelievers: possibly a temporary, or a common grace?

It was only when Asaph went to God, in His temple, that he understood what God was doing: He gave them material things, not in His grace, but in His anger. Their "good things" in life did nothing more than send them on the slippery road to hell (vs. 18). And Hoeksema found the reason for God's dealings *with sovereign grace* toward His children, and *in wrath* toward ungodly men. He drew the attention of his congregation to Proverbs 3:33: "The *curse* of the Lord is in the house of the wicked; but he *blesseth* the habitation of the just."

Pastor Hoeksema found in the Scriptures the sharp line of God's grace for His chosen people, over against His anger and His curse—not a common grace—for the unregenerated citizens on this earth. In his preaching he quoted texts such as Romans 9:18: "Therefore, hath he mercy on whom he will have mercy, and whom he wills he hardeneth," and II Corinthians 2:15, 16: "For we are unto God a sweet savor of Christ, in them that are saved and in them that perish. To the one we are the savor of death unto death, and to the other of life unto life. And who is sufficient unto these things?"

His zeal to preach particular, sovereign grace and his defense for the pure truth of the Scriptures does not mean that Pastor Hoeksema was a fire-and-brimstone preacher. In fairness to him, even his opponents agreed that his preaching was biblical and exegetical and edifying. A seminary student who was a member of his congregation said, "As I see it, his preaching was forceful, well-organized, thematic, exegetical, and generally inspiring. Here was a man who never rambled."[4]

Not all the listeners in the pews shared equal enthusiasm for his preaching. Some made it clear that they did not want such a sharp division between believers and unbelievers, the righteous and the unrighteous, especially in the sphere of the area in which these two kinds of people meet: in everyday civic life. These listeners argued that the godless man also obeys the law, is kind to the down-trodden, and often lives a morally clean life. Rather than interpret their deeds as the only way to exist on this earth (along with enhancing their self-image and self-esteem) they attributed this to a certain kind of grace, not sovereign or saving grace, but a temporal, common grace whereby a man with an evil heart can perform some good in God's sight, particularly in civic relationships. With these conflicting views of God's grace, a sharp doctrinal rift was developing, and widening. In this rather tense setting, not only in the Eastern Avenue congregation, but spreading to other Christian Reformed churches, the outspoken antagonists conducted a pamphlet war in the early twenties, which revolved around the issue of common grace.

A new publication called *The Witness* appeared in 1921. Its purpose was to be a rebuttal to the broader views of *Religion and Culture,* mentioned earlier. The Reverends Hoeksema and Danhof were two of the members of a staff of seven contributors to *The Witness.* The magazine lasted less than two years. It was hinted by some of the readers that these two leaders might bring controversy to the Christian Reformed Church if they continued their strong writing against common grace, and they were not eager to see trouble in their church.

At the same time, both Pastors Hoeksema and Danhof

---

4.   William Hendricksen: private correspondence.

realized that a major crisis in the Christian Reformed Church was developing. If there were to be a controversy, they would need time to prepare for it; and therefore they discontinued their magazine. They would not have time to publish it.

In the early twenties of this century, the synods of the Christian Reformed denomination were held biennially. At this time the Synod of 1922 was history, but the controversial issues which it had faced had not been resolved. By the time two years had passed and the synod of 1924 was ready to assemble, these same matters would again come to the meetings.

※   ※   ※   ※   ※   ※   ※

Herman and Nellie Hoeksema were comfortable in their large manse next to the Eastern Avenue Christian Reformed Church in Grand Rapids. They needed a large house, for by the year 1923 they had four children. Pastor Hoeksema was busy with his very large and active congregation. He was a popular, vibrant preacher, with audiences at the church services crowding the pews, sitting on railings, in the aisles, and even on the steps of the platform, if they could find no seats elsewhere. Most of his parishioners expressed that they enjoyed his preaching and told him that they were edified by it.

Not all the listeners in the pews were edified. Some complained. And on Saturday morning, January 19, 1924, three members of the Eastern Avenue congregation knocked at the door of the manse. After they were welcomed and seated, the pastor sensed that this was not to be a comfortable chat over a cup of coffee. It was a formal call, they said. They had objections to their pastor's views in his preaching and his writings, they said, as they handed him a formal protest.

The pastor did not have to read very far, for the protest was not addressed to him, but to his consistory.

"You are at the wrong door, brothers," he told them. His parishioners agreed; and they left. Some days later they came back with the same protest, now addressed to the Rev. Hoeksema. When the pastor agreed to discuss their grievances with each one of the signers—individually—only one of the three agreed to meet with his pastor. Soon afterward, in a short session in the pastor's study, the protester stumbled and faltered when trying to explain the grievances in his protest; and finally he admitted that he was not very well acquainted with its contents. The other two signers refused to discuss the contents with their pastor. Why? Did they not know their own protests, either? The answer was no.

The truth came out later, during public testimony at the court trial in Grand Rapids, when one of the lawyers determined that a brother of one of the three signers had drawn up the protest for the three men.

When the pastor had asked each protester to see him alone, he was following the biblical and Reformed procedure of discipline. This procedure was obedient to the passage in Matthew 18:15: "... if thy brother trespass against thee, go and tell him his fault between thee and him alone." When the three protesters saw that they were not able, and therefore not willing, to discuss and sustain their protests individually, they changed their procedure.

Instead of discussing their grievances, they charged their pastor with *public sin*. By making this accusation, the three men put themselves in the position of accusing their pastor before their consistory. In that way they were able to go to their consistory to lodge a complaint against their pastor. The complaint accused him of sin in his preaching; and the three men asked that the ruling elders discipline their pastor for this sin.

After studying the protest, the consistory told the protesters that they were begging the question, for they asked the consistory to assume what must still be proven. The consistory conceded that the pastor's preaching was *public*, but not public *sin*. When the three men would not retract their accusation against their pastor, the consistory put them under discipline and asked that they refrain from taking the Lord's Supper.

Besides these troubles in the congregation of the Eastern
Avenue Church, during the last part of April, 1924, three
colleagues of Rev. Hoeksema, the Reverends J. VanderMey,
M. Schans, and J.K. VanBaalen, each presented the consistory
of the Eastern Avenue Church with a protest against Pastor
Hoeksema. The rule of church government states that they
must first deliver a copy of the protest to the person against
whom it is directed. Rev. Schans had failed to do this.

The main content of these protests was that Hoeksema's
theology was harsh, narrow, inflexible — that his *head*, not
his *heart*, ruled his theology. The following five issues sum
up the complaints of all those who protested:

1.   They objected to Hoeksema's teaching that grace is
always particular, to the exclusion of any common grace.

2.   They objected that Hoeksema put too much emphasis on predestination.

3.   They objected that Hoeksema's world and life view
precluded the social reforms, the good that the ungodly do.

4.   They objected that the invitation was lacking in
Hoeksema's preaching.

5.   They believed that Hoeksema's teaching to "hate
those that hate Thee" tended to annul the second table of the
law.[5]

All of these protests, challenging weighty matters of the
interpretation of the Scriptures and of the Reformed creeds,
came perilously late — in April — and the classis was
scheduled to meet on May 21. Why was this situation so
serious?

According to the rules of church government, a matter
must be finished in the local consistory before it can be
brought to the broader church court, the classis; and the
classis was only a month away! There was not enough time
to treat all these matters before the deadline.

By definition, the classis is the broader gathering of
delegates from neighboring churches having the same faith,

---

5.   Herman Hoeksema, *The Protestant Reformed Churches in
America,* p. 34, 35.

who enter into a voluntary union to cooperate in discussing and deciding on matters (also appeals) for the good of the churches.

In the tradition of Reformed church government, there is no hierarchy of lower, higher, and highest bodies of ruling powers. It is an orderly method of church government, with checks and balances to avoid tyranny or dictatorship. "Pure Reformed Church polity knows of no lower and higher judicatory bodies. It acknowledges the consistory as the sole ruling power over the local congregation. A classis possesses no power over the local churches whatsoever. Whatever power it possesses is derivative, secondary, limited, advisory."[6]

The broader gatherings of the churches treat only matters which have been finished in the consistories of the local congregations and are appealed to the broader bodies. Therefore those ministers who had protested near the end of April were dangerously near the deadline. They did not give the consistory the time they needed to treat these protests before the scheduled meeting of classis on May 21, 1924.

The Eastern Avenue Church was the host church for the meetings of Classis East. As the delegates to Classis East gathered there on the morning of May 21, they seemed confused and unsure of the procedure and treatment of the mass of protests and counter-protests. They seemed unprepared, uneasy, or unwilling to go into the contents of the protests. It may have been a reluctance because of the weighty contents in these protests; or their problem may have been concern for the correct ecclesiastical procedures, governed by their church polity.

Why should these delegates to Classis Grand Rapids East be so uncomfortable? After all, they knew the history of the controversy. The church papers and even the newspapers were keeping them informed. And most of these men were veteran office-bearers who understood the polity of

---

6. *Ibid.*, p. 42.

their church. The reason that these men were so uneasy was exactly that they were painfully aware of all this.

1.   They *knew* that the protests of the three pastors were not finished and could not be ready to be treated at the gathering of Classis East.

2.   They *knew* that the Rev. Schans had not rectified his error of bypassing Pastor Hoeksema with his protest against him, and that therefore the consistory of the Eastern Avenue congregation had not yet been able to deal with it.

3.   They *knew* the rules of their church order: that they were not allowed to treat material which had not been finished at the local level.

What could the classis do at this point? The answer is simple: postpone the matters which had not been finished by the consistory and re-convene when the consistory had finished its work. The controversy of sovereign, particular grace versus common grace was not a matter which required haste. In fact, the issue was so fundamental to members who confessed the Reformed faith that it would determine the future course of the Christian Reformed denomination. The doctrinal dispute needed much study, definition, and clarification; and these important issues would take *time* to develop and mature.

In this setting Classis Grand Rapids East began its work. It is not in the scope of this history to follow the many suggestions and tentative motions which were offered on the floor of the classis, but rather to show the determination of the majority of the delegates: their intention to try to avoid discussion of the protests, along with the issue which prompted those protests: common grace.

The intention of the majority of the classis was to pass the untreated material to the broadest court, the synod, rather than face an open discussion. Not all the delegates to the classis were satisfied with this procedure; for it was clearly contrary to their church order. One of the delegates made the suggestion to the classis that they pass the material to the synod and ask that body to appoint a committee to search the writings of the Reverends Danhof and Hoeksema.

Reverend Hoeksema had a counter suggestion: to ask the synod to discuss the burning issue at its meetings, to determine the doctrinal soundness or the heresy of the teaching of these pastors. The former motion passed. The latter did not.

Then the consistory of the Eastern Avenue Church was allowed to have its say. These men urged the classis to let them finish their work first, in an orderly way, and present it to another meeting of classis.

In this confusion of suggestions, a delegate made the motion that the classis treat the matter of the protest of the Rev. Schans. The motion carried. The consistory of the Eastern Avenue Church objected. Through the debate which followed this objection — during an afternoon and evening session — the classis met in a private, executive session, which excluded Hoeksema's presence.

About that session Pastor Hoeksema writes:

> Finally, after well-nigh the entire forenoon of May 23 had been devoted to a continuation of the discussion of the previous afternoon and evening, the classis reached the following remarkable decision: it expressed that it had never decided to treat the protest and enter into its subject matter![7]

The morning of May 23, when the classis re-convened, they met in the Sherman Street Christian Reformed Church. They sent a delegation to Pastor Hoeksema to relay to him the decision which they had made the previous afternoon in their private session, and to tell him he was welcome to come back to the meetings of the classis. The pastor did not go.

Finally, in its last session, the classis passed a motion that the protests of the three ministers, whose treatment had not been finished in the Eastern Avenue consistory, were to be referred back to that consistory.

---

7. *Ibid.,* p. 55.

It had been a long session, filled with wranglings, uncertainties, confusion, and contradictions. The settlement of the common grace controversy had proceeded no further.

A few days after Classis Grand Rapids East convened, Classis Grand Rapids West began its meetings in the LaGrave Avenue Christian Reformed Church. The First Christian Reformed Church of Kalamazoo, Michigan belonged to the group of churches which sent its delegates to Classis Grand Rapids West; and the pastor of this congregation was the Rev. H. Danhof, who agreed with and who supported Herman Hoeksema on the subject of common grace.

Only one protest was submitted to Classis Grand Rapids West: the protest of the Rev. J.K. VanBaalen, which protest had already appeared at Classis Grand Rapids East, and which was directed against the consistory of the Eastern Avenue Church. VanBaalen had filed the same protest with the consistory of First Kalamazoo. The protest lodged the same complaints, this time against Pastor H. Danhof, and asked the consistory to discipline their pastor because of his erroneous preaching. The consistory of First Kalamazoo could not censure their pastor because they agreed with him. They appealed the protest to Classis Grand Rapids West.

After much discussion, Classis West decided to make arrangements for a personal conference, without witnesses, in which the two pastors, VanBaalen and Danhof, could discuss their disagreements. If they came to no satisfactory conclusions, the Rev. VanBaalen (contrary to the rules of the church order) had the option of calling a special meeting of Classis Grand Rapids West on June 10, 1924.

Because the classis had made no provision for witnesses, when the two men claimed opposite outcomes of the conference, there was no one to prove who was right. Danhof insisted that VanBaalen had no more grounds to accuse him; and VanBaalen said that Danhof's views in private were different from his views in his public writings.

The two men were at an impasse; and the Rev. VanBaalen called a special meeting of classis on June 10. The classis, not knowing what to do, asked that VanBaalen take his protest directly to the coming synod. Thus Classis Grand Rapids West, along with Classis Grand Rapids East, solved nothing.

During these two classes, which met in the planting time of May, 1924, there were grave disagreements concerning the *kinds* of seeds they should plant in the garden of Reformed plantings. They could not agree, so they waited until June.

Chapter 4
The Synod of 1924

The Church Order of the Christian Reformed Church stipulated that their synods be made up of six delegates from each classis. There were thirteen classical districts in the denomination: and seventy-eight delegates reported on June 18, 1924, to the host church, First Christian Reformed Church of Kalamazoo, Michigan, where Reverend Henry Danhof was currently the pastor.

Judging by this synod's procedures and decisions, this was not what one might call a "packed synod": a synod with delegates who had strong opinions on the issues they were to treat and who tried to railroad their decisions. The Synod of 1924 was the opposite: an ill-prepared, and therefore a tentative synod, especially from the point of view of its formal procedure.

From the start the synod had problems with the Scriptural admonition: "Let all things be done decently and in order" (I Cor. 14:40). Many of the delegates were overwhelmed with the mass of material, in the form of protests, which lay on its official table. Worse still, most of them did not understand the theory of common grace, much less the doctrinal implications and the practical results of this common grace. At this point in history they did not quite know what to do with it.

In the interest of orderly procedure, it was the custom in the synods of the Reformed churches to appoint committees of pre-advice, to give their synodical meetings a basis and to follow this basis with logical procedure in their deliberations. It was the duty of these committees to read and discuss the materials they were given, determine their legality, compose a report, and draw conclusions.

The chairman of the Synod of 1924 appointed a committee of five ministers and three elders to give guidance in the

common grace controversy. It was also customary that the
chairman appoint one of the seminary professors as advisor
to each committee. For this committee the chairman appointed Professor L. Berkhof, who was not the logical choice
for an advisor. The logical choice would have been Professor
F.M. TenHoor, who held the chair of Dogmatic Theology at
the seminary. With his doctrinal knowledge and background, he was best equipped to give guidance to the
committee on this crucial doctrinal issue. The reason that
Professor TenHoor was by-passed was that he had made the
statement that he "felt quite sure that there was such a thing
as common grace, but he did not know what it was!"[8]

This committee of pre-advice had an overwhelming
mass of material to study. They were given eight protests
from local individuals or from consistories, including one
which Classis Grand Rapids East had referred back to the
consistory of the Eastern Avenue congregation. Due to the
time element, this protest had not as yet been treated by the
consistory, but the protesters had appealed it to the synod
anyway. There were also four protests from the classes of
Hackensack, New Jersey; Hudson, New York; Sioux Center,
Iowa; and Muskegon, Michigan.

During the days in which the committee met, they did
not call in the two men, Herman Hoeksema and Henry
Danhof, with whom so many pastors and elders disagreed.
The committee did not ask the two pastors for *their* interpretations of God's grace. They did not ask for enlightenment,
explanations, or viewpoints. This was a highly unusual
procedure, even for the secular courts of the land; but this
was the broadest court of the *church,* to which the brothers in
Christ appealed their grievances. The Synod of 1924, however, was a closed court, which did not allow a hearing for
those who were on trial. One reason seemed to be that the
majority of the delegates had their minds made up that they
wanted to adopt the concept of common grace as dogma in
the Christian Reformed denomination. A second element

---

8.   *Ibid.,* p. 67.

was that they were afraid of what Herman Hoeksema had to say in his defense. They were afraid of defending their stand for common grace against the doctrine of God's sovereign, particular grace.

For two weeks the synod recessed so that the committee could formulate its advice. On July 1, the synod re-convened. The Reverend Danhof was a delegate to the synod, and the chairman could not deny him the floor. Herman Hoeksema was not a delegate and was not allowed to ask for the floor. Neither did the synod ask him to testify in his own case. They ignored his presence while they discussed the protests against him. Three times in the course of the discussions of the protests against him Pastor Hoeksema asked for the floor to furnish an explanation, and three times he was denied the privilege of speaking. The synod gave the following reason for denying this privilege: that the pastor had nothing to do with the matter being discussed.

The matter being discussed was painfully pertinent to the two pastors: for the synod was discussing three points of doctrine, drawn up by the advisory committee. These points were the foundation and defense of the so-called threefold doctrine of common grace, with proofs from the Scriptures and the Reformed confessions.[9]

Meanwhile the discussion of the newly-formed three points of common grace continued on the floor of the synod. Stymied and frustrated because he was not allowed to have a voice on the all-important issue of God's grace, the pastor tried one final time to get permission to speak. He asked that the synod allow him to speak at the session to be held that evening; and in order to get a favorable answer, he promised he would not ask for the floor again. The synod gave him permission, and he spoke to a large audience that evening.

For more than two hours Pastor Hoeksema spoke on the subject of God's grace, His sovereign grace, which God shows only to His chosen people, the ones He loves. An

---

9. The contents and proofs for these three points will be discussed in the next chapter.

eloquent speaker, Hoeksema showed from the pages of the
Scriptures that God *always* has grace for His chosen people,
and *never* has grace — not even a common, temporary grace
— for those He has reprobated. He drew the sharp line of the
antithesis between the church and the world; and he emphasized that the denial of common grace was the only position
the churches might adopt, for it was the position of the
Scriptures.

No one knows, of course, how these words fell on the
hearts of the delegates to the synod. He may have set his
audience to thinking. However, the following episode gives
another clue. It was in a later session, when the synod was
confused by the contents of their newly-formulated first
point of common grace that Pastor Hoeksema offered to give
an explanation. He was denied the floor on the ground that
he had promised not to ask for the floor again. The synod did
not want to discuss these important biblical doctrines with
him. Were they afraid of his biblical arguments? Only God
knows. Because he could not testify in his own case in the
broadest court of his denomination, there was no reason
anymore for him to attend the sessions, and the pastor left the
synod.

During the two weeks in which the committee had dealt
with the issue of common grace, they formulated explanations of *three aspects* of this common grace: the general grace
of God, the restraint of sin, and the ability of the natural man
to do good. They formulated these ideas into three points, or
three theories of common grace. The committee cautioned
the synod not as yet to accept these formulations as official
doctrine, but to consider them to be the truth of the Scriptures, which needed more study.

Accompanying this three-point document was a testimony which the committee urged to be sent to the churches
in the Christian Reformed denomination. It was a warning
not to misuse these newly-formulated doctrines of common
grace.[10] Although the synod felt it necessary to draw up

---

10. This testimony is reproduced in the next chapter.

these words of caution, and although it passed a motion to send this warning to all the churches, the testimony was never circulated in the denomination. The records of the synod do not show that the synod decided not to send the testimony to the churches as a warning. The only clue to the mystery is the testimony of Dr. H. Beets, the stated clerk of the synod, that this testimony had been "blue pencilled." It seems that the decision not to send the testimony is covered with the dust of history.

The committee of pre-advice also had a word of partial understanding for their colleagues, Danhof and Hoeksema. They declared: "First, because the brethren, according to their own repeated declarations, do not intend or purpose anything less than to preach the Reformed doctrine as contained in the Holy Scripture and the Confessions, we will gladly assume that they erred in good faith. Secondly, because it cannot be denied that they are Reformed in respect to the fundamental truths, even though it be with an inclination to one-sidedness."[11]

The committee also asked that the president of the synod give the following advice to the Reverends Danhof and Hoeksema: that its president

> 1. Seriously admonish the brethren with respect to their departures and demand of them the *promise* that in the future they will abide by the three points declared by synod.
>
> 2. *Urge* the brethren Danhof and Hoeksema that they refrain from making propaganda for their dissenting views regarding the three points in the churches.
>
> 3. Point out to the brethren that if it should appear, either now or in the future, that they will not abide by the decisions of synod, the latter to its profound regret will have to *make the case pending* with the consistories.[12]

---

11. Herman Hoeksema, *The Protestant Reformed Churches in America,* p. 77.
12. Herman Hoeksema, *ibid.,* p. 78.

The reader will note that these three warnings start with a *mild rebuke,* increase to an *urging,* and end with the *threat of discipline.*

After the synod had explored the committee's lengthy advice, the delegates met for nine sessions to discuss and decide the implications of adopting the first point of common grace, as formulated by the committee. The issue of God's grace to the reprobate, ungodly person was not so clear to the synod as it was to the committee of pre-advice. The confusion on the floor of the synod is demonstrated by the following contradictory motion presented to the synod: "Synod declares that according to Scripture and the Confessions it is established, not only that God is filled with wrath against the reprobates because of their sin, but also that He is favorably inclined and bestows blessings upon those whom Scripture calls the ungodly and unrighteous, which, of course, includes the reprobates."[13]

The Reverend Manni made a substitute motion. He put into words what some of the delegates to this synod felt in their hearts: "Synod having duly considered the advice of the committee of pre-advice in the matter of the protests and objections against the views of the Reverends H. Danhof and H. Hoeksema, decides to drop the common-grace case for the present, with the earnest admonition that thorough study be made of this matter, in the spirit of brotherly and mutual appreciation.... The time is not yet ripe for a more definite expression on the problem before which it was placed by the protestants."[14]

This motion showed the way out of the controversy: to give the issues time to be researched, reflected on, and discussed. The Reverend Manni showed a better way — the way of forming mature, Scriptural insights and decisions. But the synod rejected his motion.

The synod adjourned for a few days and went back into session on July 7. When they re-convened, the members of

13. *Ibid.,* p. 78.
14. *Ibid.,* pp. 81, 82.

synod adopted the doctrinal statements of the three points of common grace, with Scriptural proofs, along with the Testimony which was never sent to the churches.

The Synod of June, 1924, was ill-prepared for cultivating and planting in the garden of Reformed plantings. They did not want to examine the biblical qualities of the seeds nor the sproutings of Reformed plants. Rather, they favored the tares of common grace.

Chapter 5
The Doctrinal Issues at the Synod

In order to understand the historic impact which the formation and the adoption of the three points of common grace caused, it is necessary to know the *contents* of these points of common grace. In this chapter the three points will be stated, analyzed, and briefly criticized, as they stand in opposition to the teachings of the Scriptures.

It is necessary to know the contents of these points, to understand them, and to refute them, in order to explain and to justify the separate existence of the Protestant Reformed Churches in America. *Why* was this rift necessary? Why, in the Lord's wisdom, was a new denomination born from the pastors and members who were expelled from the Christian Reformed Church? Can their right of a separate existence be defended?

In order to answer this question, the reader must become acquainted with the content of these three points of common grace and with the alleged proofs which the Synod of 1924 offered to justify their validity — that the three points were biblical and confessional. In this chapter, the proofs and criticisms following the statement of each of the three points of common grace are not exhaustive, but merely a brief sampling.[15]

The first point of common grace reads as follows:

> Relative to the first point which concerns the favorable attitude of God towards humanity in general and not only towards the elect, synod

---

15. See the following references for further reading on these issues: H. Hoeksema, *Reformed Dogmatics,* R.F.P.A., 1973; H. Hoeksema, *The Triple Knowledge,* R.F.P.A., 1976.

41

> declares it to be established according to Scripture
> and the confessions that, apart from the saving
> grace of God shown only to those that are elect
> unto eternal life, there is also a certain favor or
> grace of God which He shows to His creatures in
> general. This is evident from the Scriptural pas-
> sages quoted and from the Canons of Dordrecht,
> II, 5 and III, IV, 8 and 9, which deal with the general
> offer of the Gospel, while it also appears from the
> citations made from Reformed writers of the most
> flourishing period of Reformed Theology that our
> Reformed writers from the past favored this view.[16]

A restatement, in less technical language, written by
Herman Hoeksema, is as follows:

> Firstly, the view that the grace of God in relation
> to the things of this present life, is not particular,
> not for the elect alone, but that it is received in
> common by all men head for head, by righteous
> and unrighteous, by elect and reprobate alike.
> God, that is, sustains a certain covenant of friend-
> ship with natural man.[17]

The first point of common grace posed two theories. The
first part of this point teaches a certain type of general, or
common grace, distinct from saving grace, shown to all
creatures in general, including the ungodly wicked people in
this world. God's grace may be defined as His unmerited
favor to His children, who, because of sin, are undeserving.
The delegates to synod knew that those whom God reprobated were excluded from God's favor, for He hates them.
He has not chosen them, and He has no saving grace for
them.

Yet the delegates to the synod thought they faced a
dilemma. They witnessed what was happening in the

---

16. H. Hoeksema, *The Protestant Reformed Churches in America,*
p. 309.
17. Gertrude Hoeksema, *Therefore Have I Spoken,* R.F.P.A., 1969,
p. 148.

natural, earthly lives of both the righteous and the evil people on this earth. Those who were unbelievers, who did not believe in God's sovereign rule, who did not thank Him, nor repent, received just as much — and sometimes more — of the good things of this earth. Examples of these "good things" are the gifts of God in nature: rain, sunshine, crops, and prosperity. The delegates to the synod also saw that evildoers often enjoyed good health, good times, and good outward behavior.

They saw that godless men on earth enjoyed God's bounty; and they were trying to find a reason to justify these apparently good gifts which God allowed reprobate sinners to enjoy; and the synod thought they had found the answer in positing a temporal, non-saving, common grace, or goodness of God, which He gave to reprobated men, those whom He in reality hated.

After stating their *idea* of a common grace, the next step of the committee of pre-advice was the finding of biblical and confessional proof for this theory. For the first part of this point, which read, "a certain favor or grace of God which He shows to His creatures in general," they furnished eight proof texts. Three of the texts, followed with criticisms of the use of the text as a proof for common grace are as follows:

1.   Psalm 145:9: "The Lord is good to all; and
his tender mercies are over all his works."

This psalm is a song of praise to God as sovereign Ruler of the universe. In His sovereignty He rules all things: His plants and trees, storms and sunshine, and the lives of men. In this psalm the word "all" is the living, organic creation which God has created, for "the Lord is ... holy in all his works," verse 17. The psalm teaches that God is good in all His works, even in the gifts He sends to the wicked.

Another word for God's sovereign rule is His providence. God's providence may be defined as His almighty power, as Creator and Ruler of the universe, to guide all things — His creatures and His creation — to the goal which He has decreed. In His providence, God controls the so-called natural phenomena, such as rain and sunshine, and

He leads the lives of all men — godly and ungodly — in the way He has planned. Therefore, on this earth the godly and ungodly share alike in the good things and also in the disasters which God in His providence sends. Often, in God's wise plan, He sends more material prosperity to unbelievers and evil men than He does to His humble saints. Asaph's words in Psalm 73:3-7 reflect this truth: "For I was envious at the foolish, when I saw the prosperity of the wicked. For there are no bands in their death: but their strength is firm. They are not in trouble as other men; neither are they plagued like other men. Therefore pride compasseth them about as a chain; violence covereth them as a garment. Their eyes stand out with fatness: they have more than heart could wish." Asaph thought that God treated evil men better than His chosen ones, until he went into the sanctuary of God, and "understood their end." Their end was that the Lord set them in slippery places, in order to make them slide into the destruction of hell.

✳ ✳ ✳ ✳ ✳ ✳ ✳

   2.   Luke 6:35, 36: "But love ye your enemies, and do good, and lend, hoping for nothing again; and your reward shall be great, and ye shall be the children of the Highest: for he is kind unto the unthankful and to the evil. Be ye therefore merciful, as your Father also is merciful."

It is quite possible that the committee of pre-advice did not read these verses very carefully, for Jesus spoke these words immediately after He spoke the beatitudes. He spoke those beatitudes to His *children*, those whom He loved and for whom He was soon to die. His own people on earth were sinners, too. They had enemies, also believing enemies whom Jesus said they must learn to love. Jesus gave them His reason: their Father is kind to them, even though they are unthankful and evil. He is good to them because they are His children; and He forgives them. Jesus taught them to do the same: to be merciful to sinners because their Father is merciful to them. Compassion is God's gift to them in their hearts. In these verses there is no hint of a common grace for those whom God has not chosen.

✳ ✳ ✳ ✳ ✳ ✳ ✳

3. Acts 14:16, 17: "Who in times past suffered all nations to walk in their own ways. Nevertheless he left not himself without a witness, in that he did good and gave us rain from heaven, and fruitful season, filling our hearts with joy and gladness."

For this text, Herman Hoeksema has the following interpretation:

This text does not teach that God is gracious to the reprobate ungodly. It merely teaches that God did not leave Himself without a witness to the heathen world even in the old dispensation. He revealed Himself as the One that must be thanked and served, filling them with food and gladness. And, naturally, by means of these testimonies the heathen knew that God is to be thanked and served....

Though they knew God and received His witness, they received no grace; and with their rain, fruitful seasons and food and gladness they served sin and were objects of His wrath and damnation. Fruitful seasons, food and gladness with material things are not grace, neither are they a manifestation of grace.[18]

✳ ✳ ✳ ✳ ✳ ✳ ✳

While the committee of pre-advice at the Synod of 1924 was defining and defending the concept of common grace, they slipped into a more serious error, their second erroneous theory, that of "the general offer of the gospel." The committee did hasty, superficial work in formulating this

---

18. H. Hoeksema, *The Protestant Reformed Churches in America*, p. 320.

first point, especially in the second element. They had no time for careful research, study, and exchange of opinions. The delegates were confused by the concepts of a grace which was not saving, and yet a temporal good for those whom God had not chosen as His own. In their haste and confusion of concepts, they formulated another concept, which was really unrelated to the first concept. This phrase, "the general offer of the gospel," which was slipped in at the end, was a shift in the perspective of the first part of this point, which "concerns the favorable attitude of God towards humanity in general." In the latter part of this point, general grace suddenly changes to the "general offer" of the gospel to all who hear God's Word. This short phrase, which was the insertion of the Arminian heresy of a general offer to all, is what the members of the Dutch-speaking churches of 1924 called "het *puntje* van he eerste punt," or "the *heart* of the first point." This was the doctrine of the heretic Jacobus Arminius, against whom the Reformed churches in The Netherlands battled at the Synod of Dordt in 1618-19, and from which was born the Canons of Dordrecht. The irony of it is that the authors of the first point of common grace tried to give proof of God's general offer of the gospel to all people by citing a passage from the Canons, which was a *rebuttal* to the heresy of the general offer of the gospel!

The following is the passage from the Canons of Dordt which the synod quoted, and which was a rebuttal to the general offer of grace:

> Canons II, 5: Moreover the promise of the Gospel is that whosoever believeth in Christ crucified, shall not perish but have everlasting life. This promise, together with the command to repent and believe, ought to be declared and published to all nations and to all persons promiscuously and without distinction, to whom God out of his good pleasure sends the gospel.[19]

---

19. *Ibid.*, pp. 308, 309.

In refuting the synod's claim that Canons II, 5 proves a general offer of the gospel, Herman Hoeksema maintains:

> a.   That the promise of the gospel must be preached promiscuously to all nations and men without distinction.
> b.   That it is, however, the good pleasure of God that determines even where that gospel shall be preached.
> c.   That, as to its contents, this promise of the gospel is that whosoever believeth in Christ crucified shall not perish, but have everlasting life.
> d.   Surely, this presents the promise of the Gospel as strictly particular, for it is to them that believe in Christ, that is, the elect.   The Gospel is not presented here as a general offer.   Still less does this part of our Confession teach, that the preaching of the Gospel is grace of God to all that hear it. Synod was utterly mistaken.[20]

※   ※   ※   ※   ※   ※   ※

In contrast to the confusion and inconsistencies of the theory of common grace drawn up at the Synod of 1924, both as a temporal, or common grace, and as a general offer of the gospel, the teaching of God's Word is clear and simple. Instead of a common grace, the Scriptures clearly teach God's *providence,* as He rules every detail of His universe. As to the first part of this first point — that of general grace — Psalm 65 tells of David praising God, the sustainer of the universe He had created. In this psalm, God visits His earth and waters it. He makes the hills rejoice and clothes the pastures with flocks. Psalm 65 explains that God *cares for His creation.* The psalm praises God's providence in which all His creatures share: the inert sand and seas, all His creatures, with the people whom He had created as the caretakers for His creation. This is a psalm of praise and a shout for joy that God cares for His universe in His righteousness, without a hint of some kind of common grace for reprobated men.

---

20. *Ibid.,* p. 329.

The words of Matthew 5:45 explain what God *does* to the world in His providence. "He maketh his sun to rise on the evil and on the good, and sendeth rain on the just and on the unjust." In His providence He treats all His creatures alike.

Psalm 92 adds a further dimension to God's providence. God's children "show forth thy lovingkindness in the morning, and thy faithfulness every night," verse 2.

However, this psalm also states that for evil men — the unbelievers — there is no grace, not even a common grace, to enjoy His gifts nor to thank Him for all the good gifts of His providence: for "when the wicked spring as the grass, and when all the workers of iniquity do flourish, it is that they shall be destroyed forever," verse 7.

King Solomon, in Proverbs 3:33, goes to the heart of the matter: by divine inspiration he says that when God sends His gifts in His providence, He curses the reprobate evildoers and blesses His chosen ones, for "the curse of the Lord is in the house of the wicked, but he blesseth the habitation of the just."

Asaph, in Psalm 73, had heart-rending problems with the seeming prosperity of those who hated God. Not understanding, for a little while he went even farther than a common grace. He *envied* wicked men, until God showed him how foolish he was; for in the way of His providence, God was sending the prosperous, evil people of this world on a slippery slide to hell: "Surely thou didst set them in slippery places: thou castest them down to destruction," verse 18.

These few quotations demonstrate the strong theme of the stark antithesis between God's chosen people, to whom God has given sovereign grace, and to the children of the devil, to whom God gave none, not even a common grace.

✳   ✳   ✳   ✳   ✳   ✳   ✳

As has been stated, the second part of this point was a heresy with more far-reaching consequences; for the Synod of 1924 found a general offer of the gospel to all people.

The Scriptures never speak of an *offer* to believe and repent, but of a *command:* "God ... commandeth all men everywhere to repent," Acts 17:30. Not all men *do* repent, but their calling still stands. Even when the Scriptures use the terminology of the word "come," it is always with the sense of a *divine command* to come to Him. When Jesus said, in Matthew 11:28, "Come unto me, all ye that labor and are heavy laden, and I will give you rest," He said it in the context of the woes which He had just called down over the unbelieving Jews. These Jews had no grace to heed His call, but they were nevertheless *commanded* to come. Those who obeyed His command were drawn by sovereign, irresistible grace — not by an offer. They were those who knew they were "heavy laden" with sin.

By telling the parable of the wedding feast in Matthew 22:1-14, Jesus further explained that the call to believe and repent comes to *all* men, but not all men answer it.

The king in the parable made a wedding feast for his son. He sent his servants to call men from all areas of his dominion to his feast. This call was the king's command. But the men refused to come to the feast. The explanation of this parable is that all men in God's world — from all areas of life and from every era of history — are *commanded* to come to the wedding feast. But they refuse, for though they have the responsibility and duty to come to Jesus, they cannot, for they are not God's chosen guests. Their responsibility remains, yet they do not have the ability nor the will to obey, for God has not put His grace into their hearts. Jesus explains it with these words: "For many are called, but few are chosen," verse 14. This call is no offer, for Jesus cannot offer a seat at the wedding feast if He has not chosen the man to be there. This parable is an illustration of God's general proclamation of His particular calling.

Jesus further explained why there can be no general offer of the gospel: for "my sheep hear my voice, and I know them, and they follow me," John 10:27. The reason is that they had already been drawn by sovereign grace, "and no man is able to pluck them out of my Father's hand," verse 29.

To those for whom Jesus has no salvation, He does not issue a "general offer of the gospel," but "He hath blinded their eyes and hardened their heart ... that they should not ... be converted, and I should heal them," John 12:40.

These words of Jesus do not nullify God's command that the church must preach the gospel world-wide: "Go ye into all the world, and preach the gospel to every creature," Mark 16:15. God's promise is "that whosoever believeth in him should not perish, but have everlasting life," John 3:16b.

To summarize: In formulating the first point of common grace, the synod began to dig a hole in the garden of Reformed plantings and planted an error there. One error led to another, and the synod had to dig deeper. The initial error was the confusion of providence and grace. The subsequent error became the teaching of a general, well-meant offer of the gospel to all.

※　※　※　※　※　※　※

The second point of common grace reads as follows:

> Relative to the second point, which is concerned with the restraint of sin in the life of the individual man and in the community, the synod declares that there is such a restraint of sin according to Scripture and the Confession. This is evident from the citations from Scripture and from the Netherland Confession, Art. 13 and 36, which teach that God by the general operations of His Spirit, without renewing the heart of man, restrains the unimpeded breaking out of sin, by which human life in society remains possible; while it is also evident from the quotations from Reformed writers of the most flourishing period of Reformed theology, that from ancient times our Reformed fathers were of the same opinion.[21]

In simpler form, the second point may be stated as follows:

---

21. H. Hoeksema, *ibid.*, p. 346.

> Secondly, the theory contains the view that immediately after the fall in paradise, and subsequently through history, a certain operation of grace has entered in whereby sin is retarded in its permeation of the human nature. This grace which does not regenerate a man, nevertheless so rules the mind and will, that that man does not become so corrupted as he would have become without this operation of grace.[22]

The second point was built on the premise of the first point, which teaches that God has a non-saving grace for all non-saved humanity — a certain common grace for all. Having stated this theory of a general, common grace in their first point, the synod followed the logical consequence of this theory in the second point of common grace. In this point there are really three elements.

First, the synod assumed by observing the outward decency and order in the lives of some ungodly people around them that they possess a remnant of natural good in their hearts. Their proof of this decency was the "natural good" which remains in men after the fall in Paradise. The synod offered no Scriptural proof for this "natural good." Neither did synod comment on the Fall and God's words in Genesis 2:12: "...in the day that thou eatest thereof thou shalt surely die."

A second element which synod prepared for this point of common grace is that the Holy Spirit in the heart of the natural, ungodly man, works a restraining operation of a general, not a saving grace, in his heart. The result is that his wickedness is not as great as it would have been without this general grace.

A third element in this point is that the sin of those who are not regenerated by sovereign grace will be slowed down or impeded by the influence of the Holy Spirit in their hearts. Therefore the remnant of good which still is in them will enable them to do some natural and temporal good.

---

22. G. Hoeksema, *Therefore Have I Spoken,* p. 149.

Where did the Synod of 1924 find proof for this general operation of God's Spirit in the hearts of ungodly, reprobate people? They could not find any. They did, however, list seven Scriptural proofs. Three of them are as follows:

> 1.   Psalm 81:11, 12: "But my people would not hearken to my voice; and Israel would none of me. So I gave them up unto their own hearts' lust: and they walked in their own counsels."
> 2.   Acts 7:42: "Then God turned, and gave them up to worship the host of heaven; as it is written in the book of the prophets, O ye house of Israel, have ye offered to me slain beasts and sacrifices by the space of forty years in the wilderness?"
> 3.   Romans 1:24: "Wherefore God also gave them up to uncleanness through the lusts of their own hearts, to dishonour their own bodies between themselves."

Not one of the proof texts which the synod furnished was a proof of a restraint of sin in a non-regenerate man by God' Spirit. The synod was aware that they could find no proof from the Scriptures.   Herman Hoeksema asks and then answers the following about their dilemma:

> But how could synod quote passages that are so evidently in contradiction with its own declaration in the second point?
> It understands the phrase "God gave them up" or "He gave them over" in the sense of "ceasing from restraining them any longer." Thus synod would read all these passages as if they merely signified that whereas God formerly restrained the mad course of the ungodly, He now let them go and allowed them to run their own way to destruction. In this way they arrive at the conclusion that, although these passages do not directly speak of a restraint of sin, they do presuppose such a restraint on the part of God as preceding the moment of the giving up.[23]

---

23. H. Hoeksema, *The Protestant Reformed Churches in America,* p. 364.

If the synod had not been so occupied with proving a restraint of sin based on God's common grace, the delegates would have seen the folly especially of quoting from Romans 1. The gross sinners mentioned in this chapter, whom God describes as objects of His wrath from heaven (verse 18) knew they were rejecting God's law. Their reason was that "they did not *like* to retain God in their knowledge," verse 28.

These evil men knew the huge measures of sin they were piling upon themselves, and they enjoyed their sin, as Romans 1:32 plainly shows: "Who knowing the judgment of God that they which commit such things are worthy of death, not only do the same, but have pleasure in them that do them." In this verse there is not even a hint of God's intervening with a restraint of these sins of the unregenerate sinners in His common grace.

Again, as in their formulation of the first point of common grace, the Synod of 1924 confused providence and grace. In His providence, God not only lets evil men share in the good things He has furnished for His world, but He lets them build fortunes with His goods. He also allows them to lead outwardly moral lives, to train their children in outwardly good behavior, and to live in obedience to the laws of the land. The reason that the unregenerate evildoers advance rather slowly in their *degree* of sin throughout history, and that they are not as evil as they possibly *could* be, is not due to a restraint of sin by common grace in the natural man.

The reason lies in God's eternal plan. Just as God created the natural brilliance of the sun as a contrast to the blackness of a cloudy night, so He created the blackness of sin as the stark background against which the brightness of His salvation shines. God used that figure as a type of the creation of the people on this earth. He created many kinds of people on this earth, and separated them into just two classes: those whom He loves and saves and those whom He hates and rejects.

God created all men outwardly alike. He gave them fairly equal abilities and told them to share His earth. God's created people share everything in His world except grace.

The main theme of the Scriptures plainly demonstrates this: God created an evil Ishmael as the dark background against which Isaac would shine as the covenant child, an ancestor of the Christ. He rejected Esau as the dark figure against which Jacob shone, as the father of the twelve tribes of His covenant people. God purposed that His holy light would shine against a very black background of evil so that His work of salvation would stand out rightly to glorify Him, Who is the only Light.

Therefore the phenomenon of the godless sinner not rushing to his full measure of sin until the time of the end of this world is due to God's sovereign plan of salvation, not to common grace. The Synod of 1924 not only failed to find God's sovereign will with His world; it also lost the sharp line of the antithesis in the Scriptures: the sharp division between God's children, the elected ones, and the children of Satan, those whom God reprobated.

❋   ❋   ❋   ❋   ❋   ❋   ❋

The third point of common grace reads as follows:

> Relative to the third point, which is concerned with the question of civil righteousness performed by the unregenerate, synod declares that according to Scripture and the Confessions the unregenerate, though incapable of doing any saving good, can do civil good. This is evident from the quotations from Scripture and from the Canons of Dordrecht III, IV, 4, and from the Netherland Confession, Art. 36, which teach that God, without renewing the heart so influences man that he is able to perform civil good; while it also appears from the citations from Reformed writers of the most flourishing period of Reformed Theology, that our Reformed Fathers from ancient times were of the same opinion.[24]

---

24. H. Hoeksema, *ibid.*, p. 369.

In simpler form, the third point is stated as follows:

> Thirdly, and closely related to the foregoing point, the theory teaches that by this general operation of grace upon the natural man, he can in the sphere of earthly life do very much that is good. He leads a relatively good life in his earthly sphere and relationships.[25]

The relationship between this point and the other two is that the third point is the inevitable conclusion to the theories in points one and two. The first point teaches that God has a common, general grace for non-regenerate sinners — a certain relationship of friendship with them.

The second point goes further, teaching that by the action of this common grace, the sin of ungodly, unregenerated men is restrained.

The third point takes the final step and states that evil men, apart from sovereign grace, can do positive, civic good. They are not so evil as they otherwise would be.

Two of the five texts which the synod cited are quoted and criticized as follows:

> 1.   II Kings 10:29, 30: "Howbeit from the sins of Jeroboam, the son of Nebat, who made Israel to sin, Jehu departed not from after them, to wit, the golden calves that were in Bethel and that were in Dan. And the Lord said unto Jehu, Because thou hast done unto the house of Ahab according to all that was in mine heart, thy children of the fourth generation shall sit on the throne of Israel."

In the account of Jehu's executing God's commands, in II Kings 10:29, 30, the fact that he obeyed God's commands and did well in executing them is plainly stated in this text. What is *not* stated in this passage is that Jehu did good in God's sight, through an operation of common grace. The synod

---

25. G. Hoeksema, *Therefore Have I Spoken,* p. 149.

again ignored the distinction between Jehu's *outward, formal* accomplishment of God's command, which the Scriptures state, and the carrying out of God's commands by the influence of the Holy Spirit on him, by which he received a certain *common grace* to do good.   Without any Scriptural basis, they pulled common grace out of this text.

> 2.   Luke 6:33: "And if ye do good to them that do good to you, what thank have ye? for sinners also do even the same."

Even on the surface, it will be evident to the reader that Luke 6:33 surely is no proof for common grace.   It is the opposite: a sort of "scratch my back, and I'll scratch yours." Instead of teaching the influence of the Holy Spirit on these reprobate persons, the text portrays their *selfishness*.   There is no mention of a reward, and certainly not a reward of common grace.

From the confessions, the synod chose Canons III, IV, 4 as a proof of the theory that natural men do civic good.

> There remain, however, in man since the fall, glimmerings of natural light, whereby he retains some knowledge of God, of natural things, and of the difference between good and evil, and discovers some regard for virtue, good order in society, and for maintaining an orderly external deportment. But so far is this light of nature from being sufficient to bring him to a saving knowledge of God, and to true conversion, that he is incapable of using it aright even in things natural and civil. Nay, further, this light, such as it is, man in various ways renders wholly polluted, and holds it in unrighteousness, by doing which he becomes inexcusable before God.

This article states the truth that after the Fall the people on earth retained some glimmerings of natural light — the light of reason: they had some knowledge of God and of the earth around them, of the differences between right and wrong and between good and evil.   They had a sense of orderly government, so that God's world could be ruled in decency and good order. They had a sense, at least outwardly — of virtue, an outward morality. They knew what they *ought* to do, even if they were unable because of sin to live it. This article describes the outward and orderly structure — the outward housekeeping — for a sinful, fallen world.

The synod quoted this article of the Canons only half way through, to the word "deportment." They omitted the ending of the article, which states that the natural, unregenerate men pollute even their glimmerings of natural light which God gave them. This article proves the *opposite* of what the synod tried to prove; for it states in so many words that "he (natural man) is incapable of using it aright even in things natural and civil." And the conclusion of this article is that ungodly men are *inexcusable*, not blessed with the glimmerings which God has given them.

When the reader studies these proofs, he will likely come to the conclusion that this was a feeble attempt on the part of the synod to prove that "God, without renewing the heart so influences man that he is able to do civil good." Instead, this attempt proves that evil men do not even do good to one another. The citing of these improbable references leads one to think that the committee of synod which furnished these proofs was desperate for proof of the civil righteousness which the unregenerate sinner can do — and they could not find any.

What, then, is the biblical, Reformed perspective of the relationship between those whom God has chosen in His love to be His children and the unregenerate, natural men whom God has sovereignly rejected? It is a relationship of antithesis between God's people and those who are children of Satan and of sin. The Scriptures teach that to those who are His chosen ones, God gives His sovereign grace. For the children of the devil He has no grace. The synod must have sensed something of this truth, because they prepared a cautionary Testimony. This Testimony reads as follows:

Now synod expressed itself (should be: "Now that synod has expressed itself" — GH) on three points that were at stake in the denial of Common Grace and thereby condemned the entire disregard for this doctrine, she feels constrained at the same time to warn our Churches and especially our leaders earnestly against all onesided emphasis on and misuse of the doctrine of Common Grace. It cannot be denied that there exists a real danger in this respect. When Doctor Kuyper wrote his monumental work on this subject he revealed that he was not unconscious of the danger that some would be seduced by it to lose themselves in the world. And even now history shows that this danger is more than imaginary. And also Doctor Bavinck reminded us of this danger in his *Dogmatics.*

When we consider the direction in which the spirit of the time develops round about us, it cannot be denied that our present danger lies more in the direction of worldly-mindedness than of false seclusion. Liberal theology of the present time really obliterates the distinction between the Church and the world. It is more and more emphasized by many that the great significance of the Church lies in her influence upon social life. The consciousness of a spiritual-ethical antithesis becomes increasingly vague in the minds of many to make room for an indefinite notion of a general brotherhood. The preaching of the Word concerns itself largely with the periphery of life and does not penetrate into its spiritual center. The doctrine of particular grace in Christ is more and more pushed to the background. There is a strong tendency to bring theology into harmony with a science that stands in the service of infidelity. Through the agency of the press and various inventions and discoveries, which as such are, — undoubtedly, to be regarded as good gifts of God, the sinful world is to a great extent carried into our Christian homes.

Because of all these and similar influences, exerted upon us from every side, it is peremptorily necessary that the Church keep watch over the fundamentals; and that, though she also maintains the above mentioned three points, she vindi-

cates the spiritual-ethical antithesis tooth and nail.
May she never permit her preaching to degenerate
into mere social treatises or literary productions.
Let her be vigilant that Christ and He crucified and
risen always remain the heart of the preaching.
Constantly she must maintain the principle that
the people of God are a peculiar people, living
from their proper root, the root of faith. With holy
zeal she must constantly send forth the call to our
people, especially to our youth: "And be ye not
conformed to this world, but be ye transformed by
the renewing of your mind, that ye may prove
what is that good, and acceptable, and perfect,
will of God." With the blessing of the Lord this
will keep our churches from worldly-mindedness,
that extinguishes the flame of spiritual ardor and
deprives the Church of her power and beauty.[26]

This testimony breathes the misgivings and fears which
the delegates at the Synod of 1924 faced when they adopted
the three points of common grace. Although the synod
stated its fears that the fundamental truths of the Scriptures
and the Reformed faith were in danger, they nevertheless
composed, adopted, and retained these three points. In
doing so, they lost the spiritual sensitivity between spiritual
light and the darkness of sin, and between God's chosen
people and the ungodly, unregenerated seed of the devil.

Although it was decided that this Testimony be circulated through all the churches of the denomination, it was
never sent. The clerk of synod was told not to send the
Testimony. It had been "blue-pencilled." Those who lived
in the congregations of Reformed traditions never knew that
they were supposed to have been warned; and the reason lies
buried in history.

For the Christian Reformed denomination it was a tragic
omission of caution. It was an urgent matter that the
members of the Christian Reformed churches realize that

---

26. H. Hoeksema, *The Protestant Reformed Churches in America,*
pp. 90, 91.

these three points were ill-conceived, shallowly reasoned, superficially proved, and hastily adopted. They missed the warning that their denomination was initiating a new unbiblical and unreformed note into the denomination.

The Synod of 1924 inserted a wedge — a spade — in the garden of Reformed plantings, ready to root up the doctrine of sovereign, particular grace, and to replace it with the tares of common grace.

Chapter 6
The Aftermath of the Synod

Now that the Synod of June, 1924, was history, the delegates to the synod — and the members of the Christian Reformed denomination — had time to reflect on the results of that synod: the problems and contradictions which arose almost immediately after the synod had formulated the three points of common grace.

In retrospect, many leaders in the denomination, as well as members in the pews, realized how imperative it was for a synod to work slowly and responsibly when, as the broadest gathering of the denomination, the delegates studied and made new decisions about the doctrines of the holy Scriptures. On the floor of the synod, the Rev. J. Manni had urged caution: not to formulate dogma, but rather to take time to discuss the controversial issue of God's grace throughout the denomination. The synod did not listen to him. Instead, the delegates had formulated and adopted as doctrine for the Christian Reformed denomination the three points of common grace.

Then they back-tracked. First, they formulated the Testimony, a document of caution, which they never sent to the churches. At the end of their meetings, the synod adopted the following ambiguous decisions:

> At the present to formulate no statement relative to the standpoint of the Church regarding the doctrine of general or common grace in every detail and all its implications. Such a statement would presuppose that this doctrine had already been thoroughly considered and developed in all its details, which certainly is least of all the case. Preparatory study, necessary to this purpose, is almost entirely wanting ass yet. Consequently, there is in the Reformed Churches as yet no

61

consensus of opinion at all in this case.

Neither to appoint a committee to devote itself to the study of this matter, in order to reach the formulation of a dogma concerning this matter, which eventually may be received as part of the Confession.[27]

The synod also stated that they were not ready to formulate a dogma:

Because dogmas are not made but are born out of the conflict of opinions, and, therefore, it is desireable that the establishment of a certain dogma be preceded by a lengthy exchange of opinions....

Because a certain truth must live clearly in the consciousness of the Church in general, or in the consciousness of a particular group of churches, before the Church is able to profess such a truth in her Confession ... to urge the leaders of our people, both ministers and professors, to make further study of the doctrine of Common Grace; that they give themselves account carefully of the problems that present themselves in connection with this matter.[28]

The synod concluded these resolutions by stating that "it will, undoubtedly, in the course of a few years, lead to a consensus of opinion in this matter, and thus it will gradually prepare the way in our churches for a united confession concerning Common Grace."[29]

The only conclusion one can come to is that they wanted to promote the doctrine of common grace but at the same time had misgivings about the three points they had just formulated.

The result was that no one was satisfied. Besides leaving the denomination in a quandary of contradictions, the synod had made no decision to discipline Herman Hoeksema and

---

27. *Ibid.*, pp. 92, 93.
28. *Ibid.*, p. 93.
29. *Ibid.*, p. 94.

Henry Danhof if they dissented and disagreed publicly. Nor had they made provisions for the discipline of anyone else who might oppose this doctrine of common grace as unbiblical.

The Reverend I. VanDellen, in an article in the periodical *De Wachter* (*The Watchman*), criticized the synod rather severely for allowing the Reverends Hoeksema and Danhof to preach and teach against common grace. It had not been an oversight of synod, for on the floor of synod Rev. Danhof had told the synod that he would not abide by these three points, but that he would rather oppose them with every means at his command. The synod did not seem to think that there was a cause at this time to discipline the pastor, possibly because the synod had already testified that he and Herman Hoeksema were basically Reformed. The Synod of 1924 left many loose ends. Nothing in connection with their newly-formed dogma had really been settled.

The protesting members of Eastern Avenue Christian Reformed Church wanted their censure by the consistory lifted. These men had not been disciplined for their *doctrinal stand*, but for accusing their pastor of *public sin*. Although it had not entered into this matter of the accusation of public sin, the synod had implicitly upheld Pastor Hoeksema, for that body had given him the testimony that, although he had a tendency to one-sidedness, he was thoroughly Reformed. Yet there could not be two official conflicting evaluations of their pastor in the denomination.

Because the charges of these three members of the Eastern Avenue congregation still stood, and because they would not confess it to be sin, the consistory could not lift the censure of these accusers. The only way out of this stalemate was to appeal this impasse in the Eastern Avenue congregation to Classis Grand Rapids East, which was to meet at the Bates Street Christian Reformed Church on August 20, 1924.

Earlier in the summer, when Classis Grand Rapids East had met shortly before the June Synod, it had decided to advise the Eastern Avenue congregation to lift the censure of the three men who had accused their pastor of public sin. The synod, however, had made no judgment in this matter of public sin. Nor had they condemned the pastor. This broadest gathering of the church did not ask for a confession, nor advise discipline for Hoeksema, but called him a Reformed man.

Because the protesters in the Eastern Avenue congregation persisted with their charges *after* the synod, the consistory sent a letter of information with their delegates to the August classis, giving the history of the problem and describing the growing hostility of these men. The protesters no longer attended the worship services; and the consistory asked the classis that their censure not be lifted as long as the accusation stood, and the three members continued to live in hostility.

At their gathering on August 20, 1924, the classis appointed a committee of pre-advice to meet with the delegates from Eastern Avenue Church in order to gather further background information from the delegates. Although this committee of pre-advice seemed receptive to the briefing of the Eastern Avenue delegates, when they were ready to report to the body of the classis, they advised that the censure of the three protesters be lifted on the grounds that the synod, in its decisions, had sustained the accusations of these three men. The committee of pre-advice had chosen to disregard the information from the delegates from the Eastern Avenue congregation.

In their discussion the members of Classis East leaned toward the advice of their committee. Eastern Avenue's delegates challenged this advice by asking for proof from the official Acts of Synod that their pastor was guilty of public sin. They also reminded the classis that synod had *not* advised discipline for their pastor but had instead attested that his preaching was in harmony with the Scriptures and the confessions.

None of these requests moved the classis to action. It refused all discussion and debate on the ground that the discussions belonged on the floor of *synod*. Just as he had been denied a voice at synod, Pastor Hoeksema was not allowed to speak in his defense at this classis either.

Why did the classis persist in this refusal? Because they were between a rock and a hard place. If they allowed discussion and were persuaded in these discussions that Hoeksema had committed public sin, and then condemned him, they were condemning a preacher whom the synod had not condemned, and against whom nothing had been proved. On the other hand, if the classis condemned the protesters, it would imply that the classis condemned their theology — their newly-formed doctrine of common grace, on which their protests were based. Then the grounds for the denomination's newly adopted doctrine would become untenable. And above all, the classis wanted to hold on to common grace.

Yet the fact remained that they must make some sort of decision, and they did. The classis advised the consistory of Eastern Avenue Church to lift the censure of the protesters as soon ass possible and to admit them to the sacrament of the Lord's Supper. By their decision of siding with the protesters, they implicitly condemned the pastor for public sin. This classis went further than the synod had wanted to go. It acted on the matter of common grace and gave an order which the synod had not been prepared to give.

The Synod of June, 1924, had examined the roots of Herman Hoeksema's biblical and Reformed theology, had struck a tentative spade into the roots of the Reformed plantings of sovereign, particular grace, left it there, and backed off. Classis Grand Rapids East of August, 1924, stamped on the spade and made a deeper cut into the roots.

✳   ✳   ✳   ✳   ✳   ✳   ✳

The consistory of the Eastern Avenue congregation was very disturbed. The decision of Classis East had created a painful and impossible situation for these ruling elders. If they carried out the decision of the classis, they would be compelled to take steps to depose their pastor.

Protests against Herman Hoeksema multiplied because the group which did not agree with their pastor and consistory

had also multiplied. The fact that there were two factions in
the congregation who were working at cross purposes was
now a painful reality. At the consistory meeting of October
23, 1924, a document signed by eighty-six members of the
congregation asking for an early meeting of Classis Grand
Rapids East was presented. This group complained that
they could no longer cooperate with the pastor and consistory.
Their reason was that the pastor and elders had not complied
with the decision of the classis because they refused to
promote the doctrine of common grace.

The consistory, still treating some of the protests, and
now also considering the request for an early classis, was
very busy. Before they could furnish an answer, the protesters made their own plans: they composed a letter to the
classical committee. In their letter of request they also drew
the attention of the committee to a new publication called the
Standard Bearer. The history of this publication goes back to
1922, when the Reverends Danhof and Hoeksema published
a pamphlet titled *Om Recht en Waarheid* (For the Sake of
Justice and Truth). In it they announced their intent to
publish a monthly magazine whose purpose was to develop
not only the truth of God's special grace, but the whole
spectrum of the truth of God's Word.

In this troubled summer of 1924 the members of the
Eastern Avenue congregation who were interested in pub-
lishing a witness to the Reformed truth organized as the
Reformed Free Publishing Association. The first issue of the
Standard Bearer, a successor to their earlier publication, *The
Witness,* came off the press in October, 1924, with the
editorial staff of the Reverends H. Danhof, H. Hoeksema,
and Mr. G. VanBeek, the latter a member of the Eastern
Avenue congregation.

During this summer the consistory of the Eastern Avenue congregation contacted the classical committee and
told them in writing that although there were problems — in
particular a dissatisfied group within the congregation —
they believed that the situation was not critical enough to call
a special session of the classis. The classical committee,

however, listened to the dissidents rather than to the consistory and called an early meeting of Classis Grand Rapids East.

This special meeting of the classis was called to meet in the auditorium of the Neland Avenue Christian Reformed Church on November 19, 1924. Its sessions were open to the public, and at first large crowds attended. These were men and women, and also young people, who were vitally interested in the doctrinal dispute which was disturbing their denomination.

From start to finish this special meeting of Classis East was a strange and atypical session. After the opening exercises, the first item of business was the protest containing the negative reaction of the consistory of the Eastern Avenue congregation to the necessity of this early meeting. If the classis agreed with the consistory that the matter could wait — that a special meeting of classis was not urgent — this classis would not proceed. The classis decided not to sustain the protest of the Eastern Avenue consistory but declared this to be an orderly and legal session of Classis Grand Rapids East.

The next item of business came from the group (which now numbered ninety-two persons) who had protested to the consistory of the Eastern Avenue congregation. Their communication was a combined protest against the consistory and a request for classis, in two separate documents. The Church Order of the Christian Reformed Church insisted that a local consistory be made aware of any protest or request before it was presented to the classis, in order that the consistory might examine it and have time to give its evaluation and answer. At this session of classis the consistory heard for the first time of this combined protest, and they objected to it as improper procedure.

Classis East decided to over-ride their objections and accepted both documents, even though they were aware that it was contrary to the Church Order. Later Herman Hoeksema wrote: "In this protest the 'Ninety-two' declared that the consistory of the Eastern Avenue Christian Reformed Church had severed the tie of affiliation with the denomination of the Christian Reformed Churches, because they refused to submit to the demands of the classis and to abide by the decisions of the synod. Therefore they concluded that they were no longer obliged to acknowledge the consistory of the Eastern Avenue Church as the legal consistory and informed the classis that they considered themselves the true and faithful congregation."[30]

These ninety-two people also asked that this session of classis get help from the faculty of the seminary. Although it is rather common for seminary professors to serve a classis with the broader matters of the denomination as a whole, simply in an advisory capacity, in this situation the classis asked the whole faculty to judge the Eastern Avenue congregation. These professors were asked to give advice on issues of which they had heard only one side, for the two pastors, Herman Hoeksema and Henry Danhof, were not allowed to speak in their own defense.

This meeting of classis was a closed court. Hoeksema and Danhof had no voice at this session. At this strange meeting the faculty and classis made judgments and decisions without allowing a hearing. To make the procedure still more difficult, the advisory professors refused to attend the meetings of the classis. After the classis spent some time pondering this refusal, they accepted the terms of the seminary faculty and adopted the following procedure to make such a situation fairly workable: the committee of pre-advice prepared their report, delivered their opinions in small segments to the faculty at the seminary, and after the professors approved a decision of the committee of pre-advice, someone delivered this decision to the classis meeting at Neland Avenue Church, where they adopted the advice.

As a result, there were no organized meetings, no discussions, and no airing of views on the floor of the classis. It was a silent, extraordinary, and improper classis. Classis Grand Rapids East also ignored the fact that in Reformed church

---

30. *Ibid.*, pp. 143, 144.

polity a session of classis is *advisory*, not *judicatory*. The body of classis may advise, if asked by a congregation, but may not send orders to local congregations to tell them what to do. Article 8 of the Church Order reads:

> No church shall in any way lord it over other churches, no minister over other ministers, no elder or deacon over other elders and deacons.

Therefore it was an unheard-of procedure for a classis to disregard totally the rules under which it functioned.

On the second day of their meeting (November 20) the classis sent a letter to the consistory of Eastern Avenue congregation demanding that their pastor abide by the teachings of the three points of common grace. They asked the consistory to respond by the following morning at nine o'clock. The consistory sent a rather lengthy reply, reminding the classis that it did not have the right to demand this of the consistory. In part, the letter reads:

> 1. The Synod of 1924 treated the protests that were brought against the pastor and finished the matters contained therein. The consistory received no official notification of the Synod that they, the consistory, are called in any way to treat their pastor, neither can anything of the kind be found in the Acts.
> 2. The Synod, through its committee of pre-advice, had before it the proposition to treat the pastor, but rejected this part of the report.

The letter ended by telling the classis that:

> Our pastor will gladly declare that he fully agrees with the confessions of the Reformed Churches, and the Consistory is of the opinion that this is the only demand that can be made upon our minister till this very day.
>
> For all these reasons the Consistory is convinced that the Classis, in its decision to demand of the Consistory that they place their pastor

> before the question whether he fully agrees with
> the three points, goes beyond the decisions of
> Synod. The Classis has no right to do this. The
> Consistory appeals for this opinion to the deci-
> sions of Synod of 1924. The Consistory, therefore,
> kindly and urgently requests Classis not to abide
> by its decision. If Classis should nevertheless
> maintain its decision, the Consistory must protest
> and appeal against the decision of Classis to the
> next Synod.[31]

After more maneuvers and communication, which forced
the classis to recess and re-convene several times, on December 9, 1924, at 9 A.M. Pastor Hoeksema was allowed to read a
final answer from his consistory to the gathering of the
classis now meeting at Oakdale Christian Reformed Church.
This answer was again referred to the silent committee and
the Calvin Seminary faculty.

On December 10 the committee's report was ready. The
brief document monotonously repeated its previous demand that Herman Hoeksema embrace the principles and
teaching of common grace. Now it was the turn of the pastor
and of the consistory to take up the tedious tasks of provid-
ing separate answers. Once more they gave their negative
answers. The pastor, in his letter, went a bit further: he
appealed the matter to the next synod.

For the last time in this strange and silent document
exchange, on the morning of December 11 the classis turned
the matter over to the classical committee and the seminary
faculty; and the classis adjourned until afternoon. After the
classis had heard the reply of the committee, the chairman
complained that Hoeksema was evading the issue, and he
asked — once more — that Pastor Hoeksema answer *yes* or
no on the floor of classis whether or not he would obey this
mandate of the classis.

The pastor told the classis that his answer was in his reply
to the classis, in writing, and that it was a complete and final
answer.

---

31. *Ibid.*, pp. 150-152.

Although the classis up to this moment had allowed politics to govern their procedure and unfair methods of silence and coercion, the members of this classis were not ready to face a separation in the denomination. They urged the pastor that if he could not go against his conscience by preaching common grace, he would promise to be silent on the issue.

Pastor Hoeksema was probably less eager than the classis to face a separation from the denomination; but he could not, in good conscience, be silent on the matter of God's grace, especially after he had preached the beauty of God's sovereign, particular grace through all his ministry.

He did not want a split in the church, with all its difficulties and alienations; but he knew he could not ignore the issue, for this doctrine affected all his preaching and teaching. In fact, it directed the course of his future ministry and the future lives of his parishioners and their children.

He offered a counter-suggestion. He told the classis that he was willing to sit in the seat of a candidate for the ministry again, and take an examination based on the Scriptures and the confessions. If he were found guilty of heresy, the classis could discipline him for heresy. The classis refused his offer. Then they adjourned the meeting.

On December 12, 1924, Classis Grand Rapids East met for the last time. At this last brief meeting, the committee came with the following report:

> 1. That the Reverend H. Hoeksema, in his answer to the question placed before him by the classis, had evaded the issue;
> 2. That in the afternoon session of the classis on December 11 he had refused to answer the classical questions with an unequivocal "Yes" or "No." ...
> 5. That, therefore, he was guilty of insubordination to the proper ecclesiastical authorities;
> 6. That, therefore, he was, by his own act, suspended from his office as minister of the Word of God, for the time being;
> 7. That for the time being and until final determination in the case were made by the Synod, he

should be denied all the rights and privileges connected with the office of a minister in the Christian Reformed Church.

Concerning the consistory, they ruled:

> 1.   That the consistory of the Eastern Avenue Christian Reformed Church had refused to carry out the decision of the classis with respect to the censure of the three members that had accused the pastor of public sin....
> 4.   That, therefore, the consistory was guilty of insubordination to the proper ecclesiastical authorities;
> 5.   That, therefore, by this act the consistory for the time being severed its connection with the Christian Reformed Church;
> 6.   That, for the time being and until final determination in the case was made by the synod, the consistory be denied all rights and privileges connected with the ecclesiastical connection of a consistory with the Christian Reformed Church.[32]

Then, ignoring the rule of the Reformed Church Order on the autonomy of the local congregation — that only a local congregation, with its consistory, has the power to depose its pastor — the classis voted on the committee's recommendation.   With one exception they voted to suspend Herman Hoeksema from the ministry of God's Word in the Christian Reformed denomination. This was a radical departure from their denomination's authorized procedure according to their official church order.

The reason that this was illegal procedure is that the local congregation nominates and chooses its own pastor, ordains him, and has the oversight of its pastor. If the pastor sins and will not repent, his *consistory*, with the advice of a neighboring consistory, may eventually depose him. However, this is usually a long procedure, for the Reformed Church Order

---

32. *Ibid.*, pp. 206, 207.

specifies *two steps* in this process. The first is *suspension*. If a pastor does not repent after his suspension, he may be *deposed*.

Besides, in this case the pastor and his consistory had already appealed the whole matter to the coming synod. According to Article 31 of the Church Order, this appeal must be honored. The article reads as follows:

> If anyone complain that he has been wronged by the decision of a minor assembly, he shall have the right to appeal to a major ecclesiastical assembly, and whatever may be agreed upon by a majority vote shall be considered settled and binding, unless it be proved to conflict with the Word of God or with the articles of the church order, as long as they are not changed by a general synod.

Classis Grand Rapids East followed none of these rules but chose to depose Herman Hoeksema during this session of classis.

The classis did not take its discipline quite so far when it came to judging the consistory of Eastern Avenue. The Church Order speaks clear language about deposing a consistory in one of its congregations, for no classis or synod may lord it over the local congregation. Despite the fact that the classis knew that they were not allowed to depose the consistory, they deposed that body anyway. However, they played with words. The classis did not "depose" the consistory. They used a different wording, as follows:

> And it was further decided to declare that the Consistory of the Eastern Avenue Christian Reformed Church was guilty of insubordination to the proper ecclesiastical authorities and, therefore, had *severed its connections* with the Christian Reformed Church and had forfeited all the rights and privileges of a consistory in the Christian Reformed Church.[33]

---

33. *Ibid.*, p. 207.

In actuality, both consistory and pastor were severed from the denomination by Classis Grand Rapids East on December 12, 1924.

Classis East adjourned without doing any follow-up work. They made no financial provisions for the suspended pastor, nor any arrangements for helpers to oversee and to preach for the Eastern Avenue congregation. The classis left pastor and congregation hanging until they could appeal the matter to the biennial synod of June, 1926. The congregation numbered about four hundred fifty families and needed much pastoral care. What was to be done?

Because the matter had not been finally settled, the consistory of Eastern Avenue decided to go on as usual until the broadest gathering of the denomination spoke.

Soon after Classis Grand Rapids East had adjourned, the classical committee called a meeting of those whom they deemed the faithful congregation of Eastern Avenue — the "ninety-two" and their families. They announced this meeting in the *Grand Rapids Press*. In a meeting at Sherman Street Christian Reformed Church this group was organized as the Eastern Avenue Christian Reformed Church.

Early in January a delegation from this group went to the Kent County Circuit Court to request an injunction requiring the congregation which was meeting in the Eastern Avenue church to show why they should not immediately vacate the building and surrender the property to the group of the "ninety-two."

The consistory soon received a summons to appear in court, in order to determine the property rights. The articles of incorporation of the Eastern Avenue congregation specified that if there was trouble, the group faithful to the denomination kept the property. The congregation pastored by Herman Hoeksema, which was now meeting in the church, understood this.

At the same time they had put in their appeal to the Synod of June, 1926; and they protested that there should be no secular court decision until the Synod of June, 1926, finished the matter.

They presented their reasons in court, and the judge decided as follows:

> 1. That representatives of both sides appear before him at Kent County Circuit Count, where he spoke to both sides. Then he postponed his decision for one week, to give both groups time to get together and make a friendly settlement.
> 2. If, after a week, there was no agreement, the judge ordered them to take turns — each group would occupy the building every other Sunday.

The next day the Supreme Court of the State of Michigan, for some unknown reason, reversed the judge's decision, and ruled that the consistory which had been deposed could keep the building until synod time.

In the garden of Reformed plantings Classis East dug up some of the plantings and was ready to toss them outside the garden, but the classis was forced by the court of the land to let the plantings stay and grow until the synod met. The Lord saw to it that they were temporarily re-rooted until June, 1926.

Chapter 7

Classis Grand Rapids West

The time period from August 20 to December 12, 1924, in the Christian Reformed denomination, when Classis Grand Rapids East met periodically and sporadically, was a period of the testing of the interpretations of the crucial doctrines of God's sovereign grace. It was also a glaring example of the results which followed the neglect of the classis to observe the orderly procedure of their officially adopted Church Order. The whole denomination was highly charged with interest and suspense as the classis met with fits and starts and long recesses; for their spiritual futures would be influenced by the decisions this classis made.

It may seem that because all the communication was done in writing that Classis Grand Rapids East had made decisions in a vacuum. That is not true. The progress of this classis was publicized in the church papers and by the grapevine network through the Christian Reformed denomination, as well as in other Reformed denominations. The secular press was also interested. The *Grand Rapids Press* printed more than sixty news items about the controversy, recording the drama of the dispute about common grace. Two articles about the deposition of Herman Hoeksema state the following:

COMMON GRACE

Grand Rapids has been the center within a year of two Calvinist controversies, the first the fundamentalist dispute over Dr. Fosdick and the verbal inerrancy of the Bible during the Presbyterian general assembly, the second the Christian Reformed split over the doctrine of common grace and Dr. Hoeksema.

The Christian Reformed issue is not that of fundamentalist vs. modernist. It has to do with

the question which of two interpretations of God's
grace to man during his lifetime is fundamental —
whether God maintains an attitude of wrath toward those who have not proved themselves His
elect, so that even the greatest material blessings
showered upon them are merely a curse and all
that they do is sin, or whether He showers His
goodness upon all men, checks or restrains their
sin, and holds the unregenerate capable of doing
good in human relations. In other words, it is a
dispute among fundamentalists.

Among many in other churches who do not
understand the powerful hold of complicated
theology on the minds of members of the Christian
Reformed sect, it will be almost inconceivable that
a great rift could occur through a denomination
over a theological argument on a proposition the
truth of which nothing in this life can settle.

But that would be a superficial observation.
The Christian Reformed Church in America, so
largely centered in Grand Rapids' neighborhood,
concerns itself more seriously with the terms and
interpretations of doctrine than most other denominations. Altering or attempting to add articles of faith is an act affecting immediately the
thinking of hundreds of average church members,
who in many other churches would let the theologians fight it out without knowing what the struggle
was all about, and without having their simple
essential faith disturbed whichever way the decision turned.

Religion, at least it must be said for members
of this church, is no light affair, to be undertaken
with a word or a nod of assent. Its tenets are a
matter of careful study, great earnestness and
understanding for the flock as well as the minister.[34]

The following *Press* article more directly describes the
action of Classis Grand Rapids East.

Classis Grand Rapids East of the Christian Re-

---

34. Undated clipping.

formed Church at a meeting in Creston Wednesday night formally deposed Rev. Herman
Hoeksema, pastor of Eastern Ave. church.

The classis had notified Mr. Hoeksema by
letter of the meeting of a classis committee and
requested his presence to show cause why he
should not be deposed; in other words, that he
might have the opportunity to defend himself.
Mr. Hoeksema sent reply to the committee that in
the notification there were no charges or grounds
why he should be deposed, therefore he refused to
appear and defend himself. Classis East considered a second notification unnecessary because
the consistory already had broken relations with
the Christian Reformed church.

"The consistory is out of the church entirely,"
said Mr. Hoeksema.

...The classis East committee met three times
Wednesday. The committee met again Thursday
morning at 10:30 to discuss minor matters, the
most important to decide whether the denomination desires a special synod meeting to settle the
common grace controversy which split the Eastern Ave. congregation. It is necessary requests
from more than one classis be received before
action is taken.[35]

＊　＊　＊　＊　＊　＊　＊

On January 13, 1925, shortly after the judge's decision
that the group pastored by the Rev. H. Hoeksema would
keep the building until the case was settled at the next synod
which was scheduled to meet in June, 1926, Classis Grand
Rapids West convened. Now the members of the denomination would be watching the second trial concerning the
doctrine of God's sovereign, particular grace. In this classis
were two congregations whose pastors and many of their
parishioners disagreed with the newly adopted theory of
common grace. The two pastors were the Rev. George

---

35. Undated clipping.

Ophoff, pastor of the Hope, Riverbend congregation, north-west of Grand Rapids, and the Rev. Henry Danhof of the First Kalamazoo congregation.

Although there were no protests at this session, there were letters from eight of the congregations in this classis, each with a similar request. This is the way the consistory of the Bethel congregation worded its communication:

> 2. *Bethel.* The consistory of Bethel requests the classis to ask the consistories of Hope and Kalamazoo I whether they have asked their respective ministers to declare themselves in agreement yes or no with the "three points" of the Synod of Kalamazoo. In case this has not been done the consistory requests classis to require of the two aforesaid consistories that they require such a declaration of their respective ministers and requests classis to take all further steps as conditions may demand, that shall guarantee unity of doctrine in our classis and proper submission to the doctrinal deliverance of Synod.
>
> Grounds:
> 1. Ample justification for such a request to minister or consistory is found in the Formula of Subscription.
> 2. The "three points" of Synod are automatically binding on all the ministers of our churches. See Art. 31 of our Church Order.
> 3. The editorial policy of the *Standard Bearer* is that of plain and open insubordination to Synodical authority.
> 4. The peace and unity of the church demanded decisive action in this matter.[36]

Classis Grand Rapids West accepted these requests. The delegates approved the contents of these letters from the eight congregations and acted on them. They also adopted the silent communication similar to the policy which Classis Grand Rapids East had used and sent identical letters to the

---

36. From the type-written copy of the minutes of Classis Grand Rapids West, p. 17.

consistories of both the Hope and the Kalamazoo congregations. The communication to the consistory of Kalamazoo
reads as follows:

> Grand Rapids, Mich., January 16, 1925
> To the Consistory of Kalamazoo I
> Christian Reformed Church:
>
> Dear Brethren:
>   The Classis Grand Rapids West hereby re-
> quires you to require of your minister:
> 1.   That he declare himself unequivocally whether
> he is in full agreement, yes or no, with the three
> points of the Synod of Kalamazoo, *Acts Synod*,
> 1924, Article 132, page 145 to 147.
> 2.   An unconditional promise that in the matter
> of the three points he will submit (with the right of
> appeal) to the Confessional Standards of the Church
> as interpreted by the Synod of 1924, i.e., neither
> publicly nor privately propose, teach or defend
> either by preaching or writing any sentiment con-
> trary to the Confessional Standards of the Church
> as interpreted by the Synod of 1924 and in case of
> an appeal that he in the interim will acquiesce in
> the judgment already passed by Synod of 1924.
> The Classis further requests you to furnish the
> Classis by 10:00 Wednesday morning, January 21,
> 1925, with a definite written answer of your pastor
> to the twofold requirement of the Consistory.
>   Fraternally yours,
>   Classis Grand Rapids West
>   (was signed) W. Stuart, Pres.
>   J.P. Batema, Secretary[37]

Both the pastor, Henry Danhof, and his consistory answered the letter. Pastor Danhof wrote as follows:

> Dear Brethren:
>   I hereby do state and declare unequivocally
> and definitely that I am not in full agreement with
> the three points of Synod of Kalamazoo, *Acta
> Synodi*, 1924, Art. 132, p. 145-146.

---

37. H. Hoeksema, *The Protestant Reformed Churches in America*,
pp. 232, 233.

I hereby further state and declare that Synodical decisions, which according to my sincere conviction are settled and binding, ought not to suffer
violation.

Therefore, if informed correctly, viz.: that
charges of violation of Synodical decisions against
me were brought to the attention of Classis Grand
Rapids West, I hereby implore and request the
Consistory to require of said Classis: —

a.   That either said Classis herself lay such
charges before the Consistory, or that she require
of the plaintiffs to do so.

b.   That such accusations or complaints be
laid before the consistory in unequivocal and
definite language, and in writing.

c.   That your pastor be granted an opportunity to answer such complaint or charges before
the consistory.

Very sincerely yours,
Henry Danhof[38]

The consistory of the Hope, Riverbend congregation sent
a rather lengthy letter to the classis, which ends as follows:

1.   Be it resolved that consistory of Hope Christian Reformed Church do not request its pastor to
answer questions of Classis Grand Rapids West.
2.   To appeal to Synod for the interpretation of its
decision.
3.   To request Classis Grand Rapids West to
defer any and all action said classis might contem-
plate against the consistory of said Hope Christian
Reformed Church until such time as Synod shall
have acted upon said appeal of said consistory of
Hope Christian Reformed Church and rendered
final decision of the matter.[39]

The reason for the negative answers of both pastors and
consistories was the fact that they had not been accused of

---

38. *Ibid.*, pp. 234, 235.
39. The typewritten copy of the minutes of Classis Grand Rapids
West, p. 45.

any heresy or wrongdoing. The whole procedure ended in a stalemate. What was to be done? According to the Church Order, the classis should have appealed the matter to the broader gathering of the denomination — to the Synod of 1926.

What did Classis Grand Rapids West do? The minutes of this session state that the committee of pre-advice recommended the following:

> In consideration of the absolute refusal of Rev. G.M. Ophoff to submit to the requirements of classis in re submission to the doctrinal decisions of the Synod of Kalamazoo and secondly in consideration of his defiant stand and of the strong language used by the brother, and thirdly in consideration of his own statement that he needs no more time to consider and fourthly in consideration of the serious situation that has arisen in our church demanding positive and immediate action over against ceaselessly active propaganda, your committee herewith submits to your honorable body advice that shall lead, if accepted, to final action in the case of Rev. G.M. Ophoff.
>
> Your committee naturally considered the possible advisability of less drastic action at this time, deferring the final steps till a later date. After careful and prayerful consideration, however, your committee sees no good reason why suspension rather than deposition should be advised in this case.
>
> We call the attention of the Classis to the fact that there are but three reasons why suspensions should precede deposition:
> (a) When the facts are not thoroughly known, and suspension is decided on to give time for fuller investigation. This is evidently not the case in the matters now before Classis.
> (b) When there seems to be some hope that time to consider and possibly to repent is desired by the erring brother or can possibly do some good, even if not desired. Your committee feels that in this matter before us, neither is true.
> (c) When the body that has authority to depose is not in session. This is also not the case here, since

the body that has jurisdiction to depose is, according to Art. 79, the classis.

Your committee hereby advises classis to take the following action after preceding prayers.

The Classis Grand Rapids West in session on the 22nd of January, 1925, hereby deposes Rev. G.M. Ophoff from the ministry of the Word and the Sacraments in the Christian Reformed Church of America on the following grounds:

> (a) Insubordination to ecclesiastical authority — See Formula of Subscription — "being ready always cheerfully to submit to the judgment of the Consistory, Classis and Synod under the penalty in case of refusal to be by that very fact suspended from our office."
>
> (b) Public Schism. Art. 80 of the Church Order: "Furthermore, among the gross sins which are worthy of being punished with suspension or deposition from office, these are the principal ones,... *public schism.*"
>
> Through his association with the *Standard Bearer,* Rev. G.M. Ophoff participates in organized propaganda against the officially accepted doctrines of our Church, propaganda which is making inroads upon our denominational solidarity.[40]

After filling sixty-six single-spaced pages of minutes of this session, the classis had deposed not only Pastor Ophoff and his consistory, but also Pastor Danhof with his consistory. Classis Grand Rapids West had no qualms about making judgments and submitting ultimatums. Contrary to the explicit words of the Church Order in Article 84, which reads: "No church shall in any way lord it over other churches, no minister over other ministers, no elder or deacon over other elders or deacons," this classis lorded it over the consistories and individual pastors.

---

40. Type-written copy of the minutes of Classis Grand Rapids West, pp. 49, 50.

No longer did the members of Classis Grand Rapids West consider themselves to be a broader, advisory body whose duty was to deliberate and advise, but they saw themselves as usurpers of power and authority in the hierarchy of the church, to condemn and depose pastors and congregations at will.

Classis Grand Rapids West had taken a look at two parcels in the garden of Reformed plantings and had found the plantings to be too prickly to handle. Without allowing the plantings to blossom until the time of the next synod, this classis bruised these plantings with the rod of hierarchy.

Section Three: BUDDING
Chapter 8
Eventful Years

Three pastors in the Christian Reformed denomination, with their respective consistories, had now been deposed by the Classes of Grand Rapids East and Grand Rapids West. Also the larger portions of the three congregations who opted to stay with their pastors and consistories were outside the fellowship of the Christian Reformed Church, along with their office bearers.

This situation posed a strange, unresolved, and unsettled atmosphere; for although their leaders were technically deposed by the hierarchy of the two classes, they were still members of the Christian Reformed denomination — until the appeal from the Eastern Avenue consistory came to the Synod of 1926. The secular courts had also honored the appeal of the congregation of Eastern Avenue, and had given the congregation temporary use of their church building until the synod made a judgment.

These three congregations—Eastern Avenue, Kalamazoo I, and Hope, Riverbend—were separated from the Christian Reformed Church, but not finally. At the same time they could not be part of the Christian Reformed denomination because their pastors and office bearers had been deposed! How could these congregations function under these strange circumstances?

They made a start on the twenty-ninth of January, 1925, when the pastors and office bearers of the three congregations met at the Eastern Avenue Church to discuss the possibility of forming a unity of these combined consistories. They decided to appoint a committee, which was to report at the next meeting, to be held on March 6. At the March meeting, the pastors and office bearers discussed plans of drawing closer together in their common bonds, which were their belief in God's sovereign, particular grace and their obedience to orderly procedure in the courts of the church, according to their Church Order.

After discussing their unique situation, the representatives of these three congregations decided to form a temporary organization, to tide them over until the meeting of the next synod. They also drew up their *basis* for this organization, and called it their *Act of Agreement.** They decided:

> c.   That we unite as Consistories for the following purposes: (1) To unitedly bring our appeal from the actions of Classes Grand Rapids East and West to the Synod of 1926. (2) To decide on such matters as have reference to the interests of our congregations in common; (3) To decide in all matters that pertain to the furnishing of information and advice to others, outside of our own congregations.[41]

At this meeting they also adopted a temporary name: the *Protesting Christian Reformed Churches.*

Already at the time of this organizational meeting, the members discussed a plan of outreach. The reason for this early planning was the avid interest shown by many congregations in the Christian Reformed denomination. The three pastors had received several invitations from various states in which Christian Reformed churches were located. The first requests for lectures came from Iowa, Wisconsin, and Illinois. The members of the Protesting Christian Reformed Churches delegated the Rev. Hoeksema to lecture in congregations in these three states.

Because the Hull congregation in Sioux County, Iowa,

---

*   Note: For the entire *Act of Agreement* see the appendix, p. 355.
41. H. Hoeksema, *The Protestant Reformed Churches in America,* p. 251.

sent the most urgent request to the Protesting Christian Reformed Churches in Grand Rapids, the association sent Rev. Hoeksema first to Hull. Mr. William Verhil, who later became a pastor in the Protestant Reformed Churches, went along with him, primarily to promote the *Standard Bearer.* They stayed in Hull for three weeks. At the end of their visit, forty families were organized as a Protesting Christian Reformed Church.

The next Protesting Christian Reformed Church was organized in Waupun, Wisconsin, in May, 1925. However, the members of the congregation soon discovered that they had acted impulsively. They turned to mysticism and disowned the Protesting Christian Reformed Churches.

Although the appeal of the three deposed pastors and consistories was in limbo until June, 1926, the reality of the situation in the Christian Reformed denomination was that the two groups were speedily pulling apart. They no longer had a common ground for unity; and both sides recognized the widening of the rift. Although the appeal of the Protesting Christian Reformed Churches had not yet come to the Synod of the Christian Reformed Churches in reality, each group already lived a separate ecclesiastical life.

The group pastored by the deposed ministers recognized the reality of the fact that the Christian Reformed Church in its broadest gathering was not going to change its position on their adopted dogma of common grace. By honestly facing the rift which was already present in the denomination, the deposed pastors knew that the breach would not be healed, even though they were determined to try for justice in the broader ecclesiastical court one more time.

It was during this hiatus, however, that letters kept coming from various areas of the country asking for more information, for lectures and preaching. The letters showed the intense interest of many groups in the denomination to understand the doctrine of God's sovereign grace. For the three pastors this interest meant that they needed more workers in the field of God's kingdom. They needed ministers!

The only way to get these ministers was to train them. The Reverends H. Danhof, G. Ophoff, and H. Hoeksema started basic seminary training courses for eight students who enrolled. For a start they taught the languages: English, Dutch, Greek, and Hebrew, along with Old and New Testament Exegesis, Dogmatics, and Homiletics. Later they would add more disciplines.

＊　＊　＊　＊　＊　＊　＊

According to the ruling of the Circuit Court of Kent County the group faithful to the denomination would be granted the Eastern Avenue Church property, with the following provision: that the Protesting Christian Reformed Churches keep it until the appeal to the Synod of 1926.

The group faithful to the denomination had appealed this decision to the Supreme Court of Michigan. They wanted to occupy the building immediately. Suddenly, without any previous private notice, on Tuesday, December 22, 1925, the day of the winter solstice, the news was published in the *Grand Rapids Press* that the Supreme Court of Michigan had sustained the verdict of the Circuit Court of Kent County. This decision meant that the Supreme Court reversed itself after studying this latest appeal. (See page 75.)

In the January, 1926, issue of the *Standard Bearer,* Editor H. Hoeksema wrote on page 118, "Most of our readers are, no doubt, by this time acquainted with the fact that the long expected decision of the Supreme Court of Michigan in re the property of the Eastern Ave. Church was rendered. To many it will also be of interest to read the opinion of the court in the matter and become acquainted with the grounds on which the opinion is based. For that reason we here publish it."

Then follows a long legal document, one paragraph of which reads:

> In the freedom of conscience and the right to
> worship allowed in this country, the defendants
> and the members of this church undoubtedly

possessed the right to withdraw from it, with or without reason. But they could not take with them for their own purposes, or transfer to any other religious body, the property dedicated to and conveyed for the worship of God under the discipline of this religious association; nor could they prevent its use by those who choose to remain in the church, and who represent the regular church organization. If complainants maintain the allegations of their bill — that they represent the regularly organized body of the church, and are its regular appointees — they are entitled to the relief prayed.[42]

This decree meant that the Supreme Court of Michigan gave the possession of the building to the group faithful to the Christian Reformed denomination. The deposed pastor and consistory and congregation had lived with the impression that they would keep the use of the building until the following July, when their protest was to be treated by the broadest body of the denomination. Suddenly they read in the newspaper that they had no meeting place; and Friday, three days away, was Christmas Day!

After thinking about the published decision in the newspaper, however, Pastor Hoeksema and his consistory were not unduly alarmed, for they had no official notice as yet. They would have time to look for another meeting place and time for making some long-range plans. They would prepare themselves to be ready when the official notification arrived. They reasoned that they had a little time to prepare. With the Christmas holidays so close, it would be difficult to make a sudden move; and the court would take this situation into consideration. As it turned out, the official decree was not issued until several weeks later.

But Reverend Hoeksema and his consistory were too optimistic. The group faithful to the denomination abruptly

---

42. "Opinion of the Supreme Court," *Standard Bearer,* Vol.. 2, p. 119.

interrupted all their plans and their peace of mind. These people would not wait until the verdict was officially issued in an orderly manner. Immediately "they hired deputies and broke into the buildings, supplied windows and doors with new locks, and stationed their deputies in the basement of the church to guard against an attempt to recapture the church by violence."[43]

The group pastored by Rev. Hoeksema, which to the present time had been the Eastern Avenue congregation, was forced to find another meeting place immediately; and in God's goodness, they found that the Franklin Community House in Franklin Park, near the corner of Fuller Avenue and Franklin Street, not very far from Eastern Avenue Church, was available. Many of the members of the congregation who volunteered to help get the Community House ready for the Christmas service carried folding chairs and materials for a temporary pulpit through the uneven terrain and the snow of Franklin Park. Although their accommodations were far from ideal, their spirits were joyful.

They had a reason for happiness. This congregation was in its first love: the love of the close ties of those who were experiencing the trials of a reformation in the church and the joys of the pure preaching of the Word of God.

The ousting of Pastor Hoeksema, the consistory, and the congregation had taken place a half year before the Synod of the Christian Reformed Church was to meet and where they would treat the appeal of the deposed pastor and consistory. However, by the time the June Synod was constituted, the group had six months of existence outside the denomination.

Most of the minutes of the church courts were still in the Dutch language at this time. In the *Acta der Synode* (the Acts of Synod) which met in June, 1926, are two very brief notations about the rift in the denomination. Translated, they read:

---

43. H. Hoeksema, *The Protestant Reformed Churches in America*, pp. 259, 260.

5.   Protest from the consistory of the "Eastern Avenue Protesting Christian Reformed
Church" against the resolution of Classis G.R.
East as to the lifting of the censure imposed on
three brothers.[44]

Three pages later, along with other protests in the same
category, the synod gave its decision about the admissibility
of this document of protest. They listed two reasons why
they refused:

a)   These protests are not addressed to the
synod.
b)   The protesters of these weighty matters
are outside our denomination. This advice was
accepted.[45]

The break with the Christian Reformed denomination
was final. The congregations of the Protesting Christian
Reformed Churches, with their pastors, were now a separate
denomination. The pastors and members of these three
congregations had anticipated this decision of the synod,
especially since the previous December, when the Eastern
Avenue congregation had been forcefully put out of its
church building.

While this congregation met temporarily in other meeting places, among which was the St. Cecilia building, near
downtown Grand Rapids, they had been making plans for a
new church building. They started to look for property
immediately, and soon bought a lot on the corner of Fuller
Avenue and Franklin Street. Very soon they broke ground
and workmen started excavating by leading teams of horses
through the snow-covered, frozen soil to dig a foundation.
By the first Sunday of April, 1926, the basement of the church

---

44. *Acta der Synode* van de Christelijke Gereformeerde Kerk,
1926, p. 110.
45. *Ibid.*, p. 113.

was finished far enough so that the members of the congregation could worship there.

In November of the same year the combined consistories of the three Grand Rapids area congregations met to organize a classis, to choose a name officially, and to define the basis for the new denomination. From the two choices — *Reformed Protestant Churches* or *Protestant Reformed Churches* — they chose the latter. They declared their doctrinal basis to be the Three Forms of Unity and the Church Order of Dordtrecht. Herman Hoeksema commented on the bases of this federation of churches as follows:

> The name Protestant Reformed Churches was adopted. By this name the churches meant to express that they stand on the basis of the Reformed Churches of the Reformation of the sixteenth and seventeenth centuries, officially adopt the Reformed Standards as their basis of unity and are devoted to the maintenance and positive development of the Reformed truth as embodied in those Standards.[46]

Exactly one year after the congregation had been forced from their church building on Eastern Avenue, on December 22, 1926, this same congregation dedicated the building of the First Protestant Reformed Church on the corner of Fuller Avenue and Franklin Street. Because so many of the members at that time still used the Dutch language, the program that evening was entirely in the Dutch language. On the next evening the dedication was in the English language.

> There was an enthusiasm among the leaders and laymen which was infectious and which made both the speakers and the listeners more effective. These were days of rebirth, of re-dedication, days of a first love.[47]

---

46. H. Hoeksema, *The Protestant Reformed Churches in America,* p. 278.
47. G. Hoeksema, *Therefore Have I Spoken,* p. 163.

Next door to the church, a large brick parsonage was being built. Soon Pastor Hoeksema was able to leave his interim rented house on Sherman Street and move with his family into the manse next to the church.

Although the Lord blessed this new denomination by giving them a large church building along with the pure preaching of the gospel, this joy was tempered by internal trouble for a short time.

The three Danhofs — the Reverends Henry, and his nephews Ralph and also student Ben — had become disillusioned, dissatisfied, and troublesome. Although these men met with the other pastors and had their parts in the decision-making, their problem was personal jealousy, especially of the leadership of Herman Hoeksema. In view of these personality conflicts these two pastors and the student decided to withdraw from the newly established Protestant Reformed Churches. Already on the November evening on which the denomination of the Protestant Reformed Churches was instituted, they had left the group. An appointed committee held many meetings with them to try to resolve the trouble, but the Danhofs separated themselves and went their independent ways. The Rev. H. Danhof's congregation in Kalamazoo became an independent congregation. Some years later the group went back to the Christian Reformed Church and became Grace Christian Reformed Church.

At the same time, this rift caused an emptiness and a sadness to the new denomination, and especially to Pastor Hoeksema, who was a close friend of Henry Danhof. Writing about this period of history, he said: "Always there is bright sunshine and there are gloomy shadows."[48]

The "bright sunshine" was the joy that many Reformed people, from various areas of the country, sent calls for help

---

48. H. Hoeksema, *The Protestant Reformed Churches in America*, p. 257.

and instruction. This instruction took the form of lectures, preaching, and extra copies of the new monthly magazine, the *Standard Bearer*.[49] In the year 1926, as a result of the outreach of the Protestant Reformed denomination, six congregations were organized: Byron Center, south of Grand Rapids; Roosevelt Park (now called Southwest) in Grand Rapids; Hudsonville, Michigan; Doon and Sioux Center in Iowa; and South Holland, Illinois.

In the year 1927 some of the members of the congregation in Kalamazoo, Michigan, of whom the Reverend H. Danhof was pastor, left his congregation and were organized as a Protestant Reformed congregation. Other new Protestant Reformed congregations established in that year were Oak Lawn, Illinois; and three congregations in Iowa: Rock Valley, Pella, and Oskaloosa.

The Holland, Michigan, congregation was organized in 1929 with eleven families. Their first meeting place was a bakery, from the floors of which they often had to scrape dough before they could have services. The members said they did not mind.

Many other of the new Protestant Reformed congregations struggled to provide adequate temporary meeting places until they were able to build their own church buildings. But their love for the sound, biblical preaching which they heard each Sabbath more than compensated for less than ideal meeting places. All the newly-organized congregations seemed to have the enthusiasm of a first love — of a unity and harmony in the preaching and teaching of the pure truths of the Scriptures.

In His garden, the Lord supplied His bruised plantings with the rain of the knowledge of His sovereign grace. He gave His sunshine in the rays of joy which followed the

---

49. This magazine was, and is to the time of this writing, published by a group of people in the denomination: the Reformed Free Publishing Association. The Protestant Reformed Churches have never had an official church magazine.

experience of that grace. The Lord gave the Reformed plantings a time to bud and to spread.

Chapter 9
Early Expansion

During the decades of the 1930s and 1940s, the Protestant Reformed Churches came of age. The churches had outgrown their infancy and advanced to the period of growing up; and these two decades were broadly the period of the maturing of the Protestant Reformed Churches. The congregation of First Protestant Reformed Church now numbered almost five hundred families.

Most of the congregations organized in these decades were formed as the direct results of the controversy of 1924. The members of the Christian Reformed denomination who were interested in further instruction in the Reformed doctrine of the grace of God asked for information: they asked for the writings, the teachings, and the preaching from the Protestant Reformed denomination. The problem in this young and small denomination was the lack of ministers to do this work. Until the denomination had more trained ministers, the leaders had to shoulder double loads. During the beginning of this period — in the early 1930s — the consistory of First Protestant Reformed Church released the Reverend Herman Hoeksema for temporary periods to answer calls for help from various areas of the country. As Protestant Reformed churches were organized, at times Hoeksema had the help of another Protestant Reformed pastor who lived in the general area to which he was called.

While working in a mission field (probably better stated as church extension area) Pastor Hoeksema did his work as he did everything else in the various spheres of his life — intensely. During his stay of five or six weeks he usually spoke some twenty to thirty times, preaching and giving lectures and conducting informal meetings for instruction.

99

Sometimes during that short period of work it was possible to make plans to organize a congregation. The reasons were that the people who had asked for help were already acquainted with the controversial issues and had studied them. Now they wanted to live from the principles of sovereign grace. The people in these areas felt drawn to the biblical and Reformed exposition of the doctrine of God's grace. They were *eager* to listen. Most of them also subscribed to the *Standard Bearer* and had read and digested the issues of controversy. Often the people who asked for help had already made up their minds to be organized as a Protestant Reformed congregation.

In 1932 the congregation of Creston, in northwest Grand Rapids, and Redlands, California, were organized. In 1934 Orange City, Iowa, was organized, along with Los Angeles, California. The congregation of Los Angeles later disbanded. The organization of the Bellflower, California, and Grand Haven, Michigan, congregations, followed in 1935 and 1936.

Although Pastor Hoeksema gladly admitted that his church extension work was inspiring and rewarding, he knew his calling was to be the pastor of five hundred families — no mean task, even without his church extension jaunts. Besides, at times his family called themselves "missionary orphans."

The denomination started to see the need for a full-time home missionary; and in 1931 the Mission Committee of the Protestant Reformed denomination was organized. At first this committee worked with the board of the Reformed Free Publishing Association to promote the distribution of the publications of the denomination. Then in 1936, the mission committee called its first home missionary: the Rev. Bernard Kok. His first call for help was from Edgerton, Minnesota; and in 1938 the group was organized as a Protestant Reformed congregation.

A congregation in Randolph, Wisconsin, very small at first, was organized through the work of the mission committee, who sent pastors from the Grand Rapids area to instruct the people there and to preach for them. An article written by the Rev. M. Schipper, a member of the mission committee, describes these efforts:

> On the evening of August 17th, 1943, another congregation was added to our Protestant Reformed Denomination. In the neat little Congregational Church building of Randolph, Wis. where our Mission Committee had sponsored services for over a year, eight families were organized into a congregation.
>
> Small indeed is the beginning of this little group, but we believe there is promise that this new addition to our Churches will grow and ripen into a stalwart in our ranks....
>
> We congratulate you, sister congregation at Randolph, and welcome you into the fellowship of our churches. May the Lord prosper you in the way of faithfully living the truth you have learned to love, and shall be called upon to continually profess in your community.[50]

These fast-sprouting and budding congregations in the early history of the Protestant denomination needed pastors; and they would soon have them; for the leaders had already started some theological training of interested young men in the summer of 1925. At first Herman Hoeksema, George Ophoff, and Henry Danhof were instructors. After Henry Danhof left, Hoeksema and Ophoff handled the load of instruction. These men realized the importance of training their own ministers immediately, for they understood that a denomination cannot continue without its own source of ministers.

Gerrit Vos and William Verhil were two of the earlier students who had attended classes in 1925. Because the needs in the newly-organized churches in Iowa were so urgent, the seminary released these two men temporarily — before they had completed all their seminary work — to the

---

50. "Randolph Organized," *Standard Bearer,* Vol. 19, Sept. 1, 1943, p. 493.

congregations of Hull and Sioux Center, Iowa. These men finished their training later, after some of the other students in the seminary had graduated and could take their places in the pastoral ministry.

The students made it known that they enjoyed their seminary training with the two ministers, Herman Hoeksema and George Ophoff, as instructors; and the two professors were fast and loyal friends even though they were completely opposite in appearances and natures.

Herman Hoeksema was organized, concise, logical, and orderly in his life; and his teaching in the seminary reflected these characteristics.

On the other hand, George Ophoff's large physique invited the students to call him "the lumbering giant." A ponderous man, with flowing white hair, he was not interested in the fine details of life, such as spotless ties, knife-creases in his trousers, or being on time. This man of great talents was also absent-minded and seemingly unaware of his picturesque language unique humor. His students called him "guile-less," and he was always unsuspecting of their pranks. In fact, a legacy of these pranks is still living at the time of this writing.

A man with intelligence and vision, he was totally dedicated to the cause of the preaching of the truth of the gospel. He was a loyal minister — sincere and dedicated to the cause of the pure preaching of the Word of God from the pulpits of the denomination.

In 1929 the first class of six students had graduated. Now the students Vos and Verhil could come back to school and complete their training. After these two men graduated, the small Protestant Reformed denomination could boast of ten pastors — two of them functioning also as instructors, and eight of them having received their theological education in the basement rooms of First Church!

The curatorium, or board of trustees, had the oversight of the theological school. This body met when the classis of the denomination met — three times a year. They also conducted the examinations of these new candidates.

It is important to note that all of the growth and development in the early life of the new Protestant Reformed denomination took place during the great depression of the 1930s. The severity of the depression changed people's lives, and people from every area of life were affected. There were no available jobs, and most people had little or no money. Even though a loaf of bread in these years cost only ten cents —eight cents on special—it was a struggle for many families to get enough for their families to eat. People in these years lived with the tensions of trying to obtain the bare essentials of surviving.

Because they had scarcely enough to live, it was a struggle for God's people to support their churches and Christian schools. The church budget in those lean days was one dollar per week, but many families did not have that dollar.

The Christian schools also suffered. Tuition was two dollars per week per family, whether that family had one child in school, or six. Many could not scrape up those two dollars. A support organization called the C.S.B.A. (Christian School Benevolent Association) distributed pint ice cream cartons to help collect the nickels and pennies of the congregation, so they could give to those who were not able to pay their two dollars per week tuition.

Besides being a struggle, life was *simple* in the decade of the thirties. Because they did not have and could not get the luxuries of life and because life was a severe struggle against poverty, the priorities, particularly of God's people, were changed. It has always been true in history, and it was true in this period of history, too, that when God's people live in abject poverty, the result is that they have a vital interest in spiritual realities. The luxuries of this earth do not seem very important. In the Protestant Reformed congregations during this period of the depression, the members showed a hearty dedication to the truths of God's Word, particularly of His sovereign grace, during their trials; and they were diligent to teach these truths to their children.

During these years of the Great Depression, which were also the years of the development of the Protestant Reformed denomination, the Christian Reformed Church gave them the silent treatment. For the most part they ignored the new denomination and refused to recognize its existence. In their church magazines they paid little or no attention to the Protestant Reformed denomination and flatly refused to discuss any doctrinal issues.

Also in the decade of the Great Depression, and strange as it may seem, among the Hollanders who had immigrated from The Netherlands as early as the turn of the century, many held to their native language. Even in the latter part of the 1930s there were still distinct "Dutch" areas in cities such as Grand Rapids, Los Angeles, and also Chicago. These people, from the same cultural backgrounds, settled in the same areas, even to the degree that the various *provinces* from The Netherlands were transplanted in the United States. For example, in Grand Rapids there were distinct areas: *de Groninger buurt,** de Drente buurt,* and *de Zeelanders.*

In most of the churches the Dutch language was predominant. First Church in Grand Rapids had two Holland and two English services each Sunday. Some of the smaller congregations conducted services only in the Holland language.

Slowly, toward the end of the decade of the 1930s, as the hardships of the Great Depression lessened, the native Dutchmen started to move toward their adopted culture and language of the United States. One of the younger pastors, eager to prove his point that the Dutch immigrants — some of them second generation — must drop their native language, gave his congregation a lesson.

In many of the congregations the young children still learned the answers to their catechism questions in the Dutch language, even though they did not understand what they were learning. They merely memorized rote answers, which they did not comprehend. When the pastor deliberately put the catechism questions out of sequence, and asked

---

*   neighborhood

a young boy, *"Wie heeft de hemel and aarde gemaakt?"*** he had the prompt answer: *"Moses en Aaron!"*

That was the end of teaching the young children rote answers which they did not comprehend. From then on that congregation had catechism in the English language. And the other churches in that denomination soon joined them.

However, the ties to their native land were still strong among the immigrants of Reformed backgrounds. At the same time, the decade of the 1930s was a period of transition, a period which often caused struggles in the congregations. Near the end of the decade the writings in the *Standard Bearer* were still at least fifty percent Dutch; some enjoyed the dual languages and some bemoaned them.

During this decade of the thirties, the members of the Protestant Reformed Churches were still Netherlands-oriented. Many of these were first-generation immigrants, who were also leaders in the denomination. Because almost all of the members of the Protestant Reformed Churches at that time were of Dutch ancestry and had carried their ecclesiastical backgrounds with them across the ocean, they still had an interest and concern for the Reformed churches in their homeland across the sea.

During the common grace controversy, and later when their small group was organized as the Protestant Reformed Churches, the leaders wanted the theologians and the churches in The Netherlands to understand and evaluate this doctrinal dispute in the states. All the writings of those years, which included the *Standard Bearer* and the polemic brochures criticizing common grace and the offer of the gospel, were faithfully sent to The Netherlands. The Protestant Reformed Churches wanted their friends in the homeland to understand the doctrinal position of their denomination, and to be recognized as Reformed churches, true to the doctrines of the sixteenth-century reformation.

The mother churches in The Netherlands paid close

** "Who made the heaven and the earth?"

attention to the writings of their daughter churches in the states. During the decade of the 1930s, the pastors and theologians in The Netherlands reviewed books and the *Standard Bearer* articles written by Protestant Reformed men; and some of the Dutch leaders were very sympathetic to the Protestant Reformed Churches. They publicly recognized that their daughter churches were Reformed.

One more aspect of the correspondence between the Protestant Reformed Churches in America and the Reformed Churches in The Netherlands during this decade was the keen interest of the Protestant Reformed Churches in the theological developments overseas at this time. In their magazine, the staff of the *Standard Bearer* wrote about the current theological issues in The Netherlands and analyzed them for the benefit of the Protestant Reformed Churches and also for the benefit of their friends overseas.

Since the birth of the Reformed Church in The Netherlands, there had been two wings: the Reformation of the *Afscheiding* of 1834 which had been led by Hendrick DeCock, and the *Doleantie* of 1886-7, led by Abraham Kuyper. (See page 4.) Each wing supported a theological school. Dr. V. Hepp was the professor of dogmatics at the Free University of Amsterdam, which was the theological school developed from the Secession of 1834. Dr. K. Schilder, a scholar well-known not only in The Netherlands, but also in other countries, was the professor of dogmatics at the Free University at Kampen, the school developed from the Doleantie of 1887.

During the 1930s the professors at the University of Kampen began the development of a Christian philosophy of life; but the five ideas of this development of a Christian philosophy of life led to conflict in the Reformed churches in The Netherlands. Dr. Hepp from the *Afscheiding* did not agree with this philosophy of the men at Kampen, and he objected in writing. Soon a pamphlet war started. Strikingly, the two main issues in this dispute were *common grace* and the *covenant of grace*, the issues with which the Protestant Reformed Churches had recently struggled and which had led to their organization as a separate denomination.

These were not official disagreements in The Netherlands. The issues were being studied and criticized infor-
mally as yet. The disagreement was still at the discussion
stage.

Then in 1936, at the General Synod of the Reformed
Churches of The Netherlands, and without previous notification, the synod took these five matters, made statements
about them, and made them official doctrines of the churches.
A committee was appointed to study these decisions and
decide whether the synod's elevation of these matters to
official status was proper.

At that time the Dutch synods met every three years. At
the next synod — in 1939 — the delegates made no decision
on the propriety of the decisions they had made at the Synod
of 1936.

Then came the rumblings of World War II. Soon the
Lowlands were overrun by the Germans. Although a synod
was held in 1942 — in the middle of the war — and a report
of the study committee came to this synod, the delegates did
not act on it. These were the days of the German occupation,
which eclipsed the whole of their lives. Finally, near the end
of the war, in 1944, they took a decision on these issues,
which led to a split in the Dutch churches.

This synod took decisions on the covenant of grace and
the doctrine of baptism with which Dr. Schilder, the professor from the Free University at Kampen, disagreed; and he
and his followers organized themselves as the *Liberated
Churches.* This division in the churches would have far-
reaching results in the next decade, also in America.[51]

Back in the year 1939, at the time of impending war in The
Netherlands, and also at the time of the beginning of the
doctrinal conflict in the Reformed Churches in The Netherlands, Dr. Schilder had made a trip to the United States. This
visit was sponsored by a Mr. Hamstra from New Jersey and

---

51. The doctrinal history of this controversy will be treated in the
next chapter.

Mr. William Eerdmans of Eerdmans Publishing House. It was Dr. Schilder's intention — and the purpose of his visit — to lecture and to preach in the Christian Reformed Churches in America. The Christian Reformed Church and the Reformed Churches of The Netherlands had been sister churches in full correspondence for many years. Dr. Schilder was fully confident that the pulpits of the Christian Reformed Churches would be open to him.

Dr. Schilder's confidence was misplaced. The leaders in the Christian Reformed Church were very much afraid that Dr. Schilder might say something which would be contrary to their interpretation of common grace. At the same time they must have remembered that in 1887 Dr. A. Kuyper had spoken and written about "gemeene gratie," a "general grace." They knew, too, that Dr. Kuyper's concept of a general, or common, grace was different from the interpretations in the three points of 1924. Dr. Kuyper, in the preface of his book, explains:

> Among the virtues of God is His forbearance which in this "general grace" is never exhausted, but in a forceful way glorifies God.... For because the Lord is our God, not only holy, but in His holiness is *patient*, it is from this patience (or forbearance) with which the godly patience of the Almighty bears their sins *in time*, that the term "general grace" was born.[52]

This concept of a "general grace" as God's "bearing with the wicked in time" is really related more closely to the concept of God's *providence* and does not have a resemblance to the common grace of 1924.

On the basis of their church relationships — for Dr. Schilder was a minister in the mother church of the Christian Reformed denomination — and on the basis of their Re-

---

52. Abraham Kuyper, *De Gemeene Gratie,* Vol. 1, Amsterdam, Hoveker & Wormser, 1902, p. 6, (translated from the Dutch).

formed beliefs and confessions, all the pulpits of the Christian Reformed Church should have been open to Dr. Schilder. However, the editors of their official denominational magazines, *De Wachter* and *The Banner,* bluntly advised their readers to boycott Dr. Schilder. They knew he was a Reformed man, a sharp polemicist, and a capable fighter. They did not dare risk his tongue and his pen.

The reason that the leaders in the Christian Reformed Church boycotted Dr. Schilder was that they were afraid that he agreed with the doctrines of the Protestant Reformed Churches. He did not agree initially. In exchanges of *De Reformatie* and the *Standard Bearer* across the ocean, the two editors, Schilder and Hoeksema, found that they were not in total agreement.

After the Christian Reformed Church spurned him, the Protestant Reformed Churches invited Dr. Schilder to lecture in their churches. They publicized their invitations. The Protestant Reformed denomination also assured him that he was free to state his doctrinal convictions.

The boycott which the Christian Reformed Churches imposed did not succeed, especially in the Grand Rapids area. Many members, and even leaders of the church, admitted that they were ashamed; and several Christian Reformed congregations invited Dr. Schilder to preach and to lecture. Large audiences listened to him — in the Dutch language, of course.

On the evening on which Dr. Schilder lectured in First Protestant Reformed Church (which seated twelve hundred people), the auditorium was quickly filled. The ushers then put chairs wherever they could find room, even on the platform; and the lecture committee had provided speakers for the overflow audience in the church basement.

Excerpts of Editor Hoeksema's evaluation of this lecture are as follows:

> First of all it may be said without fear of
> contradiction, that the view of common grace, as
> presented in Dr. Schilder's lecture, differs on

important points from that of the Christian Reformed Churches as expressed in the "Three
Points."

First of all, and this is the main point, Dr.
Schilder denies that one may conclude from the
fact, that the ungodly have many things in common with the godly, to a gracious disposition in
God toward the ungodly.

To my mind, this is the very heart of the
question. It certainly is the very heart of the First
Point of 1924.

Secondly, when Dr. Schilder speaks of "offer," "aanbod," it is very evident that he means
something quite different from "the well-meaning
offer of grace on the part of God to all" of which the
Christian Reformed Churches speak.... To them
also this "offer" is proof of the gracious disposition in God to all that hear the gospel. To Dr.
Schilder it means no such thing.

Thirdly,... when Dr. Schilder speaks of restraint of sin, and also of grace, he has in mind
something quite different from a general operation of the Holy Spirit outside of regeneration in
virtue of which the natural man is enabled to do
good in this world....

I feel that in substance I can agree with the
main thoughts of Dr. Schilder's lecture. There are,
indeed, differences. I would not speak of common
grace at all; he still does.[53]

The leaders, and also the laymen, of the Protestant
Reformed Churches began to have personal contact with Dr.
Schilder. He was a personable and attractive man; and as a
result of this pleasant contact, all the Protestant Reformed
ministers were invited to a conference held in the manse of
First Church, with Pastor Herman Hoeksema as host.

Among the doctrinal issues they discussed was, of course,

---

53. "Dr. Schilder's Lecture on Common Grace," *Standard Bearer*,
Vol. 15, March 1, 1939, p. 245.

the issue of common grace, particularly as it affected the birth and the development of the Protestant Reformed Churches. As they discussed, Dr. Schilder volunteered that the ministers of the Protestant Reformed Churches, and their Reformed stance made a favorable impression on him.

It may be that Dr. Schilder told his friend, Mr. William Eerdmans, his impression of the Protestant Reformed leaders. At any rate, in April of 1939 Mr. Eerdmans brought up the idea of having a large conference with ministers of both the Christian Reformed and Protestant Reformed denominations, to be held at the Pantlind Hotel in Downtown Grand Rapids (now the Amway Grand Plaza), with the leaders — pastors and professors — of both denominations invited to attend. Dr. Schilder stipulated that he wished to be there, too, for the subject to be discussed was: The Reunion of the Christian Reformed and Protestant Reformed Churches.

In the nature of the case, not all the ministers of the Christian Reformed churches were able to attend; but most of the pastors of the small Protestant Reformed denomination attended the conference. The Rev. Hoeksema had prepared a thorough conference paper. Under the title, "The Reunion of the Christian Reformed and Protestant Reformed Churches," he asked three questions:

1. Is it demanded?
2. Is it possible?
3. Is it desireable?

The paper from which Pastor Hoeksema spoke was written in the Dutch language, and was later translated into English and published in pamphlet form.*

Pastor Hoeksema was the only one who had prepared a position paper for this conference. The Christian Reformed ministers admitted they had not prepared anything. After the presentation of the paper, Dr. Schilder was given the opportunity to make remarks. He admitted that he was stunned — that at this meeting he had heard things about the

---

*   Some of the points he made in this paper are listed in the Appendix.

common grace controversy which he had never heard before; and he told the audience of ministers that the position of the Protestant Reformed Churches was Reformed.

It was noon when Herman Hoeksema finished his paper; and from noon until late afternoon, when the conference adjourned, he tried to persuade the Christian Reformed men to discuss the issue of God's grace. He *urged* them to talk about it, but they would not take part in a discussion. The conference could do nothing but adjourn and meet in the future, after one of the Christian Reformed delegates prepared himself to speak on the issue of common grace. That meeting never took place.

The conference adjourned. Dr. Schilder had another engagement that evening. When, late in the evening, he came to the door of the Hoeksema manse, he greeted the pastor in his broad Dutch brogue: "Ik heb de smoren!" ("I'm stifled!" "I'm thoroughly disgusted!")

This conference helped to open Dr. Schilder's eyes to the common grace question and the roots of the Protestant Reformed Churches. He publicized, both in the United States and in The Netherlands, after he went home, that he had a good impression of the Protestant Reformed denomination and their biblical stance on God's grace. He began to write about the controversy over common grace in his church's official paper, *De Reformatie.*

※   ※   ※   ※   ※   ※   ※

Suddenly in the next year — 1940 — World War II was upon the tiny Netherlands. Along with the German occupation came the censorship of all incoming and outgoing mail; and the contact between the United States and The Netherlands was greatly reduced. Word *did* get through to the states, however, that after 1941 Dr. Schilder who was outspokenly anti-Nazi, had been in hiding and was put in prison for a time as a result of his Christian testimony. After he was released, he was forced to go underground until the end of the war.

On December 7, 1941, on Pearl Harbor Day, the United States became involved in World War II. After that day, there was no contact at all between The Netherlands and the States. All that Dr. Schilder's friends in this country knew was that a *doctrinal battle* involving Dr. Schilder was also going on during this time of war with Germany. News slipped through that Dr. Schilder was tried and condemned by the ecclesiastical courts of The Netherlands — without a hearing; for he had been underground and was not able to defend his doctrinal position. That is all the churches in the states knew until the end of the war.

Meanwhile, in America all church life was affected by the war, too. After all the able-bodied young men had been drafted, the older men — up to age forty-five if they were single — were called, too. At the worship services were many empty seats. There were the urgent congregational prayers for the boys, and grief when one of the boys was killed and would never worship God again on this earth. There was the tension of war even in the routine lives of God's people: the new government rules, the rationing and shortages, the loyalty to the United States, the anxieties as the boys were called to war — all these factors created a completely different atmosphere in the lives of the people.

Even though the atmosphere of war pressed heavily during these years, and also *because* of this atmosphere, God's children called on Him often and urgently; and the life in the communion of saints prospered during these years. Also in this time of war there was some development in the Protestant Reformed Churches. In 1939 First Church of Grand Rapids called a second pastor to help Pastor Hoeksema with his work load. The congregation called the Reverend Richard Veldman; he accepted and became second pastor.

In the year 1939 the leaders of the denomination decided to divide the churches into two classes — east and west — with the Mississippi River as the dividing line between them. In 1940 the denomination held its first general synod, with delegates from the two classes. Now the churches had completed the structure of a Reformed denomination.

During the war years there was very little external growth in the churches. In many areas, especially travel, the events of these years interrupted and impeded the normal ways of life. Another factor in the small external growth was the fact that the Protestant Reformed Churches had no home missionary between 1942 and 1947. During World War II one new congregation was organized and one congregation had a daughter church. It was during the wartime that the Rev. C. Hanko, who was at that time pastor of the Oak Lawn, Illinois, congregation, with the help of Rev. Hoeksema, organized the congregation in Randolph, Wisconsin, in 1943.

In 1944 the First Church congregation realized they were getting too large. Even though there were two pastors to shoulder the oversight of the congregation, they found the work load too heavy for them. Some of the members complained that because of the large number of members the congregation was losing its closely-knit ties and was becoming impersonal. It was time to have a daughter church. Thirty-five families volunteered to leave First Church and organize Fourth Protestant Reformed Church. In March of 1944 these families left First Church, and using the gift of money from their parent church, they remodeled a former two-story garage building on nearby Kalamazoo Avenue, near Boston Square. For nine years this building was their meeting place, with Rev. R. Veldman as their first pastor. The members used the upper story for their weekday meetings.

The garage-church was only temporary. As the congregation grew in numbers, they started plans for a new church building. In the winter of 1951 the builders started work on a church building on Kalamazoo Avenue, south of their present location. They worked through the year 1952 and in 1953 they were ready to have services, with Rev. Veldman as pastor, in their new church building.

This congregation did not keep its name, Fourth Church, however. In 1957, due to the legal problems which stemmed from the split of 1953, they were obliged to take the name Southeast Protestant Reformed Church.

Meanwhile, back in First Church the members could not tell that a new congregation had left them. The church was filled each Lord's day. All this growth was internal growth.

In 1947 the synod of the churches decided to call two missionaries, with the purpose of having them work together. They called the pastors W. Hofman and E. Knott, and both men accepted. There was one problem with this choice of missionaries: neither spoke the Dutch language fluently. The reason that this was a handicap was that at this period of time a rather massive Dutch immigration arrived at the docks of America, and most of the immigrants settled in Canada. The war had ended in 1945, and there was a steady immigration to that country, especially in the early 1950s. Many — probably most — of the immigrants chose to settle in Canada because this country welcomed a larger population and made it easier for immigrants to enter their country and settle there.[54]

In these two decades, in contrast to the intense preoccupation of polemics of the 1920s, the Protestant Reformed Churches not only sent out missionaries with the purpose of establishing new congregations, but the denomination also worked to enrich the organic life of their churches, the lives of the members of their congregation. In 1941 some members of the denomination were suggesting a weekly radio broadcast, as a Protestant Reformed witness. At that time, when the synod of the churches was still in its infancy, that body was not ready to take the responsibility of the project. So the Young Men's Society of First Church, a group of eighty to one hundred members, volunteered to underwrite the project.

They investigated many stations throughout the country. Then, with a budget of more than $16,000, they started their program with live broadcasts — the only kind in those days. A radio choir was organized, and Rev. Herman Hoeksema was asked to be the main speaker. Because these were live broadcasts, every Sunday afternoon all the partici-

---

54. The next chapter will furnish a detailed account of this immigration.

pants in the program went to Station WLAV in downtown Grand Rapids for the forty-five (and later thirty) minute broadcast.

Later a telephone connection between the station and First Church was hooked up. The program was still broadcast live, now with the speaker in the consistory room and the choir in the auditorium, at 4:00 P.M. each Sunday.

* * * * * * *

During the decade of the 1940s William B. Eerdmans, the publisher, expressed interest in Herman Hoeksema's writings. He was interested in publishing any Reformed writings which he considered worthwhile. Among the first books which he published were *The Amazing Cross,* a series of Lenten sermons; *Wonder of Grace,* an exposition of the truth of sovereign grace; and *In the Sanctuary,* sermons on the Lord's Prayer.

Next Mr. Eerdmans published the Triple Knowledge series which Herman Hoeksema had written in the *Standard Bearer.* This was a series of articles on the Heidelberg Catechism. Originally these expositions were published in a ten-volume set.* In a later publishing, they were consolidated into three volumes, with the title *The Triple Knowledge.*

Also in this decade of the 1940s, Herman Hoeksema began to develop an English version of the Dutch lessons he had developed in the field of dogmatics for his seminary students. Mr. Eerdmans then published the English version, written in popular style, with the title *Reformed Dogmatics.*

This was the era when the Protestant Reformed Churches became an English-speaking denomination. The last student who preached in the Dutch language was Hoeksema's son, Homer, in his charge in the rather provincial area of Doon, Iowa.

In 1944 the Reverend G. Ophoff left the pastoral ministry

---

* See the appendix for the titles.

to devote all his time to his work in the seminary, which was still holding classes in the basement of First Church. As professor of Old Testament studies, he developed his own classroom materials in this field; and they are still being used at the time of this writing. The textbooks which he wrote are works with scholarly and valuable insights into God's revelation in Old Testament times.

In the decade of the 1940s, the churches and the *Standard Bearer* gave more attention to developments in the *American* Reformed church-world rather than turning to their homeland across the ocean. Starting with the *Standard Bearer* of January 15, 1944, Editor Herman Hoeksema wrote a series about the doctrinal issues in the Orthodox Presbyterian Church, particularly in the Presbytery of Philadelphia. In this presbytery a problem had developed concerning the ordination of a Doctor Gordon Clark to the ministry. The presbytery seemed to find four reasons why Dr. Clark should not be ordained. Especially the third and fourth complaints are interesting.

> The third part accuses Dr. Clark of maintaining "that the relationship of divine sovereignty and human responsibility to each other presents no difficulty for his thinking and that the two are easily reconciled before the bar of human reason.
>
> And the fourth part is an elaboration upon the statement that "in the course of Dr. Clark's answers it became abundantly clear that his rationalism keeps him from doing justice to the precious teaching of Scripture that in the gospel God sincerely offers salvation in Christ to all who hear, reprobate as well as elect, and that He has no pleasure in any one's rejecting this offer but, contrariwise, would have all who hear accept it and be saved."[55]

---

55. " 'The Text of a Complaint,' " *Standard Bearer,* Vol. 21, p. 174.

Herman Hoeksema adds the editorial comment that "Especially in view of the last alleged error of Dr. Clark, the reader can readily understand that we are rather interested in this controversy, and that we cannot refrain from making a few remarks about the complaint."[56]

This error of a well-meant offer of salvation was not the only issue, but stemmed from the main problem: the complainants in the presbytery questioned whether revelation itself is intelligible to us, a heresy which would undermine the foundation of the church. For at least a year Dr. Clark argued his cause at his presbytery and Editor Hoeksema discussed the issue in the *Standard Bearer* in defense of Dr. Clark. In the end Dr. Clark left the Orthodox Presbyterian Church and took the Chair of Philosophy at Butler University. And Hoeksema kept his contact with Dr. Clark for many years.

* * * * * * *

In October, 1945, delegates from the Protestant Reformed denomination, and also interested visitors and seminary students, joined members of the Evangelical and Reformed Church in Kassel, South Dakota, for a conference. This denomination was a merger of the German Reformed Churches in the United States and the Evangelical Lutheran Church. To an average audience of one hundred listeners, delegates from each denomination gave position papers on subjects such as "The Idea of the Covenant" (by Herman Hoeksema); "Imputation" (by Rev. R. Grossman of the German Reformed Churches); "The Fundamental Principle of Reformed Church Polity" (by Rev. G. Ophoff); and "The Confession" (by Rev. D.E. Bosma of the German Churches).

In the *Standard Bearer* of November 1, 1945, the Rev. W. Hofman concluded the article about the conference as follows:

---

56. *Ibid.*

Although there are points of difference, mainly of emphasis, both groups revealed that they are always ready and willing to submit in love to the criterion of the truth — the Word of God. Finally, therefore, we believe that the Conference moved definitely in the direction of finding that unity of faith concerning which the moderator spoke in his opening remarks. Personally, we believe that continuing in the spirit of truth and love that marked the proceedings of the Conference, the expression of unity in the faith through Church union is a definite future possibility.[57]

The interests of the Protestant Reformed Churches were broadening. They were looking over the ecclesiastical scene, particularly the scene of the churches of Reformed beliefs, and evaluating what they saw. In come of the churches of Reformed persuasion they found basic compatibility, interest in discussions, and therefore new friendships.

❋   ❋   ❋   ❋   ❋   ❋   ❋

As early as the end of the decade of the 1930s, groups of parents in the Protestant Reformed Churches started to realize that if the future generations in the churches were to love and to cherish Reformed preaching and Reformed living in its purest manifestation here on this earth, they must train *their children* in the truths and beauties of these God-glorifying doctrines in their grade schools.

In the 1920s and 1930s the children from Protestant Reformed congregations had attended the established Christian grade schools in their areas. These were schools staffed mainly by Christian Reformed teachers, with a few teachers from the Reformed Church of America and the Protestant Reformed Churches.

In the early forties some of the leaders in various Protes-

---

57. "The Conference," *Standard Bearer,* Vol. 22, p. 69.

tant Reformed congregations tried to organize groups of
parents as members of a society to plan for future Protestant
Reformed grade schools. In many areas there was not much
support at first. An example was First Church: only twenty-
four men from a congregation of five hundred families
initiated the movement in the congregation. The movement
for distinctively Reformed schools had trouble getting off the
ground.

Pastors and leaders in the various congregations spoke
and wrote about the necessity of having the consistency of
Reformed training for their covenant children in their *homes,*
their *churches,* and their *schools.* Under the title, "The Ideal of
Protestant Reformed Schools," the Rev. R. Veldman wrote as
follows:

> That Protestant Reformed instruction for our
> Protestant Reformed children by Protestant Re-
> formed teachers, sincerely dedicated to and thor-
> oughly equipped for that task, in Protestant Re-
> formed Schools would be *ideal* no Protestant Re-
> formed person, it seems to me, would care or dare
> to gainsay....
>
> Until now and still we support the Christian
> Schools as they are today. We can and may do
> nothing else as long as our ideal is not yet real-
> ized....
>
> This does not mean, however, that we support
> the present schools as wholeheartedly and enthu-
> siastically as we should like....
>
> The Christian schools of today are *Christian
> Reformed* schools.... Christian Reformed men and
> women teach in these schools. A few exceptions
> to this rule do not alter the same. As a result, the
> doctrine of the Christian Reformed churches, the
> doctrine as these teachers see it and believe it,
> forms the basis and contents of the instruction....
>
> In the light of all this, how can we Protestant
> Reformed people be fully satisfied with the present
> set-up? How can we consider it ideal, that our
> children whom we pledge to bring up "in the

aforesaid doctrine," are instructed and trained in
this atmosphere 5 hours each school day, 25 hours
each school week, some 1,000 hours each year?
Remember, it would take our children 40 years to
spend as much time in catechism under the present
set-up, as they spend in the day school in one year.
The 12 years our children spend in school are
equivalent, as far as the time element is concerned,
to 480 years in the catechism class. It would
certainly be ideal, that those 12 years, those 12,000
hours be spent in a school of our own, a school
where the truth we confess and love is maintained
and applied wherever possible....

    This importance of the school for the welfare
of the child as well as the home and the church has
always been recognized by Reformed educators.
Therefore I stated above, that even our Christian
Reformed brethren will grant us that our ideal can
be no other than the one defended in this essay.
Always they have stressed the point, that Reformed doctrine, the principles of "Calvinism,"
must permeate all the instruction our children
receive.[58]

Almost two years went by. In February of 1944 the Rev.
H. Veldman gave a speech urging parents to establish Prot-
estant Reformed parental schools. Under the title "Why Our
Delay?" he said:

    ...It is my opinion that my subject tonight is
    timely. This child, that of our own school move-
    ment, is now some four years old. It seems to me
    that its growth is painfully slow, that it has not
    advanced very far beyond the state of infancy. I
    have consequently resolved to ask you this ques-
    tion tonight: Why our delay?...
        Is it because it is not sufficiently important?...
        Because we have an abundance of time?...

---

58. *Standard Bearer,* Vol. 19, Nov. 1, 1942, pp. 65-67.

Already 4 years we have waited; during those years our children have received instruction, instruction in the very things we have learned to hate and flee; these years constitute half of a child's instruction preparatory for high school — these years are gone, and, as far as these children are concerned, can never be recalled or replaced. Therefore, I ask: Why do we delay? Why do we wait? Time does not wait for us....

How urgent therefore, how extremely timely comes to us the exhortation that we lose no time, that we delay not, but that we work while it is day and instruct our children in the fear of God, in the doctrine of the antithesis, so dear to us and our only comfort in the midst of a world which lieth in darkness. Let us therefore not wait, but go forward — there is no time to loose....

Because we lack the means to go ahead?...

Permit me to say in this connection that God does not demand of us the impossible — He does not command us to do something which, *by His grace* cannot be done. And God surely commands us to instruct our children in the truth of His Word and testimony, does He not?...

Let us then proceed and go on. Do we lack the means here? I am sure that we in Grand Rapids are certainly in the position to make this project a reality and instruct our children in the way they should be instructed.[59]

One may ask the following questions. Why was this urging for schools consistent with the doctrine of the Protestant Reformed Churches so necessary? Why did many — perhaps the majority in the churches — resist parental schools from their own denomination? The answer is that ominous negative developments were starting to show themselves. There were rumblings of discontent over one matter or another. Rumblings of dissatisfaction were starting to be

---

59. *Standard Bearer,* Vol. 20, Feb. 15, 1944, pp. 216-218.

heard about too much doctrine, about being too sharp and too strict. An undercurrent of opposition and discontent was invading the churches. Pastor Hoeksema recognized the feelings of dissatisfaction when he wrote in the *Standard Bearer:*

As To Our Moral Obligation

Of all the arguments and would-be arguments the opponents of the movement for schools of our own wherever possible adduce for their position, that concerning the moral obligation to the existing schools is the weakest of all....

It runs as follows: We have no moral right to organize our own school movement and to establish our own schools as Protestant Reformed people, until we have done our utmost, and exhausted every means at our command, to improve the existing schools....

But what does this cooperation mean, as far as we, Protestant Reformed people, are concerned?

It means that we may, perhaps, protest against certain evils found in the existing schools, such as the singing Arminian hymns, the introduction of plays and dramas, the teaching of evolutionist conceptions or of grossly Arminian tenets, encouragement of movie attendance, etc.... We may request that the "Three Points" shall be carefully avoided.... It means not only that in biblical instruction all questions concerning particular and common grace, concerning total depravity and the ability or inability of man to do any good before God, must be carefully avoided; but it also implies that the same attitude of neutrality be assumed in the instruction in many other subjects that pertain to our view of the world, history, civil government, the unions, and other matters.

It should be quite plain from all this, that the opponents of the movement to establish schools of our own, by their argument as to our moral obligation to cooperate with the existing schools, do not care for, are not interested in, do not see the need of specific Protestant Reformed education for our children.[60]

The need for Pastor Hoeksema to call the members of his own denomination to teach the riches of the Reformed faith in their own schools was an ominous sign of the trouble which was sure to come. In spite of the opposition of many members of the denomination, some positive development of parental Protestant Reformed schools went on. The Redlands, California, members established a grade school already in 1933. Hope (Walker) in the Grand Rapids area was next in 1947, and Adams Street School in southeast Grand Rapids was started in 1949.

＊　＊　＊　＊　＊　＊　＊

In the year 1940 the denomination celebrated the twenty-fifth anniversary of Reverend H. Hoeksema's ordination as minister of the gospel. An announcement on the first page of the September 15, 1940, issue of the *Standard Bearer* reads as follows:

> This September 15, 1940 number of our *Standard Bearer* is dedicated to Rev. H. Hoeksema in commemoration of his ordination as a minister of the gospel on September 15, 1915, just twenty-five years ago.
> The Reformed Free Publishing Association and the 25th Anniversary Committee have cooperated in bringing to you this memorial number containing all the speeches delivered at the celebration held in Rev. Hoeksema's honor on August 15, 1940 at John Ball Park.[61]

In an account of the celebration, the Rev. H. Veldman wrote:

60. *Ibid.*, Vol. 20, May 15, 1944, pp. 348, 349.
61. "Rev. Hoeksema's Anniversary Celebration," *Standard Bearer*, Vol. 16, p. 505.

The setting of our celebration was ideal. Firstly,
the Lord gave us a beautiful day, partly cloudy
and warm. Then, in John Ball Park we enjoyed a
beautiful layout, particularly if we bear in mind
the nature of the day. We had the Park practically
to ourselves.... The committee had made arrangements for 1,500 seats between the speakers' stand
or band-stand and the pavilion. This number of
seats, however, proved to be far from sufficient.
For, although the celebration was sponsored by,
proceeded from the consistory of our Fuller Ave.
Church, it was truly a Protestant Reformed affair,
also in the sense that many of our churches, inasfar
as possible, took part in it.[62]

In honor of this anniversary the committee — and the
members of the denomination—had shared a secret. Through
the previous weeks they had all signed their names in a large
book. On the day of the anniversary, the members of the
churches presented Reverend and Mrs. Hoeksema with an
eighteen by twelve-inch leather autograph book set in a
cover of a beautifully grained maple case.*

In the same issue of the *Standard Bearer* mentioned
above, the Rev. H. Veldman commented on "Rev. Hoeksema's
Anniversary and our *Standard Bearer*." Although his speech
(recorded in the *Standard Bearer*) was positive and hopeful,
he, too, sensed the winds of change which were starting to
blow in the denomination. He said:

If now we are gathered here today truly to
celebrate Rev. Hoeksema's 25th anniversary in
the ministry of the Word of God, we can do so by
rededicating ourselves to our wholehearted support of our *Standard Bearer*. This we will do, this
we must do if we truly appreciate that which he,

---

62. *Ibid.*, p. 505.
*   This beautiful tribute, along with Hoeksema's diploma of June,
1915, is now in the archives of the Protestant Reformed Churches.

by the grace of God, had meant and still means to us.... Today we remember Rev. Hoeksema not merely as a man, but as one who by the grace of God has led us into a clearer insight of the truths of God's Word. If then this appreciation lives in our hearts, the *Standard Bearer* will indeed remain our standard, our emblem, our bearer. I do not say this merely because I would speak a good word for our paper. But I do say this because it is well at this time that we pause and reflect and rededicate ourselves unto the principles for which we fought some 16 years ago. At that time we demanded this paper because it was our desire to be witnesses to the truth so precious to us. At that time we were filled with enthusiasm to such an extent that the financial burden connected with our own paper was a mere trifle.... I am afraid that conditions among us have changed. The *Standard Bearer* today has at times a hard row to hoe. The financial obligations appear at times a burden. This should not and need not be. Hence, let us on this occasion repledge ourselves to the cause we hold dear, rededicate ourselves to the *Standard Bearer,* as our emblem in the midst of the world and of Zion. Let us support our paper, not only financially, but also as the symbol of our faith and struggle, that God's Name may be glorified and we may continue to be an actively protesting people in the midst of the world.[63]

Pastor Veldman was right. Winds of change were blowing in the denomination. Through the decade of the forties there began to be ominous negative developments among some of the leaders and members in the Protestant Reformed denomination.

The garden of Reformed plantings had budded in the decade of the 1930s. In the decade of the 1940s it had started

---

63. *Ibid.,* pp. 507, 508.

to blossom and to spread. The blossoms developed into flowers and fruits, and other Reformed gardens enjoyed the beauties of this little garden of Reformed plantings. Then a small fungus found an opening in the garden of Reformed plantings, and it crept in.

Section Four: PRUNING
Chapter 10
Rumblings of Trouble

The previous chapter described the lives of God's people as they lived through a great financial depression. Another upheaval in their lives was looming in the background. America entered World War II and suddenly most of the young men and boys, also from the Protestant Reformed churches, left the safety and security of their homes and the activities in their churches and were suddenly thrust into the company of total strangers, among whom were very few godly men, and still fewer Reformed Christians. Life in the sphere of the church was different without the energetic enthusiasm of the young men.

In the communion of the Protestant Reformed churches there was also a change during these war years especially among some of the pastors. It was a change of atmosphere. Gradually these pastors began to preach a softening — a muting — of some of the cardinal doctrines of the Scriptures and the Reformed faith, especially those of God's sovereign, particular grace, the doctrines for which they had fought in 1924 and which were the foundations and heritages of the Protestant Reformed denomination. They were losing their first love and their zeal to preach the full gospel of grace as revealed in the Scriptures.

On the other hand, these men did not want to preach overt heresy, either. Their preaching began to be bland, colorless, and not distinctively Reformed. They made no secret of saying that they made deliberate attempts *not to be* distinctively Reformed.

These pastors were heard to sneer: "We don't wear the label 'Protestant Reformed' on the lapels of our coats."

In itself, the statement was true, but the spirit behind it

was the attempt to caricature the devotion of the pastors who were devoted to the doctrines which made the Protestant Reformed Churches distinctive. There was also a lethargy among those who sat in the pews. Many members of the churches seemed to have lost their first love and enthusiasm for Scriptural and Reformed preaching. They had little interest in developing the Reformed truth, and little initiative to live within the guidelines of the Reformed faith in their family lives and the organic life of the church. This was a foreboding change hovering over the unity of the denomination, a special problem which God had sent to the churches during World War II; for these rumblings surfaced during the war and immediately thereafter.

In the Protestant Reformed denomination were other concerns caused by the war. Many of the members of the various congregations, who were transplanted Hollanders, had great concern for their relatives and friends in the old country. During the earlier stage of the war, before the fighting had accelerated, it was still possible to send relief to the citizens of that war-torn country. In the June 1, 1940, issue of the *Standard Bearer,* Editor Hoeksema published the following information:

> What, for a long time we feared, what, according to the reports in the last papers we received from the old country, the Dutch more and more, especially since the "protective" possession by the Germans of Denmark and Norway, has now become history: old Holland was invaded and overcome by the German war-machines!
>
> And we, no doubt, were all shocked and filled with indignation because of this brutal and wholly unjustified attack upon the lowlands.
>
> Without provocation on the part of the Dutch, though the German government concocted several reasons and excuses for this wanton disregard of international relations and Holland's neutrality, the Germans drove their smashing hordes into The Netherlands....

In the meantime, there was fierce fighting. Holland was the scene of a terrible combat, so that according to official estimates one out of every four of Dutch soldiers was killed in action. One hundred thousand young men were slaughtered in a conflict that lasted no longer than five days. And who can say how many are wounded, and those that are maimed for the rest of their life?

And now the Germans have occupied Holland.

I shall not attempt to draw a picture of the suffering and agony, the sorrow and grief, that is endured at present by the Dutch as a result of this brief and impossible conflict....

There must be concerted and centralized action. Relief must be brought to war-torn Holland through some agency that knows through what channels our gifts can be sent to the Dutch, so that we may be reasonably sure it will not fall into wrong hands.

For this purpose a relief committee was organized in Grand Rapids under the leadership of Mr. J. Steketee, consul for The Netherlands, to collect funds for the destitute and needy over there. And they will put forth every effort in their power to see to it that the relief-money or materials will reach the Dutch people.

The *Standard Bearer* appeals to all our people to help in this cause!

Not only our people in Michigan, but everywhere.

It is the least we can do....[64]

Also in the early part of the war Dr. Schilder's friends in America were very concerned about his personal safety, for he had made many friends during his visit in 1939. Rumors had spread through the churches until the following was published:

---

64. "Hatred and More Hatred," *Standard Bearer,* Vol. 16, p. 388.

Regarding Dr. K. Schilder

While I was at the sea-coast the Hon. Bartel J. Jonkman, our representative from Michigan, tried to get into connection with me by long distance telephone from Washington, to inform us about the safety of Dr. Schilder. I understand, that as he found me absent, he established connection with Mr. LaGrange to whom he imparted the information that Dr. Schilder was safe and well. This information was promptly announced from the pulpit of First Protestant Reformed Church of Grand Rapids, and, perhaps, in other churches. At all events, it may be considered quite generally known by this time, that Dr. Schilder is well, and that all the rumors concerning his imprisonment or death were without basis in fact.[65]

Soon the war escalated and all correspondence between The Netherlands and the United States was censored or prohibited. The silence — especially of the last two years of the war — was painful for friends and relatives on both sides of the ocean. The friends and relatives in the states knew that the Netherlanders were not only suffering severe hardships and sorrows in this war, but that they also were living through a time of serious controversy in their churches. It was not until the end of the war, in the middle of the summer of 1945, that the anxious friends and relatives of the Hollanders received any news.

The church news from The Netherlands for which the members of Reformed denominations in America were eagerly waiting was printed in American periodicals as soon as it reached the states. Already in the *Standard Bearer* of August 1, 1945, Editor Hoeksema wrote an early and scanty news report titled "The Separation in the Netherlands":

From a very reliable source in the old country

---

we learned a little about the deposition of Dr.
Schilder and others, and the split that occurred in
the Reformed Churches in The Netherlands.

A brother wrote me that the Synod of the
"Gereformeerde Kerken" in the old country
adopted the Kuyperian view of "Presupposed
regeneration," that is, the theory that infants are
baptized on the ground of the presupposition that
they are already regenerated; that Dr. Schilder
and others disagreed, came into trouble with the
Synod, not only because of this question, but also
because of certain questions concerning church
polity; that he and others were deposed; and that
many churches "have liberated themselves from
the yoke of Synod."

These are still scant details. But the writer
promised that he would send me all the available
literature on the matter as soon as possible. And
we hope to keep our readers informed.[66]

In the September 1, 1945, issue the readers of the *Standard Bearer* learned that Dr. Schilder, who was still underground, did not agree with the "presupposed regeneration" adopted by the Synod of the Reformed Churches of The Netherlands. Because he did not agree, the synod deposed him without a hearing — while he was still underground. Only the following scanty news was available at this time:

> March 23, 24. Doctor Schilder was suspended,
> both as professor at the Kampen Theological
> School, and as emeritus minister of Delftshaven.
> The ground of this suspension: alleged schism in
> the churches.
>
> May 31. On this synod there appeared several
> requests to retract the decision concerning the
> suspension of Dr. Schilder, and the binding force
> of the doctrinal declarations of 1943. Synod main-
> tained its former decisions, decided to seek con-

---

66. *Standard Bearer*, Vol. 21, p. 454.

tact with Dr. Schilder (who was underground)
and for this purpose lengthened the suspension-
term from three to four months.[67]

When the censorship of the mail was finally lifted, hundreds of people penned news letters from The Netherlands
to America with news about the war time, and especially
about the details of the breach in their churches. In quick
succession, all the details of the controversy in The Netherlands came pouring into the churches in the United States;
and the leaders in the various Reformed churches in the
States were able to piece together all the accounts of the
Dutch controversy during World War II. They studied all
aspects of the church trouble and learned the details. Many
of these details had an important bearing on the developing
conflict in the Protestant Reformed denomination.

They learned that the problem lay in the interpretation of
God's promise, particularly in the statement in the Form for
the Baptism of Infants of Believers, which reads, in part, as
follows:

> And although our young children do not
> understand these things, we may not therefore
> exclude them from baptism, for as they are with-
> out their knowledge, partakers of the condemna-
> tion in Adam, so are they again received unto
> grace in Christ; as God speaketh unto Abraham,
> the father of all the faithful, and therefore unto us
> and our children (Gen. 17:7) saying, "I will estab-
> lish my covenant between me and thee, and thy
> seed after thee, in their generations, for an ever-
> lasting covenant; to be a God unto thee, and to thy
> seed after thee. This also the apostle Peter testifieth,
> with these words (Acts 2:39), "For the promise is
> unto you and to your children, and to all that are
> afar off, even as many as the Lord our God shall
> call."[68]

---

67. "The Liberated Churches in The Netherlands," *Standard Bearer*,
Vol. 21, p. 476.
68. The *Psalter*, Grand Rapids, Eerdmans, 1988, p. 86.

The trouble in the churches of The Netherlands started because of their different interpretations of this promise of God to infants of believers. These doctrinal differences in their congregations had been surfacing through the years of the war; but due to the upheavals in their country, no firm decisions were taken by the Synod of the Reformed Churches of The Netherlands during these stressful times. These issues *were* on the agendas of the war-time synod, however.

Already at the meeting of the continuing Synod of 1942, the members followed the *B* wing of the Reformed Churches — the wing favored by Dr. A. Kuyper's interpretation of God's covenant with His people. Herman Hoeksema explains as follows:

> The synodical decisions of 1942 follow, in the main, the view of Dr. A. Kuyper, Sr., with respect to the baptism of infants.
>
> This theologian ... approached the question concerning the validity and meaning of the baptism of infants from the aspect of the question concerning the sacraments. Sacraments, he argued, are signs and seals instituted by God in His Church for the strengthening of the faith of those to whom they are administered. They are means of grace, means whereby it pleases God to impart grace to His people through the Holy Spirit.
>
> It follows, then, that they presuppose faith in those that receive and partake of them.... In fact, according to Kuyper, through baptism little infants receive a very special kind of grace, which, it would seem, they cannot receive in any other way, although in just what this "baptismal grace" consists he does not succeed to make clear. Well, then, in this way it becomes very clear that infants as well as adults have a right to baptism, and that, when they are baptized, there is a very real administration of a very real sacrament. Infants are baptized on the ground of their "supposed regeneration."[69]

---

69 "The Liberated Churches in The Netherlands," *Standard Bearer*, Vol. 22, Dec. 1, 1945, p. 101.

When the Reformed Synod in The Netherlands adopted this theory of presupposed regeneration, they were taking a "wait and see" attitude: will my child grow up to be one of God's children who has been given the promise of salvation, as I have supposed?

Dr. Schilder and his followers could not agree with this interpretation of the baptism of the children of believers. Through the leadership of Dr. Schilder, his followers began to develop their own interpretation of God's promise to the infants of believers. They insisted that God gave a *promise* to infants of believers, not a *presupposition*. The promise is "that they are *sanctified* in Christ...." Therefore they objected as follows to the decision of their synod:

> The authors can accept the synodical declaration that the children of the covenant must be considered as sanctified in Christ and regenerated, until the contrary appears, as a practical definition of the rule according to which in the life of the church the children of the covenant must be treated.... They cannot accept the theory of presupposed regeneration.[70]

The group led by Dr. Schilder was correct. God's promise is not a *presupposition*. What, then, was Dr. Schilder's interpretation of the promise of God to the children of believers? Dr. Schilder and his followers had not as yet stated their interpretation of the baptism of infants of believers.

Herman Hoeksema expressed the hope that Dr. Schilder had denounced *suppositions* in the covenant, and had insisted that God gave a *promise* to infants of believers, and that he and his followers had come to a solid Scriptural interpretation of covenant theology. The readers of the *Standard Bearer* had their answer in the next issue.

When the news came in the mail at the Hoeksema manse by way of *De Reformatie,* the periodical of the Reformed

---

70. *Ibid.*

Churches of The Netherlands, Pastor Hoeksema read the decision which Dr. Schilder and his followers had adopted. He was stunned. He paced the floor of the living room, reading and re-reading the article, meanwhile exclaiming, "I can't believe it!"

The Rev. Hoeksema was shocked because of Dr. Schilder's non-reformed interpretation of God's promise to the infants of believers. Although Dr. Schilder and his followers knew it was not a presupposition as the synod had defined it, and although he believed in the *promise* "to you and your children," Acts 2:39, he and his followers defined that promise as a *conditional* promise, a clause that said, "You will receive God's promises *if* you believe."[71]

Hoeksema called this interpretation "pure Heynsianism." Dr. William Heyns had been one of Hoeksema's professors at Calvin College, and one of the professors who had pressed for the adoption of the theory of common grace. Dr. Heyns' view of God's covenant as a *pact*, with stipulations and conditions, is as follows:

> The essence of the covenant is the promise in the sense of a conditional offer. On His part, God promises, that is, He offers, to all who are born in the covenant that He will be their God, on condition that they also accept that promise of God and consent to the covenant. That conditional relationship in which God placed Himself to the seed of the covenant, the realization of which depends on the consent and acceptance of the covenant-member — that is for Prof. Heyns the essence of the covenant.[72]

This was the doctrine which Dr. Schilder and his followers (the Liberated Churches) adopted. Dr. Schilder was a descendant of the Afscheiding of 1834, led by Hendrik

71. "The Liberated Churches in the Netherlands," *Standard Bearer*, Vol. 22, Oct. 1, 1945, p. 6.
72. H. Hoeksema, *Believers and Their Seed*, R.F.P.A., 1971, p. 22.

deCock. This wing of the Dutch churches was doctrinally weaker than the group which came from the Kuyperian reformation.

Herman Hoeksema, on the other hand, was a son of the Doleantie of 1887, led by Abraham Kuyper (but born of Afscheiding parents). The movement of 1887 was generally more solidly Reformed. As a son of the Doleantie, Hoeksema had given much study to the development of these Reformed tenets according to the guidelines in the Scriptures, especially in defining and developing the biblical view of God's covenant, which he defined as "a bond (or relationship) of friendship between God and His people." A brief summary of Herman Hoeksema's interpretation of God's covenant with His people is as follows:

> 1. The idea of the covenant is neither that of a pact or agreement, nor that of the promise, nor that of a way of salvation; but it is the eternal and living fellowship of friendship between God and His people in Christ, according to which He is their Sovereign-friend, and they are His friend-servants.
>
> 2. By friendship we mean a bond of most intimate fellowship, based on the highest possible likeness of nature by personal distinction.
>
> 3. The deepest ground of this covenant relation is the life of the triune God Himself, of which it is the highest revelation.
>
> 4. This covenant is established with Christ, as the Servant of Jehovah *par excellence*, and with the elect in and through Him.
>
> 5. Historically this covenant is realized in the line of the continued generations of believers. These generations receive the sign of the covenant, circumcision in the old, baptism in the new dispensation, and, in general, are addressed and treated as the real covenant people of God; yet, God's election and reprobation cut right through these generations, and "God is merciful to whom He will be merciful, and whom He will He hardens."

6.   This covenant of God is eternal, and will
be realized in its heavenly perfection in the new
creation, when the tabernacle of God will be with
men.[73]

Although Dr. Schilder's theology stemmed from the
Afscheiding and Rev. Hoeksema's from the Doleantie, and
they did not agree on many doctrinal issues, yet these men
were attracted to one another.   Herman Hoeksema liked
Klaas Schilder.   He enjoyed Schilder's personality and his
basically Reformed convictions.   Both men agreed on the
issue of church polity: that the classis and the synod are
broader—not *higher*—ruling bodies in the church. Hoeksema
sympathized with Schilder because of the way he had been
put out of his office without a hearing by the hierarchy of the
Dutch Synod. He — as Hoeksema twenty years earlier —
had been deposed from office without a hearing. These two
men had many things in common. On the other hand, they
had sharp differences in the area of man's free will in the
sphere of the covenant.

The importance of this historical background in The
Netherlands is the "Dutch Connection," a term which was
coined later.   It meant generally that the doctrines and
practices in The Netherlands were transported to America,
and these doctrines and practices had great influence on the
churches of Reformed origin in the United States. Also in the
states the differences in the slants in the theology of the *A* and
the *B* groups kept surfacing and causing friction.   The
problems and results of this schism in The Netherlands were
transported into the various Reformed churches in America
through the great post-war influx. Netherlanders by the
thousands emigrated in the late '40s and during the '50s.
These immigrants came in great numbers both to Canada
and the United States; and it was through this massive
immigration that the Protestant Reformed Churches began

---

73. "The Liberated Churches in The Netherlands," *Standard Bearer,*
Vol. 22, March 15, 1946, p. 269.

to have close contact especially with members of the Liberated Churches of The Netherlands.

In the garden of Reformed plantings across the sea, two different kinds of seeds had been planted: the seeds of the *prerequisites* of the growth of the Reformed plantings, and the seeds of *conditionality* — that *if* they planted the seeds the plants would take on the responsibility to believe that they would sprout and bear fruit in the gardens of Reformed plantings in America.

Chapter 11
Winds of Change

World War II was over. In America life began to be more peaceful and normal. The countries of Europe were busy cleaning up and rebuilding their war-torn lands and adjusting to the aftermath of war. In The Netherlands, in the peace of the post-war life, Dr. K. Schilder started to think about visiting his friends in America; and the May 1, 1947, issue of the *Standard Bearer* informed its readers that Dr. Schilder had made plans. Titled "The Coming of Dr. Schilder," the article reads as follows:

> Many of us must have heard a rumor that Dr. Schilder is planning to visit us, and to speak for us in behalf of the cause of the liberated churches in The Netherlands.
>
> There was basis for this rumor. Some time ago undersigned received a cablegram from him to that effect with the addition: "Letter follows." Considerable time elapsed before that letter arrived. When it came, the brother informed me that he intended to come during the summer. I hastened to answer that letter, and to tell him that, if he intended to speak here, the summer period would be the worst to select, since it is well nigh impossible to get an audience in the hot weather. He finally replied that he would try to leave the latter part of August, so that he will be with us, most probably during September and October.
>
> Dr. Schilder knows quite well what is our attitude with respect to their movement, both from a church political and doctrinal viewpoint. He knows that we do not agree with their covenant conception, and that we take the same stand as they church politically. He is assured, too, that

141

in spite of our differences our churches will give
him a hearing. He trusts that we still love him, and
that we will give him a warm reception. In this, I
think, he will not be disappointed. May I suggest
that all our churches make arrangements to receive him and let him speak?...

How about it, brethren? Is not this a splendid
opportunity to hear the other side?

The *Standard Bearer* will gladly make arrangements for you.[74]

In the churches there were mixed reactions about his
coming to America during the fall of 1947. As Herman
Hoeksema put it, the people agreed with him and they
disagreed with him. Yet Dr. Schilder was the kind of man
who disagreed pleasantly, and a man who would listen
carefully to an opposite opinion. He had a magnetic personality.

* * * * * * *

On the 17th of June, 1947, Rev. and Mrs. Hoeksema left
for a western vacation, which would also be a sort of working
vacation. They planned to stay in Bellflower, California,
where their oldest daughter Johanna lived with her husband,
the Rev. L. Doezema, pastor of the Bellflower congregation.
Father-in-law Hoeksema would be preaching some services
for his son-in-law during his stay.

Traveling with another daughter, Jeanette, and her husband, they arrived at Sioux Falls, South Dakota, the first
night of their trip. Suddenly that night Hoeksema began to
have severe pains. His children took him to the hospital.
That night he suffered a major stroke which paralyzed his
right side and impaired his speech. After a stay in the Sioux
Falls hospital, the doctors allowed him to be flown home.
The doctors in Grand Rapids immediately started therapy.

---

74. H. Hoeksema, Vol. 23, p. 343.

Hoeksema, with his determined personality, pushed himself hard to learn to speak, to read, and to walk again.

The pastor's illness, forcing him to be reduced from an able leader to a helpless invalid, shocked the members of the denomination.   Immediate arrangements were made for interim pulpit supply; and the Rev. G. Vos took over Hoeksema's duties as editor of the *Standard Bearer.* In his first editorial, titled "A Substitution," Rev. Vos ended by stating:

> Allow me to assure our readers that I have accepted this position with mingled feelings of trepidation and trust in God. However, to explain this state of mind and heart is neither edifying nor necessary. This state of affairs is thrust upon us by the hand of God Himself, and therefore, we will carry on. After all, it is His business which we are attending to in our *Standard Bearer.*
>
> I would close this introductory editorial with the expressed wish and prayer that I may soon receive word from him who is still our Editor: You may be excused from this task! I am able to resume my labors!
>
> And: may the Lord deal kindly with him and give him grace to bear his cross! This visitation is nothing but adorable wisdom![75]

The illness of Herman Hoeksema did not change Dr. Schilder's plans. By the first part of September he had arrived in Grand Rapids. His purpose was to discuss the doctrinal questions which were adopted in The Netherlands, and to lecture in Reformed churches in America: the German Reformed, the Christian Reformed, and the Protestant Reformed.

On October 16, 1947, and again on the days of November 4 to 6 an ongoing conference with Dr. Schilder and pastors

---

75. *Standard Bearer,* Vol. 23, Sept. 1, 1947, p. 484.

and office bearers of the Protestant Reformed Churches met
to discuss their respective theologies, especially their opposing views of God's covenant with His people. Although an
amicable atmosphere prevailed during these sessions, no
agreements were reached and no decisions were made. Part
of the problem was the ambivalence of Dr. Schilder. When
faced with a question or a challenge, he did not usually give
a concise answer. He was ambivalent and often answered:
"If you mean this, my answer is no; and if you mean this and
this, then probably my answer may be yes."

An illustration of his oblique answers to precise questions which he would rather evade took place in a humorous
encounter with one of Schilder's American friends. She
asked, "Dr. Schilder, I never hear you talk about your wife.
Do you miss her a lot?"

His answer is an example of a non-answer: "If I say, 'No,
I do not miss her,' you will say, 'Poor fellow, he does not love
his wife.' If I say, 'Oh, yes, I miss her very much,' you will
say, 'Poor fellow, he is so lonesome.'"

Dr. Schilder often spoke in this manner when discussing
theology. He was not concise and to the point.

Although the men at the Schilder Conference discussed
closer relationships between the Protestant Reformed
Churches and the Liberated Churches in The Netherlands,
the differences were too great. Dr. Schilder despised the
doctrine of the covenant taught by the Protestant Reformed
Churches. The Rev. G. Vos put it this way:

> It is our plan to write on the questions of the
> Covenant and related matters. And we will do so
> with the express purpose to clarify our position
> and to defend it against those views which are
> contrary to the Word of God, according to our
> convictions. Doing this, we shall also criticize the
> views of the liberated churches. For although we
> may now say with all emphasis that their view is
> not entirely Heynsian, especially as far as the late
> professor's views on the so-called subjective bap-
> tism-grace is concerned, and although Professor

Schilder constantly stated that our differences are only a matter of terminology, we nevertheless are convinced that there are elements in their covenant views, clearly expressed in their written and published treatises, and now corroborated by the spoken elucidations of Prof. Schilder which we whole-heartedly reject. And it is also our conviction that even though it were only a matter of difference in terminology, we are of the opinion that their terminology is not correct, not according to Scripture and not according to the form of baptism. We will welcome exchange of ideas in the future.[76]

Editor Hoeksema's evaluation was as follows:

The differences between the Liberated Churches and us, as they were brought out in the discussion, concerned especially the following points:

1)   First of all, the definition of the covenant. According to us the idea of the covenant is essentially that of friendship and fellowship between God and His people in Christ; the Liberated Churches, although they do not define the covenant, nevertheless, lay all the emphasis on promise and demand.

2)   In our view the promise of the covenant is for the elect only; according to the Liberated Churches the promise is for all that are born in the covenant line, although this must not be understood in the Arminian sense, since also they emphasize the truth that God Himself must fulfill all the conditions of the covenant.

3)   The Liberated Churches speak of parties in the covenant, although they admit that in the real sense man cannot be a party over against God; we prefer to speak with the Baptism Form of parts rather than of parties.

---

76. "The Schilder Conference," *Standard Bearer*, Vol. 24, Dec. 1, 1947, p. 101.

We agreed upon fundamentals, and for the
rest we agreed to differ.[77]

Shortly after Dr. Schilder went back to The Netherlands,
Pastor and Mrs. Hoeksema left for Bellflower, California,
where the pastor could recuperate in the warm sunshine. In
a letter dated January, 1948, he wrote to his congregation that
he had two pieces of good news: On January 25 he had
preached for the first time since his stroke; and he had also
been swimming in the ocean!

                    *   *   *   *   *   *   *

In the May 15, 1946, issue of the *Standard Bearer* was the
following short announcement:

> Literally thousands of Hollanders are leaving the
> old Fatherland and seeking a new home. The great
> majority are settling in the province of Ontario,
> Canada, while several are also entering the United
> States.[78]

Through a mandate from the previous synod, whose
members had anticipated this influx, the mission committee
had called two men to work as home missionaries in the
denomination. They were the Reverends W. Hofman and E.
Knott. Until the summer of 1948 they had been working,
respectively, in the Byron Center, Michigan, and the Lynden,
Washington, areas. Now, however, the post-war scene
called for a change in the mission field of the Protestant
Reformed Churches. The Synod of June, 1948, decided to
keep the Lynden area as a mission station, and designated
the area of Ontario, Canada, as a new mission field. The
Reverends J. DeJong, pastor of the Hull, Iowa, congregation,

---

77. "Our Conference With Dr. Schilder," *Standard Bearer*, Vol. 24,
p. 103.
78. J. DeJong, "Periscope," *Standard Bearer*, Vol. 24, p. 381.

and Missionary W. Hofman spent a month investigating the field in Ontario. They reported "that there is a field in Canada and that this field is increasing should be evident.... But that there are also many problems is evident. The greatest of these is the fact of the scattering of the immigrants and the unsettled situation amongst them."[79]

In these post-war years the mood of the members of the Protestant Reformed Churches was changing. Along with the contact with the Reformed Churches of The Netherlands, and especially through Dr. Schilder, there was much sympathy for the Liberated Churches among the pastors and also those who sat in the pews. Many of the ministers, mostly in the West, and led by the Reverends J. DeJong and A. Cammenga, were eager to embrace — or at least tolerate — the view of the covenant which the Liberated Churches in The Netherlands had formulated.

At the same time, in the comparatively young Protestant Reformed denomination the concept of the doctrine of God's covenant of grace with His people was not as yet fully developed; and the evaluations and criticisms of the covenant views which had been developed in The Netherlands served as the impetus for more study and development of Scripturally precise concepts by the theologians and leaders in the Protestant Reformed Churches.

Very evident also in the late 1940s and early 1950s was a change of mood in the Protestant Reformed Churches, especially among the clergy. Winds of dissatisfaction and criticism blew through the denomination. Many of the pastors were tired of living in a small, insignificant denomination, with small, struggling congregations; and they saw in the massive immigrations the opportunities to grow in number and to have an important name in the church world.

Along with these feelings was the personal jealousy of Herman Hoeksema by many of the ministers. Some of the men in the West resented the influence of "the pope" in

---

79. W. Hofman, "Periscope," *Standard Bearer,* Vol. 24, Aug. 1, 1948, p. 480.

Grand Rapids. And they complained that "Hoeksema is always right!"

That Hoeksema was a very *definite* man and a precise thinker is true. The Lord gave him that gift as a tool for the Scriptural and doctrinal concepts which he developed. He was a scholar and a born leader. He could also be brusque in insisting that he was right; and some of his sharpness seemed to be aggravated by his stroke in 1947. At times his polemics could be very sharp. And some of the pastors in the denomination wanted to shake off his leadership.

Another factor in the changing mood in the denomination was the rise of the "two-hundred percenters," or the "guillotines," as they were named by some in the denomination. These were a small minority of members of the denomination who had narrow, radical interpretations of the current problems, and who were rigidly and offensively abrasive if someone in the denomination disagreed with them on any point of doctrine, no matter how insignificant. Parallels of this phenomenon in the Protestant Reformed Churches may be found in the doctrinal struggles in many of the Protestant reformations in church history. It was not uncommon in the earlier reformations that the left wing of error gave occasion for the rise of the radical right wing. In the Reformation of the sixteenth century the anabaptists — the far right wing — developed as the radical element over against the left wing of the Roman Catholic Church. As in all reformations, the existence of the right wing — the "two-hundred percenters" — in the late forties and early fifties added a troubled atmosphere to an already unsettled Protestant Reformed denomination.

In this setting and with these undercurrents of unrest, in the summer of 1949 the Reverends B. Kok and J. DeJong made a non-official trip to The Netherlands and visited the Liberated Churches there — as tourists, not as representatives of the Protestant Reformed Churches.

During that same summer one of the immigrants from The Netherlands, who now lived in Canada, started to attend the worship services at the Protestant Reformed mission station in Chatham, Ontario. Not sure whether or not he should join the Protestant Reformed denomination, he wrote to his friend, Professor B. Holwerda, who held the chair of church polity in the denomination of the Liberated Churches in The Netherlands. He asked the professor whether, in good conscience — in view of the differences in the two denominations about the interpretation of God's covenant with His people — he could become a member of the Protestant Reformed denomination.

Professor Holwerda sent an answer to the man in Chatham. The man must have been rather surprised at the answer from his professor; for he showed the letter to the Rev. Ophoff, who was taking his turn to preach at Chatham that weekend. Rev. Ophoff had a shock. This is what he read:

> I received your letter yesterday, and a direct reply per airmail is in order. Day before yesterday we held a meeting with Rev. Kok and Rev. DeJong, the purpose being mutual discourse. We had a wholly openhearted exchange of thoughts. They said this: Indeed, we have much to be grateful for to Rev. Hoeksema. But his conception regarding election, etc., is not church doctrine. No one is bound by it. Some are emitting a totally different sound. Their opinion was that most (of the Prot. Ref.) do not think as Rev. Hoeksema and Rev. Ophoff. And sympathy for the Liberated was great also in the matter of their doctrine of the covenant. They do accentuate differently in America, considering their history, but for the conception of the Liberated there is ample room....
>
> They, that is, Rev. Kok and Rev. DeJong, also reported what is being done in their churches for handling the spiritual care of the Liberated. I must honestly say that thereby much of my fear has been removed. I still consider the method of the Amersfoort decision regarding correspondence with the Protestant Reformed Churches unfortunate. But now I see the thing thus: First, the Prot. Ref. church is the true church, be it that the lay (of

conception) regarding election, etc, is somewhat
different, considering their wholly different history. However, I am not entirely agreed. Second
the Protestant Reformed Church proves to be the
true church also herein that she truly seeks the
immigrants from Holland and consciously allows
all room for their conception. In this situation I
believe that joining the Prot. Ref. Church is calling.
And let them then as Liberated preserve their
contact with Holland by all means, and also spread
our literature. Our Liberated would be doing a
fruitful work, if they labored in the Prot. Ref.
churches to remove misunderstanding and to
deepen insight. Rev. Kok said, We can still learn
much from each other. The communication that
Rev. Hoeksema, who first was skeptical of the
immigrants, paid them a visit, and returned enthusiastic, struck me as remarkable....

If Rev. Hoeksema's conception was binding, I
would say, Never join. Now I believe, however,
that accession is calling; and then so that the
Liberated also help to disseminate the dogmatical
wealth of Holland in the Prot. Ref. Churches.[80]

In the same issue of the *Standard Bearer* Rev. Ophoff
recorded his shock and commented on the letter from Professor Holwerda, which he published. He wrote:

This is an astounding letter, especially the
statements in it that bear on the doings of Revs.
DeJong and Kok in The Netherlands and on the
state of affairs in our own communion of churches.

Do I have the right to publish this letter and
thereby make it the property of all our people? I
do have that right. Let us consider the following:

a) Prof. Holwerda's letter partakes of the
nature of a report of the acts of a conference that
was open to the public certainly.... Fact is then,

80. "Revs. DeJong and Kok in The Netherlands," *Standard Bearer*,
Vol. 25, Aug. 1, 1949, p. 470.

that I am not by my doing revealing things that were meant to be kept secret and therefore ought to be kept secret. The deliberations of that conference in The Netherlands are being spread far and wide among the Liberated in The Netherlands and among the immigrants in Canada. Our people, too, have a right to know.

b) Revs. DeJong and Kok, be it as self-appointed ambassadors—they were not sent by the Protestant Reformed — were speaking for all our people. Hence, every man, woman and child of our communion has a right to be made acquainted with the content of the professor's letter.

c) If the report of the professor is true, the brethren DeJong and Kok involved most of our people including the clergy. For the report states that most (of the Protestant Reformed) do not think like Rev. Hoeksema and Ophoff. This was said to the leaders among the Liberated in The Netherlands. It is being broadcasted far and wide. Certainly every minister, elder and deacon in our communion, and every common member must receive the opportunity of expressing himself regarding that statement, and regarding all the other statements occurring in the letter as well. This demanded the publication of this letter....[81]

Rev. Ophoff went on to lament the fact that the two ministers in The Netherlands spoke of the doctrine of God's covenant as the *private concept* of the Reverends Herman Hoeksema and George Ophoff and claimed that this doctrine was not binding — not official doctrine — in the Protestant Reformed Churches. Ophoff also reminded the churches that *if* it were true that the doctrine of the Liberated was being accepted in the Protestant Reformed Churches, then the denomination was going back to the acceptance of the three points of 1924, which also included the covenant theology of Professor Heyns.

---

81. *Ibid.*

The publishing of the letter from Prof. Holwerda, along with the comments of the Rev. Ophoff, put the Protestant Reformed Churches into immediate turmoil. Most members were shocked by the contents of the public letter. They too were angered by the misrepresentation of the Protestant Reformed stance on God's grace — that instead of maintaining God's sovereign, particular grace, the churches were portrayed as repudiating all their struggles for that grace in 1924 and embracing conditions to God's salvation in the realm of His covenant — the Heynsian error which they had rejected along with the three points of common grace in 1924. Many of the members of the denomination remembered their struggles in condemning the heresy of common grace in 1924. Now they recognized the fact that they were facing the same errors of common grace once again: only this time they were fighting the error of common grace in the sphere of the covenant of grace. They were fighting "het puntje van het eerste punt" — "the heart of the first point," which claims that it "deals with the general offer of the gospel." A general offer is *conditioned* on acceptance of that offer. And if one believes that God promises salvation to little babes on *condition* that they believe, he rejects God's sovereign, particular grace.

While many members of the denomination were heavy-hearted about this doctrinal issue, others were angry that Ophoff published the letter before he discussed the issue with the Reverends Kok and DeJong. In a subsequent issue of the *Standard Bearer,* Editor Hoeksema asked the Reverends Kok and DeJong some pointed questions about their statements as self-appointed representatives of the Protestant Reformed Churches. A sampling is as follows:

> 3.   Did you or did you not state at the conference in The Netherlands that the conception regarding election etc. maintained by the Rev. Hoeksema is not the doctrine of the Prot. Ref. Churches?
> 4.   Did you or did you not say that the above doctrine is not binding in our churches?

> 5. Did you or did you not, with evident approval, state that some are sounding an entirely different note?
> 6. Did you or did you not state that, in your opinion most, or many of the Protestant Reformed did not think as the Revs. Hoeksema and Ophoff?
> 7. Did you or did you not state that there is great sympathy in the Prot. Ref. Churches for the covenant view of the liberated?[82]

After asking his questions, Editor Hoeksema told his readers that he had advised Rev. Ophoff not to make the letter public until the return of the Reverends Kok and DeJong; and Rev. Ophoff had agreed. But Rev. Ophoff, in his total devotion to the cause of the truth of the Scriptures, saw this situation in black and white, with no doubt that he must inform the churches of these immediate problems, which were later labelled the "selling of the Protestant Reformed Churches down the river."

In the same issue of the *Standard Bearer* the Rev. Ophoff wrote a short article titled: "Open Confession to the Brethren Rev. Kok and DeJong." After a brief introduction, he wrote:

> I do believe, after having given the matter some thought, that in publishing Prof. Holwerda's letter, when I did, I failed to take you brethren into consideration sufficiently. Out of regard for you I should have waited until you had returned to make a statement and had received testimony of the brethren in The Netherlands. Your statement together with their testimony could and also should then have been published with the letter and my comments. That would have been the right way. By my hasty action I took the joy out of your homecoming and caused you unnecessary grief. And for this, too, I am heartily sorry. I see now that I sinned against love.
> But brethren, I do wish that you would per-

---

82. "The Open Letter of Prof. Holwerda," Vol. 25, Sept. 15, 1949, p. 518.

> ceive from my statements occurring in my previously published article that I did not accuse you at all and therefore I did not accuse you unheard....
>
> I do wish, brethren, that you would also perceive that I did no wrong in publishing the letter *as such*. The letter had to be published sooner or later for reasons stated in my previously published article. It had also to be published to clear your name, brethren, if you did not make the statements attributed to you by Prof. Holwerda.[83]

Although this apology may have somewhat calmed the turmoil, the correspondence about the incident continued, the issue was unresolved, and the problems in the churches persisted.

Meanwhile, two groups of immigrants from The Netherlands were organized as Protestant Reformed Churches in Canada: first the congregation at Hamilton, Ontario, on April 19, 1949, and then the congregation at Chatham, on March 23, 1950.

The winds of change were still blowing in the various congregations of the denomination. Also during this period the denomination was growing and developing. Because both the Theological School and the Reformed Free Publishing Association, along with the important standing committees of the synods, had their bases in the Grand Rapids area, the congregations in the western and southwestern parts of the country felt very far from the hub of the denomination. They were also unhappy about the uneven distribution of administration between the East and the West.

Some of the pastors in the midwest started to discuss closer ties, at least among the area of their western congregations. They got together for a meeting and decided to publish a simple news magazine. They named it *Our Church News*. The little magazine did not prove to be a success. After more discussions, in the beginning of the year 1944 a group of

---

83. *Ibid.*, pp. 522, 523.

midwestern pastors met again. This time they decided to put out a different kind of paper. They named it *Concordia*. The goal of the editors of this magazine was that it should be a complement to the *Standard Bearer* — Western style. In the March 15, 1944, issue of the *Standard Bearer*, Editor Hoeksema congratulated the staff of *Concordia* as follows:

> It is not necessary for the *Standard Bearer* to introduce to our readers the newest arrival in the field of current Protestant Reformed literature, *Concordia*. It introduced itself in the form of a sample copy of the first issue sent to most of our readers, if not all, together with the announcement that it is willing to visit them every two weeks for the small sum of one dollar in eight months.
>
> We only write this editorial to welcome it, to recommend it to all our readers, to wish it a prosperous existence and a long life, to offer the *Standard Bearer* as an exchange paper as a matter of courtesy, and to make a few remarks about its contents and appearance.
>
> The *Concordia* undoubtedly fills a need in our churches: among our people there is room for this paper. Even though *Our Church News* did not seem to enjoy the high esteem and hearty support of many of our people, when it appeared no longer in our homes, we all felt that there was something missing, especially in the line of news from our churches....
>
> And although it may appear somewhat bold to enter everybody's home without being invited, especially when you make a charge of three cents for the privilege of being visited, *Concordia* does not have to be ashamed of its appearance, and had pretty solid reasons to think that, once having gained entrance into the homes of our people, they would invite it to stay.
>
> *Concordia* is a bi-weekly. It proposes to visit us in the weeks when the *Standard Bearer* does not appear....

> Those six ministers that designed the new bi-
> weekly did a good job. Honor to them![84]

Editor Hoeksema then went on to give the staff a bit of criticism in the areas of minor matters such as type-style, and ended with suggesting that *Concordia* be published weekly as soon as possible; and his last sentence said, "I heartily recommend *Concordia* to all our readers!"

Also in the mid-forties the churches in midwest America started their own weekly radio broadcasts. This type of growth and enthusiasm, if done in the proper way and in the right spirit would indicate a dedication to the growth and advancement of the denomination. Instead, there were sounds of discontent and murmurings about Herman Hoeksema and his position in the church from both the pastors and the members in the pews.

When the Lord sent Hoeksema his severe stroke and his consequent serious disabilities, He sent it in His perfect plan; and one facet of His plan was that it acted as a catalyst for the independent spirit which was blossoming in parts of the denomination. These people had not realized that a little more than a year after he suffered his stroke, Hoeksema would be back at work. They had thought his work as pastor and editor was ended. They were wrong, for along with his preaching Hoeksema also took up his work as editor of the *Standard Bearer*, although he never again was able to coordinate his fingers to type. All his work from 1948 until his death he put on recordings, to be typed by his son Homer.

Toward the end of the decade of the 1940s, several men in the denomination, especially pastors, began to *show* their spirit of independence. In the October 15, 1948, issue of the *Standard Bearer* Editor Hoeksema wrote about "A Tendency Towards Individualism." His message contained some criticisms, as well as a sense of disappointment.

> In the past, as anyone will be able to verify

---

84. "Concordia," *Standard Bearer*, Vol. 20, p. 252.

when he peruses the volumes of the *Standard Bearer,* we have been accustomed to direct our criticism to others rather than to ourselves....

Now, however, since we have passed the age of our first youth, and, the Lord willing, will celebrate the twenty-fifth anniversary of our churches next year, it may be well and salutary to cast a look at ourselves. No doubt, we are old and experienced enough by this time to stand a little well-meant, brotherly, and upbuilding criticism. And how could criticism passed by the *Standard Bearer* upon our own churches ever be anything but brotherly and well-meant, and positive and upbuilding criticism. Moreover, if the critical remarks of the *Standard Bearer* should be judged to be out of place and unfair, anyone can set himself to write a well-founded and well-motivated contradiction.

And then I want to subsume my remarks under the heading placed above this article, "A Tendency Toward Individualism."

By this I mean a tendency to go one's own individual way rather than to work in unison as churches. A tendency, moreover, to ignore or to forget the decisions of the churches in general, reached in their major assemblies; a tendency that is often rooted in lack of historical knowledge and a certain disrespect for historical precedent.... As an illustration of what I mean, I may point first of all to the new system of catechetical instruction that has been introduced in some of our congregations. This I read in the bulletin of my own congregation, the First Prot. Ref. Church of Grand Rapids; "For some classes the lesson material has been changed. We have planned to begin teaching doctrine at an earlier age." The proposed change is rather important. It seems that our children will be taught the biblical history only during the ages of 6 to 9 years; while from the age of 10 until the time that they make confession of faith they will be taught nothing but doctrine....

Besides, the new system is based on a mis-

taken notion of proper catechetical instruction
and of instruction in biblical history. I appreciate
the fact, of course, that the writers of those new
catechism books, as well as those that are in favor
of introducing them are motivated by the desire to
instruct our children and our youth thoroughly in
the Protestant Reformed truth; and for this I will
give them credit. I nevertheless think that it is a
serious mistake; and, as I said, it is an illustration
of individualism, when something so radically
new is introduced into our churches without the
advice of our major assemblies.

Why did the Lord give us such a large part of
His revelation in the form of history, if it was not
His purpose to instruct our children, the children
of the covenant, thoroughly in the works which
He has accomplished for our salvation in the past?
Moreover, and in close connection with this, all
the main doctrines of the church, as revealed in the
Bible, are historical and should be thoroughly
taught in this historical form, in order, before we
teach our own system of doctrine....

Looking over the new system and the proposed books for catechetical instruction, I venture
to predict, in the first place, that during the ten
years of proposed doctrinal instruction our cat-
echumens will find so much repetition of the same
things that in the end they will get weary of that
instruction. And, in the second place, I predict
that by the new system we make little dead intel-
lectualists and dogmaticians, rather than believers that live from the Bible as the living Word of
God.[85]

The Rev. Hofman, who was working as missionary in the
Lynden, Washington, area at this time, answered Editor
Hoeksema as follows:

...First of all, I would like to substantiate your

---

85. *Standard Bearer,* Vol. 25, pp. 28, 29.

> contention that catechism as it is being conducted
> in our churches generally, reveals a tendency to
> individualism. In fact I would like to add a few
> thoughts in support of your contention. In my
> very limited experience, I have already heard
> several parents complain of the lack of unity in
> respect to method and material. They deplored
> the fact that with every change of minister the
> current system was discarded and new individual
> ideas were instituted....

After several more examples of this individualism, Rev.
Hofman concluded:

> Finally, in order to bring out one more point,
> I too must confess some guilt in respect to the
> individualism you suggest. In my former charge
> we began teaching doctrine to the 10-12 year class.
> I found I was able to maintain better interest by
> teaching something relatively new. Perhaps this
> reveals a deficiency on my part in respect to the
> teaching of history but just for that reason I would
> appreciate a few suggestions. We have also found,
> in our present work, that the greatest lack does not
> lie in a knowledge of biblical facts but in a clear
> conception and line of truth; as well as almost
> complete ignorance of the contents of the Re-
> formed Confessions....[86]

Although this matter of individualism was openly discussed, it was not resolved. In fact, more unresolved problems and disagreements started to surface. These were the
disagreements about God's promise of salvation in the sphere
of His covenant with His people. Was it a conditional
promise? If so, what is God's condition? The pastors in the
West used their magazine *Concordia* to discuss conditions in
the covenant of grace, and those in the East countered with

---

86. "Periscope, *Standard Bearer,* Vol. 25, Jan. 1, 1949, pp. 167, 168.

their arguments in the *Standard Bearer.* Most of the men in the West favored the idea of conditions in God's covenant of grace with His people. They were opposed by most contributors from the East. An example is the on-going polemic between the Reverends A. Petter and G. Ophoff. Under the title of an "Open Letter to Rev. Andrew Petter" Rev. Ophoff referred to an article by Rev. Petter in *Concordia.* He quoted Rev. Petter as follows:

> You write,
> "And then it seems to me that if we remain strictly Reformed, without any pelagianizing supposition of the natural man in some way being able to meet the *conditions* of the covenant, then we need not be afraid of speaking of *conditions.* I cannot see a great importance in the question, except as it leads us back to the question, `What do we mean by the covenant?'
> "On the one hand the Scriptures plainly teach that there are conditions in connection with the covenant...."

Rev. Ophoff countered as follows:

> It is plain that in the proposition, "God saves His people *on the condition* that they believe," that is, "Salvation as a work of God is *contingent* on the faith of the believer," we deal with a heresy of the first magnitude, destructive conceptionally of God and of all true religion.
> Isn't it plain, brother, that the term *condition* as a sentence-element in the proposition, "God saves His people on the *condition* that they believe," is a dangerous one? It doesn't fit in the thought-structure of the Reformed theologian. It has place only in the perverted system of theology hatched out by Pelagius and Arminius.[87]

---

87. *Standard Bearer,* Vol. 25, May 1, 1949, pp. 350-352.

* * * * * * *

Even though these were years of disunity in the churches, the Synod of 1949 listened to the request of the mission committee "that a Holland-speaking missionary be called through the present calling church who will be available for work in Canada."[88]

The committee of pre-advice recommended this overture and the synod voted in favor of it. The Rev. A. Cammenga, who spoke the Dutch language, was elected, and he accepted the call. It was Cammenga who asked the mission committee for a statement of the Scriptural doctrine of God's covenant of grace which he could take with him in his mission work with the immigrants who came mostly from the Liberated Churches in The Netherlands.

Due to lack of time, this request of the Rev. Cammenga could not be implemented before the synod met in June of 1950; and before the time of this synod, the calendar showed another important date: the celebration of the twenty-fifth anniversary of the birth of the Protestant Reformed Churches, in March, 1949.

The celebration of this anniversary did not have the spontaneity and the joy of the twentieth anniversary of 1945; for the denomination was no longer united in its doctrines nor in its spiritual goals. A different spirit existed in the denomination. Many of the pastors and those who sat in the pews were obsessed with the idea of numerical growth, even at the expense of lowering their doctrinal principles. They were ready to adopt the common grace (in the sphere of the covenant) which they had staunchly repudiated in 1924.

Many members and most of the congregations had fallen into a spiritual lethargy. Their zeal to fight for biblical and Reformed truths had evaporated. They had developed a spiritual lethargy, an indifference to the love and study of

---

88. *Acts of Synod* of the Protestant Reformed Churches in America, 1949, p. 90.

sound doctrine. In fact, many members throughout the denomination did not hesitate to express their hatred of the doctrine of sovereign, particular grace in God's covenant with His people. They complained that the preaching was too doctrinal or that it was dead orthodoxy; and they clamored continuously for a change in the preaching.

It is no wonder, then, that the celebration of the twenty-fifth anniversary of the Protestant Reformed Churches was somber and — although Herman Hoeksema denied it — pessimistic. The very fact that the Rev. C. Hanko chose the passage from Ezra 3:10-13 as his theme for his sermon at the celebration shows that all was not well. In his sermon he contrasted the joy of those who were laying the foundation of God's house after the captivity to the "many of the priests and Levites and chief of the fathers" who "wept with a loud voice" because it could not be compared in beauty to the first temple in the former times of peace and gladness. They were weeping for their earlier days of joy in the way of obedience to the Lord.

Pastor Hanko showed a parallel in the church of Ezra's time and in the Protestant Reformed Churches in 1950. In these churches there was no longer the united and joyful defense of the truth as it had been celebrated in the first twenty years. The members of the denomination admitted openly that there was "a different sound" from the trumpets of many Protestant Reformed leaders in recent years. The trumpets were tuned to a conditional theology.

At the time of this celebration Herman Hoeksema asked and answered some questions. He asked: "Are you surprised, then, that on this twenty-fifth anniversary, I rather mourn than celebrate with rejoicing?"

He went on to say:

> But I ask, what is the heritage of the Protestant Reformed Churches? Is there any part of the truth which they have emphasized and further developed in distinction from other Reformed Churches?

To this question some, perhaps most of us, will answer: the Protestant Reformed Churches deny the theory of common grace. And that is, of course, true. But that is a mere negative answer. And we must have something positive. No church can live by a mere negation.

Others will answer more positively: the Protestant Reformed Churches teach the doctrine of sovereign grace; and that is also true. But, after all, that is not their peculiar heritage and their particular contribution to Reformed theology. Do not all Reformed Churches believe, officially, at least, the same truth? Do not even some Baptist churches confess this? It may be true that the Protestant Reformed Churches lay more emphasis upon this truth than other Reformed churches, but it cannot be said that the doctrine of sovereign grace is their peculiar heritage.

If you ask me what is the most peculiar treasure of the Protestant Reformed Churches, I answer without any hesitation: their peculiar view of the covenant.

And what is their particular conception?

It stands closely connected with their denial of common grace, and with their emphasis on the doctrine of election and reprobation.

Moreover, it emphasizes and carries out the organic idea.

Briefly stated it teaches that God realizes His eternal covenant of friendship, in Christ, the First-born of every creature, and the First-begotten of the dead, organically, and antithetically along the lines of election and reprobation, and in connection with the organic development of all things.

That is, in a nutshell, the peculiar Protestant Reformed heritage.

He that has been captivated by this beautiful Reformed truth must have nothing of anything that smacks of Heynsian theology, nor will he ever retrogress into a traditional conditional theology.

But rather than go backward, he will go forward and continue to develop the pure Protestant

Reformed truth of God's eternal covenant.

To do this is the specific calling of the Protestant Reformed Churches.

Failure to do this is our death. It is the end of our distinctive existence.

And that is the reason why, under the present circumstances, I cannot wholeheartedly join in with the joy of celebration.[89]

All was not well in the twenty-five year-old garden of Reformed plantings. Some of the gardeners were not interested in tending the garden, for winds of change and uncertainty were blowing through the garden of Reformed plantings, and seeds of thorns and thistles were beginning to sprout.

89. "Protestant Reformed," *Standard Bearer,* Vol. 26, March 15, 1950p. 269.

Chapter 12
Turmoil

The rather pessimistic celebration of the twenty-fifth anniversary of the Protestant Reformed Churches was past. The future of the denomination was not optimistic. Running through the denomination were undercurrents of dissatisfaction, disagreement, and polarization. During the years of 1949 and 1950 many of the pastors in the West wrote what they understood to be conditions in God's covenant of grace. Three examples are as follows:

> Rev. L. Doezema: Conditions are "the confrontation of God's demand which God annexes to the promise, in order to bring out clearly His unconditional grace and mercy, as well as His just wrath and man's inability to fulfill them.[90]

> Rev. B. Kok: I am seeking to show that we as Protestant Reformed Churches have always maintained that there are *conditions* in the Reformed sense of the term.... To deny that conditional element as it is so clearly revealed to us in the Word of God would be a catastrophe indeed. It would be fatal to all preaching of the gospel, and would lead our churches astray.[91]

> Rev. A. Petter: Speaking of the Liberated view of a conditional promise to all who are baptized: "And now this their presentation may have this good element that it seeks the better to emphasize

---

90. "The Synod of 1951," *Standard Bearer,* Vol. 28, Jan. 15, 1952, p. 174.
91. " 'Logical Truth,' " *Standard Bearer,* Vol. 28, Sept. 1, 1952, p. 495.

> and maintain the responsibility of man away down
> to the roots of his relation to God in the covenant....
> And I will add now that if we must all agree that
> there are no two parties in the covenant and that
> we may not speak of conditions in any sense
> whatever, *then they are on that point richer than
> we.* [92]

While most of the ministers who favored the idea of conditions in God's covenant of grace with His people wrote their views in *Concordia,* the Western paper, those who wrote in the *Standard Bearer* during these years gave strong rebuttals against any kind of condition in God's covenant which His children must — and are able to — fulfill in order to obtain salvation. An example of such a rebuttal is found in an article in the June 15, 1950, issue of the *Standard Bearer.* The Rev. H. Veldman, in an ongoing polemic with the Rev. A. Petter, made the strong statement that "the Word of God, in no uncertain terms, presents the *entire way of salvation, from the beginning to the end,* as exclusively the work of the Lord." [93]

Already a year earlier the Rev. A. Cammenga had asked for a statement from the synod to define and clarify these doctrinal issues; and at this time of crisis the whole denomination began to recognize the need for such a declaration: a declaration which would define and clarify the covenant views in the denomination and would serve to unify the churches; but no action had been taken.

This declaration was to be the main task of the Protestant Reformed Synod of June, 1950. As was customary, a presynodical service was held the evening before the synod convened. The Rev. H. Hoeksema preached, and his text set the mood for the synod which followed: Ephesians 4:14, 15 — "That we henceforth be no more children, tossed to and fro, and carried about with every wind of doctrine, by the

---

92. *Concordia,* July 21, 1949, p. 3.
93. "In Answer to Rev. A. Petter," *Standard Bearer,* Vol. 26, p. 413.

sleight of men, and cunning craftiness, whereby they lie in
wait to deceive; but speaking the truth in love, may grow up
into him in all things, which is the head, even Christ."
   Hoeksema started his sermon with a greeting:

>   Beloved in the Lord Jesus Christ:
>   This text, this part of the Word of God, con-
>   tains, as you recognize immediately, an admoni-
>   tion, an exhortation. And the exhortation is di-
>   rected to the whole church, of course: not only to
>   the officebearers.... They especially, as well as the
>   whole church, must be careful that they are not
>   tossed about by all kinds of false doctrine, but
>   must stand and be firm in the truth as it is in Christ
>   Jesus our Lord....

   He took as his theme *The Admonition to Be Firm in the
Truth.* A few pertinent statements in his sermon are as
follows:

>   The first question is answered by the words
>   that we be firm over against all kinds of false
>   doctrine. He (Paul) speaks of winds of doctrine
>   because he has in mind a ship that is crossing a
>   storm-tossed sea and that meets with all kinds of
>   winds — winds that will prevent the ship from
>   reaching the safe harbor, its proper destination,
>   winds that will drive the ship from its course, so
>   that really it gets nowhere. All kinds of winds
>   prevent the ship from getting anywhere. That is
>   the figure which the apostle uses in the words of
>   our text to characterize false doctrines in relation
>   to the church of Jesus Christ in the world.
>   And we know that indeed there are all kinds
>   of false doctrines, and that there is not a part—not
>   one part — of the doctrine, of the truth, as it is in
>   Jesus Christ our Lord that has not been denied and
>   has not been attacked in the course of the history
>   of the church, and that is not denied and is not
>   attacked today....
>   Many are the winds of doctrine that always

have been trying to prevent the church from
steering a straight course along the line of the truth
as it is in Jesus Christ our Lord.

And we may ask the question: why is it?... The
answer is in the words of our text, beloved. We do
not have to depend on our own opinion and our
own philosophy for an answer. But the apostle
himself tells us what motivates those false teachers when he says that all kinds of winds of doctrine
toss the ship because of the *sleight of men,* because
of *the cunning craftiness,* because *they lie in wait to
deceive....*

The false prophet is one, beloved, who according to the words of my text plays *hocus pocus*
with the truth. Cunning craftiness of men: what
does that mean? It means, beloved, that they twist
and twist and twist the truth in such a way that
you can no longer recognize the truth from the lie.
That's the cunning craftiness of men.... You have
but to read again, if you please — and it's well to
remind ourselves of these things; they must not be
forgotten — you have but to read again the Three
Points in order to be convinced of the truth of what
I am saying. Just read the First Point of 1924 ... and
you will find that the Christian Reformed Church
gathered in synodical session in 1924 in Kalamazoo
played *hocus pocus.*

Hoeksema went on to cite many other examples of hocus
pocus which had taken place in the history and development
of the church of New Testament times. After he traced the
history of those who played hocus pocus and departed from
the truth of the Scriptures, taking thousands of people into
the errors of heresy, he asked *why* the Lord allowed false
prophets and false doctrines in His church on earth. Then he
answered his question:

God Himself by His providence uses these
false doctrines in order to wake up the church and
in order to set the church strongly against the false
doctrine, and to cause her to develop the truth

over against that doctrine. That's her calling....
Negatively speaking, if we be tossed to and fro by
every wind of doctrine, we will lose Christ....
Outside of Christ we have absolutely nothing....

We must be firm in the truth.... That is your
calling as a synod. That is your calling as a church.
Stand firm in the truth. [94]

This synod appointed a committee to draw up a form
which would "remove all misunderstanding and aid toward
unity." Later at this same synod the committee reported that
it was ready to submit its statement concerning the doctrine
of God's covenant, particularly in the sphere of the baptism
of infants. The Rev. G. Vos read the document to the synod.
Its title was *A Brief Declaration of Principles of the Protestant Reformed Churches.*

The document started with the *basis* on which the Protestant Reformed Churches stand: the basis of God's Word and
the Reformed Confessions. The rest of the document is
divided into three parts:

A.   That election, which is the unconditional and
unchangeable decree of God to redeem in Christ
a certain number of persons, is the sole cause and
fountain of all our salvation, whence flow all the
gifts of grace, including faith.
B.   That Christ died only for the elect and that the
saving efficacy of the death of Christ extends to
them only.
C.   That faith is not a prerequisite or condition
unto salvation, but a gift of God, and a God-given
instrument whereby we appropriate the salvation
in Christ.

These three statements were supported by proofs from
the Scriptures and the Confessions. The committee which

---

94 *Acts of Synod* of the Protestant Reformed Churches of America,
1950, pp. 5-15.

composed this declaration gave the churches a thoroughly Reformed statement.*

After discussing the Declaration, the synod adopted it — almost unanimously — but provisionally. The reason that the synod adopted it provisionally — for one year — was that this time period furnished the opportunity to send the document to the congregations for study, comments, and corrections.

The provisional adoption of this important document also brought the issue of the controversy to a climax. It brought into focus and stated in concise terms what the Scriptures and our confessional and liturgical forms teach about God's covenant promises, also to the infants of believers. This document stood opposed to a covenant with conditions which God's people must fulfill. Without stating it in words, this document, with its Scriptural and Reformed stance, completely condemned Dr. Schilder's view of covenant theology — that of conditions which all baptized children must fulfill, and which fulfillment will bring them salvation. Those pastors in the Protestant Reformed denomination who sided with Dr. Schilder saw that their views — the Liberated views — were not tolerated in this statement of faith. Soon several of the pastors, especially in the West, began to build up opposition to the Declaration. Before long they were vehemently opposing the *Declaration of Principles.* This was a puzzling situation, for at the June synod the delegates had adopted it almost unanimously. Now many of the pastors became very vocal in their opposition — also from their pulpits.

Part of the problem lay in the unsolved and unsolvable doctrinal problems in the denomination. Another part was the denomination's relationship with the churches in The Netherlands in the aftermath of Dr. Schilder's visit. Also the controversy created by the visit of the Reverends Kok and DeJong in the summer of 1949 was still unresolved. Ongoing polemics between the pastors and editors of church papers in

---

* See the appendix for the complete Declaration of Principles.

both countries were still crossing the Atlantic, but the problems remained. These troubling matters were published in the church magazines in both denominations, and members in both denominations were taking sides on the issues.

In the January 1, 1951, issue of the *Standard Bearer* the Reverend B. Kok published his thoughts about *The Declaration of Principles*. He wrote:

> I am becoming more and more convinced that the "Declaration of Principles" adopted by our last Synod to be proposed to our churches was a sad mistake, and that we as Churches should reject them. I base this contention not so much because of their doctrinal content, but rather on the following grounds: First that the decision to adopt these declarations and propose them to our Churches was contrary to Article 30 of our Church Order. Secondly, that the Synod of 1950 acted too hastily in this matter. Thirdly, that this action of Synod has been, and, if God does not graciously forbid, will be the cause of dissention and schism in our Churches. Finally, that the questions involved are extra-confessional and hence may not determine membership or non-membership in the Church of Christ.

Kok objected, he claimed, not because of the document's contents, but because of *procedure*. This declaration should have come from a request of a congregation, through the classis and then the synod. He contended that the churches, in their synod, should not have agreed to the request of the mission committee that synod draw up a statement of doctrine to take to the mission field. Kok had other doubts: he wrote:

> Apart from the question whether or not this was the request of the Mission Committee, which I do not believe, (the Mission Committee merely requested Synod to draw up a formal letter to be signed by all those that desire to be organized into a Protestant Reformed Church) the Synod had no

right to violate the principles involved in Article
30 that only such matters shall be dealt with as
could not be finished in minor assemblies. [95]

In the next issue of the *Standard Bearer* Editor Hoeksema
explained why the declaration and the procedure of formulating it was proper and desirable:

> It is indeed often necessary that within the
> Confessions the Churches clearly express what
> according to their conviction is the plain teaching
> of those Confessions. This becomes necessary
> when one or a group of persons within the churches
> claim to stand on the basis of the confessions but
> nevertheless deviate from them....
>
> Now let us note — and this is my main and
> principle ground on which I based the contention
> that the Declaration of Principles should be adopted
> — *that the declaration is based from beginning to end
> on our Three Forms of Unity, as well as on our Baptism
> Form.*
>
> Some have alleged, without any proof for
> their contention, that the Declaration of Principles
> is nothing but a private theological opinion, or that
> it is at least extra-confessional. But this is certainly
> not true....
>
> The Declaration of Principles was adopted as
> a proposal to all our churches in the regular
> ecclesiastical way. No one can refute this on any
> sound church political basis. As I have repeatedly
> stated, it was adopted at the request of the Mission
> Committee. That committee is a synodical com-
> mittee and cannot send its proposals or requests in
> the way of consistory and classis to Synod, but
> must report to Synod directly....
>
> It will safeguard our Protestant Reformed
> Churches by the grace of God against the influence
> of those who claim that they adhere to the Re-
> formed Confessions, but who nevertheless devi-
> ate from them. [91]

---

95. "The Declaration, A Mistake," *Standard Bearer*, Vol. 27, p. 153.
96. "The Proposed Declaration," *Standard Bearer*, Vol. 27, Jan. 15,
1951, pp. 172, 173.

The sessions of the 1951 Synod were not tranquil sessions. It was necessary for the synod to recess and reconvene through the summer months, even until the fall of that year. Most of the days were filled with discussions and debates. When the synod at last officially adopted the provisional declaration as it had been amended, it was by a vote of nine to seven. The synod, with one exception, was split across geographical lines, with the delegates from the east voting positive and those from the west voting negative.

* * * * * * *

For all the members of the denomination, these were days of upheaval. The periodicals were bursting with new developments or disputes.

Already in January, 1951, before the official adoption of *The Declaration of Principles,* the Rev. Herman Veldman, who had been called as pastor to the newly-organized immigrant congregation of Hamilton, Ontario, Canada, and who had accepted this call and become Hamilton's pastor, was suddenly deposed from his office as pastor.

The reason for his deposition was that the congregation of Hamilton (who were former members of the Liberated Churches in The Netherlands) did not agree with the doctrinal basis of *The Declaration of Principles.* Neither could they agree with the preaching of their pastor, who heartily agreed with the declaration. Suddenly the Rev. Veldman was denied his pulpit because of his Reformed teaching of God's covenant with His people. He was not allowed to preach the Reformed doctrine of the Protestant Reformed Churches.

The majority of the consistory of the Hamilton Protestant Reformed Church charged their pastor with insubordination. They insisted that he submit to the desires of most of the members and preach the Liberated doctrines of conditional covenant-theology. These people made plain that they did not want to be Protestant Reformed.

The consistory of Hamilton, Ontario, met on Tuesday

evening, January 16, 1951, without the knowledge of their pastor or the vice-president of the consistory, Mr. S. Reitsma, an elder who agreed with his pastor. Without giving these men a hearing, the rest of the consistory of Hamilton met to decide their grievances against these two men. This "consistory meeting" of January 16 was an unusual meeting, a meeting in which the president and vice-president were "read out" of the consistory, and the decision was reached that the congregation sever connections with the Protestant Reformed Churches.

The congregation of Hamilton wanted to be Liberated, not Protestant Reformed. In an account of the history of the Hamilton congregation, the Rev. H. Veldman gave the following summation: "They surely have no interest in the cause of the Protestant Reformed Churches. They had regard for our churches only as long as they could affiliate themselves with our churches, *as Liberated.*" [97]

The Reformed Churches of The Netherlands were also taking note of the developments and the unrest in the Protestant Reformed denomination. Dr. Schilder, in the Liberated magazine *De Reformatie,* wrote an article titled "De Kous Is Af" (The Stocking is Finished), dated November 17, 1951. Editor Hoeksema's comments on Dr. Schilder's article are as follows:

> Dr. Schilder writes that the stocking is finished. But I would say that the knitting of the stocking was a complete failure, and that the failure must be blamed not on our churches, but on the churches in The Netherlands. Instead of knitting a stocking, we tangled up the whole business. And the best that can be done is to unravel that tangle and start from the beginning, that is, if the Liberated Churches in The Netherlands still desire correspondence with us....
> Dr. Schilder writes that he has clearly shown

97. "Rev. Petter Replies," *Standard Bearer,* Vol. 27, March 1, 1951, p. 254.

that the Declaration was not necessary, that it is
not the correct interpretation of the Confessions,
and that it is based on misunderstanding....

Nor was it our fault that the stocking of
correspondence was not properly knitted officially, but became one entangled mess. Let me
relate the history. [98]

Then Editor Hoeksema gave a brief resume of the history
of the correspondence between the two denominations; he
reminded Dr. Schilder and the members of the Liberated
Churches that they dragged their feet in their correspondence with the Protestant Reformed Churches; that later
they wished to use the help — financial and pastoral — of
these churches. Yet they would not embrace their Reformed
doctrines, and he noted that:

This was not knitting a stocking, surely not the
stocking of ecclesiastical correspondence, but
working on a hopeless and tangled mass.... In
conclusion, I want to emphasize once more that
the stocking is not finished. And if Dr. Schilder
feels that because of the stand of our churches as
revealed in the Declaration of Principles he does
not want to unravel the tangle and start knitting
anew, it suits me. Nevertheless, I want to state that
in that case I am disappointed in him, and for the
rest say, "Vale, Amice Schilder." [99]

✳   ✳   ✳   ✳   ✳   ✳   ✳

After the extended sessions of the Synod of 1951 and the
final adoption of *The Declaration of Principles*, many protests from all over the denomination against the declaration
arrived at the office of the Stated Clerk of Synod; but these
protests could not be treated at the next synod, that of 1952,

---

98. *Standard Bearer,* Vol. 28, pp. 149, 151.
99. *Ibid.,* p. 153.

because the Synod of 1951 had dragged on rather long, and then the printer, a sympathizer of those who did not want the declaration, worked so slowly that the documents were not ready in June of 1952. As a consequence, these many protests could not be treated until the Synod of 1953.

In the uneasy and brittle days of uncertainty in the spring of 1951, before *The Declaration of Principles* had been officially adopted, the Rev. Hubert DeWolf, one of the co-pastors with Herman Hoeksema and Cornelius Hanko in First Church, preached a sermon in the evening service of Sunday, April 15. His text was Luke 16:19-31: Jesus' parable of the rich man and Lazarus. In the last part of his sermon, Pastor DeWolf spoke of the request of the tortured rich man in hell, who asked Abraham to send Lazarus to witness to his brothers on the earth. Abraham's answer in the parable was, "They have Moses and the prophets; let them hear them," verse 29.

In connection with Abraham's reply to the rich man, Pastor DeWolf made the following statement: "God promises everyone of you that if you believe, you will be saved."

In this year of 1951, a year of heavy burdens, in an atmosphere of ecclesiastical warfare about conditions in God's covenant of grace, coming to a climax in the controversial *Declaration of Principles,* Pastor DeWolf made this controversial statement in the pulpit. It smacked of the heresy of the free offer of the gospel which was taught in the Christian Reformed Church in 1924. It was also similar to the theology of the Liberated Churches in The Netherlands, who taught that in the sacrament of baptism the promise of salvation is given to every baptized child on the condition that he accept it. DeWolf presented a combination of these two ideas — a conditional promise in two spheres — in one statement. It was a statement of a general, conditional promise, conditioned on the faith of a sinner, resulting in the conclusion that faith is the work of a sinner.

This attempt of Pastor DeWolf to water down the doctrine of sovereign grace caused uproar in the congregation of First Church. Two protests were immediately lodged with

the consistory of First Church, one of which was later with-
drawn. The treatment of the other protest dragged on month
after month without any decision, because the consistory
was deadlocked.

More than a year later, before there was any decision on
Pastor DeWolf's statement from the pulpit, on September 14,
1952, he made a second controversial statement from the
pulpit. Preaching a sermon preparatory to the administration of the Lord's Supper which was to be celebrated the
following Sunday, the pastor chose as his text Matthew 18:3:
"Verily I say unto you, Except ye be converted, and become
as little children, ye shall not enter into the kingdom of
heaven."

In the course of his sermon, DeWolf made this statement:
"Our act of conversion is a pre-requisite to enter the kingdom."

Again the congregation was in turmoil; and protests
arrived at the consistory as quickly as the next evening — the
Monday session of the consistory. The two factions existing
in the congregation started to label one another. When
aggressive members who sided with Hoeksema called these
statements "deformed," Pastor DeWolf countered by saying
that it was not necessary to carry the name "Protestant
Reformed" on the lapel of his coat. This exchange continued,
and there were still no decisions issued on the protests
against Pastor DeWolf's first statement of a year and a half
ago; and the second group of protests also met a stalemate in
the consistory.

In a personal paper Professor Herman Hanko wrote:

> Those who were sympathetic to the Liberated
> views of the covenant made every effort to intro-
> duce them into the theology of the Protestant
> Reformed Churches. This was not only true of the
> many articles which appeared in *Concordia;* it
> was also true of the preaching. Rev. DeWolf
> clearly showed that he was prepared to bring
> these erroneous views to the pulpit. Especially his
> first statement made that clear: "God promises to

every one of you that if you believe, you will be saved."

While he was speaking in this sermon of the preaching and not of the sacrament of baptism (as the Liberated usually did), he boldly stated that the promise of the gospel was for every one who heard the preaching. This made the promise even more general than the Liberated wanted to make it, for they limited the promise to every child who was baptized. Be that as it may, the statement clearly asserted that everyone to whom the preaching came could claim as his own the promise. God made His promise to every one. God, by an oath which He swore by Himself, promised every one salvation. Such a general promise clearly indicates that it is God's desire and intention to save every one who hears the preaching. He even goes so far as to seal His intention with a solemn promise.

How is it then to be explained that not all are actually saved? It is evident to any one who gives this whole matter a moment of thought that many to whom the promise comes are not in fact actually saved. How is this to be explained?

The answer is that the actual work of salvation is dependent upon the faith of those who hear. They must believe before they actually receive salvation: "...if you believe, you will be saved."

Various truths were clearly at stake. Does God actually promise to save every one who hears the gospel? Does God bind Himself to an oath that it is His desire and intent to save all to whom the gospel comes? Very clearly, this is a denial of eternal election. God, from all eternity, chooses His people and determines to save them alone. It is, therefore, impossible for God to declare solemnly by an oath that it is His desire and purpose to save all. The great truth of election, the very heart of the gospel, was denied. DeWolf and the Liberated under whose influence he had come did not want the truth of election.

The truth of Christ's particular atonement

was at stake. Did Christ die for every man: or did He die only for His elect given Him of the Father from all eternity: The Reformed faith has always maintained that Christ died only for His people. But, if God promises salvation, binding Himself to an oath, to all who hear the gospel, then Christ must have merited that salvation in order for the promise to be real. If God promises something to some one which is not obtained in the cross and for whom Christ did not die, the promise becomes an open mockery.

And because the promise is for all, but conditioned upon faith, all of salvation becomes conditional. It rests for its full realization upon man's work of faith. Man must believe. He must accept the promise. He must comply with the conditions before the promise can ever be realized. Thus God is dependent upon man's fulfillment of the condition of faith, and the worst form of Arminianism has been introduced into the church. A general promise is always conditional. And a conditional promise always makes faith the work of man.

That DeWolf had committed himself to a basically Arminian position became clear in his second statement where he clearly made the condition of salvation the work of man. He did this in a bit different context, but his meaning was clear. He stated: "Our act of conversion is a prerequisite to enter the kingdom." Man must convert himself before he can secure entrance into the kingdom of heaven. Nothing could be stated more clearly. In blatant opposition to the teaching of Scripture, DeWolf made salvation dependent upon the work of man. Scripture says that God "hath delivered us from the power of darkness, and hath translated us into the kingdom of his dear Son" (Col. 1:13). DeWolf said: "Our act of conversion" brings us into the kingdom of God's dear Son.

It is not as if these battles had not been fought before in the Protestant Reformed Churches. They were battles which were fought at the very beginning of our history. Then already, back in 1924,

Rev. Hoeksema had fought against the pernicious lie that God wills the salvation of all men and expresses His desire to save all through the general offer of the gospel. Then already Rev. Hoeksema had fought hard and long for the truth that the gospel is God's sovereign means to save His elect church through Christ. Now that truth was under attack once again. The very life of the Protestant Reformed Churches was at stake. If the views of those sympathetic to the Liberated doctrines of the promise of the covenant had prevailed, the Protestant Reformed Churches would have lost every right of existence. Although under a slightly different form, the battle was the same. The great question was: Were the Protestant Reformed Churches going to be faithful to their heritage? It was a battle for the very life of the denomination.[100]

＊　＊　＊　＊　＊　＊　＊

Finally, in February of 1953 the consistory asked Rev. DeWolf to submit to an examination by the consistory concerning his doctrinal views. DeWolf agreed to it. In the examination, he gave biblical and Reformed answers on all questions except on the issues of God's grace and His covenant. He would not state clearly what he believed. His answers were ambiguous and unclear.

The result of this examination was that the consistory voted to approve his examination; and his statements were upheld by the consistory. Some of the consistory members brought protests against the consistory's decision, and these protests were appealed to the next classis, which met the following April and on into May of 1953. Because of the deadlock in the consistory of First Church — with the result that all issues ended in a tie vote—those who disagreed with their pastor appealed the matter to Classis East. It had

---

100.   Herman Hanko, Personal Paper.

become necessary to get help from a broader assembly.

Classis East, meeting in April and extending its sessions through May, 1953, appointed a committee of three ministers and two elders to come to the classis with advice. This committee came back to the classis with a very lengthy report and with a shorter one. These were the majority and minority reports: for the committee could not agree on this matter. The majority of three ministers gave the two statements of DeWolf a positive and Scriptural interpretation. The minority of the two elders advised Classis East to condemn the two statements as neither Scriptural nor Reformed. After the opinions were read at the Classis, Pastor DeWolf himself asked to speak, and addressing the three ministers who gave a favorable interpretation to his statements, he said, "You men all know that is not what I meant by these statements."

Pastor DeWolf made it clear that he had deliberately tried to preach the doctrine of a conditional salvation — a salvation conditioned on man's response.

Classis East made two decisions:

1. That Rev. DeWolf's statements were not Reformed according to the Scriptures and the confessions.

2. That he must apologize for these statements from the pulpit. If he did not apologize, he would be suspended from office. Also the consistory members who agreed with DeWolf were told to concur in the apology or be suspended from office.

On June 1, 1953, a committee from Classis East was appointed to bring this decision to the consistory of First Church. By a majority vote of one, the consistory accepted the decision of Classis East. They did not implement the decision, however, until June 15. The classical committee warned the consistory of First Church not to give Pastor DeWolf nor his supporting elders a vote in this matter. Their reasons were as follows:

1. The classis had condemned them.

2. The consistory had decided to accept the decision of Classis East.

3. Pastor DeWolf and his supporters were in a position

in which they lost their right to vote in the consistory because they were the accused.

Next the consistory adopted a motion to request Rev. DeWolf to make the following apology concerning the two offensive sermons he had preached—those of April 15, 1951, and September 14, 1952 — from the pulpit on Sunday, June 21, 1953. If he did not apologize, he would be suspended from office, as well as the consistory members who agreed with him.

The apology which the consistory requested the Rev. DeWolf to deliver to the congregation, and to which the pastor had agreed, is as follows:

> I am sorry that in a sermon I preached on April 15th, 1951, I made the statement that, "God promises to all of you salvation, if you believe," implying a general conditional promise, which is contrary to all our Confessions. I promise henceforth to refrain from such statements and to teach that the promise of God is unconditional and for the elect only. I am sorry that in a sermon I preached on September 14, 1952, I preached the error that our act of conversion is a prerequisite to enter into the Kingdom. For this is contrary to the Word of God, John 3:3-5, Colossians 1:13, as well as to all our Confessions. Cf. especially Canons III, IV, 10-12. I promise that henceforth I will refrain from such unscriptural and un-reformed teaching.

Although the Rev. DeWolf was agreeable to these stipulations, on the evening of Sunday of June 21, 1953, he presented this apology instead:

> As far as those statements are concerned, I am ready to say that I am sorry that they were not clear and therefore left room for a wrong interpretation. I would like to explain that by the first statement I had no intention at all to teach that God promises salvation to all men and that it depends on man's own will whether or not he will be saved. I have

> never taught this and could not have intended to teach this by that statement. By the second statement I did not mean to teach that a natural man must convert himself while he is in the power of darkness, outside the Kingdom of God. Also, this is contrary to anything that I have ever preached. If therefore, I have offended anyone by not stating clearly what I meant and thus giving occasion for misinterpretation, I am sorry. [101]

Instead of making an apology, DeWolf put the onus on his congregation. He implied that his congregation did not listen very well and that he was sorry that the congregation did not understand what he was trying to say. If some did not understand what he said, he would apologize for that.

The next evening, Monday, June 22, the consistory of First Church met. One of the members made a motion to reject the apology of Pastor DeWolf, which was no apology. The vote, as it always was in those troubled days, was a tie: eleven to eleven. The chairman ruled that the Rev. DeWolf and those who supported him had no right to vote, for they were involved in the trouble. DeWolf argued their right to vote, and the meeting ended in disorder.

The following evening, Tuesday, June 23, 1953, the two other pastors of First Church, the Reverends Hoeksema and Hanko, and twelve elders met with the nearest consistory, that of Fourth Church (later called the Southeast Church). With the advice of this neighboring consistory, the consistory of First Church suspended Pastor DeWolf and deposed the elders who supported him. First Church was on the brink of a split.

* * * * * * *

While these doctrinal struggles were going on in the eastern part of the denomination, the congregations in the

---

101.   Minutes of the First Protestant Reformed Church Consistory Meetings, Art. 4, p. 20.

West were also filled with uneasiness and anxiety. Yet in the summer of 1951 the small group of five families meeting in Lynden, Washington, showed their trust in the Lord even in these difficult times. They voted to organize as a Protestant Reformed congregation. With the help of the Rev. H.C. Hoeksema who had accepted a call to the Doon, Iowa, congregation in October, 1949, this courageous group was organized and joined the western congregations of the Protestant Reformed Churches — even though the winds of change were increasing in velocity especially in the western part of the denomination.

The tendency to individualism was still active. One of the results of this tendency was the decision of the staff of *Concordia* to close their magazine to Herman Hoeksema, as editor of the *Standard Bearer.* Editor Hoeksema expressed his surprise in an article in the *Standard Bearer:*

> I think it very strange, to put it mildly, that *Concordia* first allows the Rev. Kok to attack me, permits him to announce to all our people that he intends to ask me some questions, and thereupon closes its columns so that I cannot reply.
>
> This, as far as I can remember, happened to me only once before. That was in 1923-24, when the Christian Reformed Church closed its papers to the discussion of our part on the issue of "common grace...."

Hoeksema explained why Kok's policy was an unfair policy for *Concordia:*

> He asked me to answer his questions in the *Standard Bearer.* I replied to him that I would be glad to answer his questions, but in *Concordia,* not in the *Standard Bearer.* You will realize, Mr. Editor, that it wouldn't be fair to answer those questions in the *Standard Bearer,* for the whole discussion concerning "conditions" was started by the Rev. Kok not in the *Standard Bearer,* but in *Concordia.*

Hoeksema also refuted Kok's charge that in former years

he — Hoeksema — had preached conditional theology. He wrote:

> I find it rather strange, to say the least, that the Rev. Kok so desperately attempted to ascribe to me conditional theology, to which — as the whole church well knows — I have never been addicted, but which always I have principally opposed....

Next Hoeksema quoted Kok's most recent article in *Concordia.* Kok wrote:

> It is not that I have attacked the good reputation of either the Rev. Ophoff, or Hoeksema, but they have cast suspicions on me, and that because I am defending the very truth which they have always defended, namely the truth of a general proclamation of a particular or conditional promise....

Again Hoeksema countered:

> Is this quite true? Is the Rev. Kok reproached because of the truth that the promise is particular, and therefore only for the elect?

Then he reminded Kok that in The Netherlands the Rev. Kok had told Professor Holwerda to inform the Canadian immigrants "that in our churches the sympathy for the Liberated was great also in the matter of the doctrine of the covenant, and that for the conception of the Liberated there is ample room in our churches."

He ended his reply to Rev. Kok by writing:

> I ask: it is surprising that those who love the Protestant Reformed truth received the impression that the Rev. Kok rather favors the Liberated view, and is at least in favor of throwing open our church doors to the Liberated and their conception of the covenant?... He and others have been leaving the impression that they favor the Liber-

ated view, and prefer it to our Protestant Reformed conception.... This is the history of our
churches in recent years. [102]

Following the lead of the mood of *Concordia* and its staff,
most of the pastors in the West, and parts of the congregations, continued their policies of individualism and
independentism over against the denomination to which
they belonged. The one exception was Pastor Homer C.
Hoeksema, son of Herman Hoeksema. A few episodes may
help the reader understand, at least in part, the atmosphere
in the West at this time. When H.C., as he was often called
in the denomination, accepted the call in 1949 to live in the
tiny burg of Doon, in Northwest Iowa, he came as pastor to
a soundly Reformed congregation — with a few exceptions.
The welcome to his new, and first, congregation was joyful
and sincere. The reception of the Hoeksema family by H.C.'s
fellow pastors in Classis West was courteous. At first the
young Pastor Hoeksema was made welcome by them and
was urged to attend the monthly gatherings of the pastors in
the Northwest Iowa area and to take his turn to speak on the
radio broadcast sponsored by the radio committee of Northwest Iowa.

Gradually differences between H.C. Hoeksema and the
other Western pastors surfaced. Quite soon after the family
had arrived in Doon, Hoeksema's wife was introduced to the
League of Women's Societies in Northwest Iowa. The board
of this league prepared two mass meetings a year. As a
newcomer to the area and with a background of experience
as a school teacher, she was asked to give the talk for the first
meeting she was to attend. The board stressed that a talk
about the education of covenant children would be welcomed.

Gertrude Hoeksema based her talk on the Parable of the
Two Builders, the wise and the foolish, taken from Matthew

---

102.   "The Closing of Concordia," *Standard Bearer,* Vol. 29,
Nov. 15, 1952, pp. 76-79.

7:24-27. She explained how, in their godly education of their covenant children, God's people must — and will — build their houses — also their houses of education for their children — on a rock. That rock is the Rock of Christ, and the Rock of His teachings in the Scriptures, along with the doctrines of these Scriptures, which God's church on earth has developed.

Hoeksema ended her talk by urging her listeners to build *their schools* for their children on the Rock of Christ, and to stay as close to the truth of His Word as possible in their schools. She asked, "How can this be accomplished?" And she answered, "By starting Christian day schools within the denomination, schools in which the home, church, and school all teach the truth as it is taught in our Protestant Reformed Churches."[103]

It was customary, the speaker had been told, and the chairwoman who had introduced her had promised, that there would be a time for questions after the talk. However, after the speech, the chairwoman mounted the platform with an angry face and announced that there was no time for questions. After the meeting was over, the speaker was bombarded with reprimands for advocating distinctive parental instruction for their children. Many of the women made it clear that the people in the West were very happy with the public schools or other Christian schools already established. Some made it clear that the speaker would not be welcome in their homes.

There was also a positive reaction to the speech. The reaction of those who had been struggling for solid Reformed education for their children was appreciation and encouragement.

It was not long before the skies in the West became storm clouds for the Rev. H.C. Hoeksema, too. It was customary for the Northwest Iowa Protestant Reformed Churches to have a large festival for all the Northwest Iowa Churches on the Fourth of July. In 1951 this picnic was held in the Rock

---

103.   Private notes.

Valley, Iowa, park. Large crowds came to this picnic, which included a speech, singing, games, and food. The Rev. H.C. Hoeksema had been asked to be the speaker, and he had accepted. He had lived in Doon for nearly two years, and understood the atmosphere which prevailed in the West.

The title of Hoeksema's speech was *Heart Trouble*. In his introduction he made clear that he was not speaking about heart trouble in the physical sense, but about heart trouble from a heart which controls all the issues of life, as Proverbs 4:23 teaches.

He said that the church on earth has a heart, too. There is a certain central truth which is pumped through the bloodstream of the church. Hoeksema asked, "What is it?" And he answered, "God's eternal sovereign election, together with its corollary, reprobation. The heartbeat of the church is sovereign, free, independent election — not of a mob, but of Christ's church."

Hoeksema asked: "What happens if you have heart trouble? What happens if the church of God has heart trouble?"

He answered: "The heart beats weakly or stops beating. Heart trouble may be caused by losing God and enthroning man ... or having a Christ for all and a well-meaning and conditional offer of salvation, either in general or in the sphere of the covenant. That's heart trouble."

He went on to say that if your heart beats weakly you "lose all certainty and assurance of salvation and the only comfort in life and death that you belong to your Savior."

Hoeksema gave a brief review of church history, showing heart trouble in the history of God's church on earth. The history of Jacobus Arminius was one of his examples.

Next he talked about the diagnosis of the spiritual heart, the cardiogram of the heart of the troubled child of God. The cardiogram may show that the beat of election is not heard; or that the heart has lost the beat of God's sovereignty in the election of His child; or that the heart is beating to another rhythm — that of a conditional rhythm which tends to wax and to wane.

"What is the cure for such a weak and troubled heart?" Hoeksema asked. He answered from the Scriptures: get healthy exercise by studying and teaching and holding on to this central truth of the Scripture found in II Timothy 2:15: "Study to show thyself approved unto God, a workman that needeth not to be ashamed, rightly dividing the word of truth." He urged his listeners to preach and teach it regardless of its unpopularity.[104]

From that time on there was a coolness on the part of all the pastors in Western Iowa and Minnesota. These men made it clear that Rev. H.C. was not welcome at their monthly gatherings for fellowship and discussion. He was also told that he was not on the roster for speaking on the Western radio broadcast. The other pastors made it clear that they wanted to promote their own Liberated, conditional theology.

Occasionally Pastor Hoeksema had classical appointments to the various churches of Northwest Iowa and Minnesota. In their pastor's absence, the congregation of Doon would have a visiting pastor from the area in its pulpit. In the summer of 1953, at a morning service, when many of the parents took their young children to church, one of the neighboring pastors was preaching about conditions which *we* must fulfill. He repeated and reinforced the necessity of *our* obligations: what *we* must be and what *we* must do. As the pastor paused for an expressive silence, a young child, sitting near the back, chanted in a clear, high voice — before his mother could stop him — "Wee, wee, wee, all the way home!"

Although the situation, with its background of what *we* must do to obtain our salvation was tragic, the incident was funny, and almost the whole congregation laughed!

❋   ❋   ❋   ❋   ❋   ❋   ❋

---

104.   Private notes.

Classis West, which met in the spring of 1953, received five protests against *The Declaration of Principles* from the congregations of Sioux Center, Pella, and Oskaloosa, Iowa; Bellflower, California; and from the Rev. W. Hofman. A partial report of the committee of pre-advice is as follows:

> That Classis West express to Synod that we cannot be satisfied with Synod's treatment of the Protest of Classis West since Synod did not answer said protest by positively indicating the legality of the Declaration with well-motivated grounds. Classis therefore maintains its original position that it considers the Declaration to be illegal....
>
> 1. For it separates the Confessions from their derived and inseparable context, Scripture.
> 2. It omits what the Church has done in its formulation and use of the Confessions.

Editor Hoeksema commented in the *Standard Bearer:*

> Frankly, the *Standard Bearer* cannot understand the church polity of Classis West....
>
> Let me explain.
>
> The decision of Classis West is independentistic in relation to Synod. Although the Synods of 1950 and 1951 took the stand that the Declaration of Principles was legally adopted, and although it maintained this stand even after all the protests of Classis West had been considered, nevertheless Classis West now protests against the adoption of the Declaration as being an illegal act.... Evidently the position of Classis West is that the Declaration is not legal, and that no matter what Synod may decide, it will continue to take that stand. That is pure independentism. [105]

In this atmosphere of uncertainties and of polarization in

---

105.   "Classis West versus the Declaration," *Standard Bearer,* Vol. 29, May 1, 1953, pp. 340, 341.

congregations and families, with the certainty that this tenu-ous condition could not continue, the rumors of an imminent rift in the East began to travel through the Protestant Re-formed congregations in the West.

In the garden of Reformed plantings, a crisis was arising. The fungus which had crept into the garden had quickly spread and was loosening the roots of the Reformed plantings. Many plants in the garden looked with anxiety at the fungus. Others in the garden of Reformed plantings were comfort-able living with the fungus and suggested peaceful co-existence, or as they expressed it in words: "hoeless weed-ing."

Chapter 13
The Split of 1953

As was already mentioned in the previous chapter on page 183, on Tuesday evening, June 23, 1953, the elders who supported the decision of Classis East held another consistory meeting. The meeting of the evening before had ended in chaos. Because of the weighty matters to be discussed at this meeting, the consistory had asked the elders of Fourth Church to meet with them. Article 4 of the minutes of this meeting reads as follows:

> The Chairman relates (that) the purpose of calling this meeting, together with those members present, is to consider action in re the refusal of Rev. DeWolf and those Elders supporting him to apologize per the decision adopted by this Consistory and thereby becoming a matter of discipline.

In other words, because Rev. DeWolf did not apologize, the consistory's next step was to consider his suspension. The next article in the minutes furnishes the grounds for this suspension: "the two heretical statements made in two sermons preached on April 15, 1951 and September 14, 1952...."

Next the consistory passed a motion to depose the elders who had supported Pastor DeWolf. The grounds were as follows:

> 1. Their refusal to apologize for supporting and defending Rev. DeWolf in maintaining the two statements declared by Classis to be literally heretical;

2.The advice of Classis regarding this case;
3.The decision of this Consistory made on June 1
to adopt the advice of Classis and act accordingly.... [106]

If the consistory followed its own decisions and the
advice of Classis East, this body was obligated to suspend
these men. They also understood that this action would
result in a rift — a permanent separation. If this separation
became a fact, there would be *two* congregations with only
one meeting place: First Church. Therefore the problem of
a possible alternative meeting place to worship on the Lord's
day was one which needed immediate attention, if the other
group also claimed possession of First Church. The consistory
made the following decision in Article 8.

It is moved that the chair appoint G. Stadt and G.
Vink as a Committee to contact the other group
and to notify them we intend, as the rightful
consistory, to use the pulpit on the coming Sabbath days and the purpose of this notice to them is
to avoid any misunderstanding or violence. [107]

In case the group following Rev. DeWolf, with his
consistory, refused to honor this notification, the consistory
adopted Article 11.

It is moved that the Building Committee arrange
a place for us to hold services in the event resis-
tance is expressed in our use of the pulpit. Carried. [108]

Article 10 reads as follows:

---

106.   Minutes of the First Protestant Reformed Church Consistory Meetings, p. 21.
107.   *Ibid.*, p. 22.
108.   *Ibid.*

> Motion is made that we adopt the letter proposed
> and read by Rev. H. Hoeksema which is ad-
> dressed to the Congregation and get same in mail
> this week. Carried.[109]

This letter was not circulated in the congregation until
after their first meeting in the auditorium of the Grand
Rapids Christian High School. See the appendix, p. 373.

On Wednesday, June 24, the consistory of First Church
who agreed with the decision of Classis East met again.
Article 3 of that meeting gives the following information:

> The Committee appointed last night to visit the
> DeWolf group in re the use of the pulpit brings the
> following report; they were advised by Rev.
> DeWolf to visit with S. DeYoung and W. Stuursma
> who were appointed as a Committee to see us. A
> meeting with them was held at 7:30 this evening in
> which our Committee brought our expressions of
> using the pulpit. The Committee was denied
> meeting with their entire group which they stated
> was going to be held at a later hour tonight.
> However, this Committee assured they would
> bring our message to their body and stated a reply
> could be expected from them. Received for infor-
> mation. [110]

Later that same evening the two couriers from the DeWolf
faction visited the consistory meeting of the group led by
Pastor Hoeksema with an answer. Article 4 of the minutes
reads:

> S. DeYoung and W. Stuursma enter the meeting
> and tender the following as an answer to our
> notice of using the pulpit: "We cannot possibly
> recognize your schismatic action and your illegal
> suspension and deposition of office bearers and

109.   *Ibid.*, p. 22.
110.   *Ibid.*, p. 23.

therefore cannot concede you the right to hold
meetings in our midst. We therefore notify you
that we will occupy the buildings until the proper
deposition of the buildings are (sic.) made.
(was signed, Consistory of 1st Prot. Ref. Church)[111]

As a result of this information, the consistory with
Hoeksema as president made the following decision:

Article 5. Motion is made that we hold 3 services
Sunday at the usual time in either Ottawa Hills or
Christian High School auditoriums and empow-
ering the Building Committee to make the decision upon gathering the necessary data.
Article 7. Motion is made that we make an
appendix to the letter previously approved to be
forwarded to the Congregation consisting of our
meeting place and reasons for going there as well
as asking those that attend to bring along their
own *Psalter* books. Carried.
Article 8. It is moved that the Classical Committee
be notified of our request for a reconvening of
Classis East at the earliest possible moment for
them to receive and sustain our actions. Carried.[112]

After the leaders in First Protestant Reformed Church
had lived through the busy and almost unreal week of
meetings, tensions, and decision-making, it must have seemed
that Sunday, June 28, 1953, arrived very quickly. Not only
were the leaders of the two factions of the split congregation
tense, with a sense of unreality, but the *members* of both
groups had also lived that first week in an unsettled atmosphere. Families were already divided, friends found themselves in opposite groups, and all the members of the congregation were especially anxious about the Sunday morning

---

111.   *Ibid.,* p. 23.
112.   *Ibid.*

service. Who would be with each group, and who would not? Could they keep their composure in the sad atmosphere?

On that first Sunday after the split, the faction with Pastor DeWolf took over the First Church building. They not only held services in First Church, but they changed the locks so that none of the opposition could get into the church and take possession.

The group pastored by Herman Hoeksema went to Grand Rapids Christian High School for services. The atmosphere was tense, with many unspoken questions: Who will be in church? Will our friends of many years be here? Will we see our in-laws? We just do not know!

Reverend Hoeksema preached that first Sunday morning after the split on the passage from John 6:67 and 68: "Then Jesus said unto the twelve, Will ye also go away? Then Simon Peter answered him, Lord, to whom shall we go? Thou hast the words of eternal life."

Pastor Hoeksema explained that Jesus spoke the words of this text just after a great wonder. He had fed the five thousand with bread, and then had preached the gospel of Himself as the Bread of Life. When many of the people in Jesus' audience would not listen to that gospel and walked away, Jesus asked His disciples, "Will ye also go away?"

With the theme: Christ the Choice of Faith, he divided his sermon into three parts: The Question, The Choice, and The Faith.

In the first part of his sermon he drew the attention of his audience to the fact that Jesus' question was *negative;* and he asked, "Was this a reckless question?" His answer was "No! It was a correct question."

The pastor explained that the reason was that Jesus' asking whether they wanted to leave the Bread of Life posed no danger to the faith of His people in the audience. Rather, it strengthened those who were wavering. It made them face the issue: Believe or go away! It was either or!

When Hoeksema applied the words of Jesus to the situation in June of 1953, he asked his audience, "Which is it?

Either a promise for all *or* a promise to God's elect? Either salvation by faith *or* on the condition that *you* believe?

Next Pastor Hoeksema noted that the disciples of Galilee gave a spontaneous answer: "Lord, to whom shall we go? Thou hast the words of eternal life," verse 68. In applying this answer to his congregation, the pastor explained that this was also the answer of the members meeting in the Grand Rapids Christian High School on this unsettled day.

Finally Hoeksema told his audience that the *reason* for the answer of the godly Galileans and those sitting in front of him on this sabbath day was the gift of *faith* and *trust* from God. At the end of his sermon, he asked: "Will you also go away? From the Protestant Reformed truth? From Christ, the Bread of Life?" [113]

In the evening Pastor C. Hanko preached on the last part of Revelation 2:10: "Be thou faithful unto death, and I will give thee a crown of life," a fitting and beautiful ending for a sad and difficult day.

*   *   *   *   *   *   *

The trouble in the other congregations of the denomination had not as yet led to any splits. In the August 1, 1953, issue of the *Standard Bearer*, Editor Hoeksema gave a brief summary of the upheaval in First Protestant Reformed Church:

> After almost thirty years of Protestant Reformed Church life, the falling away from the Protestant Reformed truth which, already for some time, corrupted our churches, has officially become a reality and the split in our churches has begun.
>
> It became a reality in the mother church, the First Protestant Reformed Church of Grand Rapids which together with our Hope Church and the

---

113.   From a hand-written sermon.

Protesting Christian Reformed Church in Kalamazoo formed the beginning of all our churches.

No doubt, if all signs do not fail, the split in the First Church is only the beginning, and it will have its repercussions in some of the other churches.

Already the Rev. A. Petter took sides with those that apostatized and severed, with them, his connection with the Protestant Reformed Churches.

The same may now be said of the Rev. A. Cammenga. He also preached for those that severed themselves from the Protestant Reformed Churches, and refused to recognize the legal consistory of the First Protestant Reformed Church of Grand Rapids that called him as missionary for our churches. The Mission Committee has, for the time being, relieved him of his labors as missionary.

For the time being, to avoid a church fight for the buildings, the First Church meets in the rather large and convenient auditorium of the Christian High School. This does not mean that First Church repudiates its right to the property. But if at all possible it would like to settle this matter outside of the worldly court. [114]

Immediate practical problems followed the split in First Church. The summer would soon be over and the seminary would start its fall classes. However, the professors and students could not meet in their accustomed classrooms in the basement of First Church because they had been locked out. The answer to the problem came from the Adams Street grade school. Due to the rift, the school was losing many pupils; and they suddenly had a couple of empty classrooms. The school board invited the staff and students of the seminary to make Adams School their temporary home; and the Theological School accepted the offer. Until the question

---

114.   "The Split," *Standard Bearer,* Vol. 29, p. 436.

of the rightful ownership of the First Church property was settled in court, the seminarians studied under the same roof with the kindergartners. Many of the catechism classes and societies also found temporary homes at Adams School.

※　※　※　※　※　※　※

The troubles of the split did not remain in the congregation of First Church. For a long time the simmerings of discord had been present in most of the other Protestant Reformed congregations. The impetus to bring this simmering trouble in these congregations to a head was the July, 1953, session of Classis East. Both the group pastored by Hubert DeWolf and the group pastored by Herman Hoeksema and Cornelius Hanko sent delegates to this classis. Even before this classis could constitute itself as a proper classis, it had to treat the problem of credentials: this means that before the classis may take on its duties, it must determine that all delegates are legally and properly at this meeting of classis. At this July Classis the chairman announced that there were two separate groups from First Church, and also two sets of credentials: one from the "DeWolf group," as it was called, and one from the "Hoeksema group."

Because of the undercurrents of discord connected with some of the upheavals in the denomination, it took the classis a long time to determine which pair of delegates to seat. Finally the classis decided that the consistory of which Herman Hoeksema and Cornelius Hanko were presidents was the rightful consistory of First Church, and that the consistory of which Hubert DeWolf was president was not the consistory of First Church. The Hoeksema contingent was seated.

Reverend DeWolf and his delegates then left the classis, along with some of the delegates from other congregations of Classis East who supported DeWolf. Delegates from Holland, Second (now Southwest) and Kalamazoo congregations walked out with DeWolf. This action immediately led to an open split in each of these three congregations.

This summer session of Classis East, due to its volume of work, was forced to recess and reconvene. By the time of its last meeting on October 6, 1953, most of the congregations of Classis East had split.

The groups who joined the DeWolf faction sent protests to this session of classis. Creston congregation in northwest Grand Rapids and the Fourth (Southeast) congregation did not split but were plagued with internal disagreements. The congregations of Hope (Walker) and Hudsonville, Michigan; Randolph, Wisconsin; and South Holland, Illinois, did not have a split. Most of the members stayed with the denomination; and some of their members left the congregations either to join the DeWolf group or the Christian Reformed Church.

The members in the two opposite groups in the congregations of Classis East reacted with varying degrees of sadness and anger, fear and frustration, and even hatred. As in all conflicts — probably especially because this conflict touched the interpretation of God's Word — there were extremists on both sides of the dispute concerning the interpretation of God's sovereign grace in the line of the generations of His covenant children. Some of these extremists from the Hoeksema group, the "two hundred percenters," as they were named, spoke more harshly in the conflict than they should have. Others, on both sides, resorted to slander, adding resentment and bitterness to the deep sorrows already hurting the churches.

Would it not have been better and easier to soft-pedal the differences and live either with a compromise or different interpretations of God's promise to His covenant children? The leaders answered no. All these trials were necessary; for the pastors and members of the Protestant Reformed Churches who upheld the doctrine of sovereign grace were fighting a battle which in essence had been fought before — the common grace controversy in 1924. In that battle almost thirty years earlier, the emerging Protestant Reformed Churches had fought the battle to hold on to the doctrine of God's sovereign grace instead of teaching a doctrine of a general common grace along with a general offer of the gospel to all people who hear the gospel.

In 1953 the battle for God's sovereign, particular grace was fought again. This time the Protestant Reformed Churches fought a battle against a certain common grace to infants of believers in the sphere of God's covenant promises along with a conditional promise of salvation depending on their acceptance of the promise. The leaders and members of the churches understood that if they lost God's sovereign, covenant promises in the sacrament of baptism and made the general promise conditional, depending on the will of the baptized child, to be saved, they would lose their salvation in their generations, for no baptized child of himself can fulfill the condition of gaining salvation through his act of believing.

When the Reverend DeWolf was suspended by the consistory of First Protestant Reformed Church, the consistory of that congregation notified all the churches of the denomination of this suspension for, according to the Church Order, the denomination is a federation of churches; and the logical conclusion adopted by the denomination was that if a pastor is suspended in his own congregation, he is not allowed to minister in a sister congregation unless or until he is cleared of wrong-doing. When the pastors in Classis West read the notification of Pastor DeWolf's suspension, they were, with one exception, very angry. They did not agree with this principle of the Church Order nor with the consistory of First Church. At the same time it was not the business of the pastors in Classis West, as individuals, to judge this situation. They would have done well to follow the orderly way of taking their grievances to the consistory of First Church.

Instead, these pastors and their consistories, with the exception of Pastor H.C. Hoeksema and his consistory from Doon, took action. They brought their grievances directly to the next meeting of Classis West (which met on September 2,

1953) with the accusation that First Church in Classis East had acted improperly and had done wrong in suspending Rev. DeWolf. If classis agreed with these grievances and acted on them, its decision would put Classis West on the side of the Rev. DeWolf.

At the meeting of Classis West on September 2, all the delegates except the delegates from Doon agreed to accuse First Church of wrong-doing and to notify First Church *as classis* of their disapproval. Again, as pastor, Rev. H.C. Hoeksema stood alone in Classis West. Earlier in the conflict he had expressed his objections to Classis West; but these meetings had been times of discussion and debate. Now the churches had come to a crisis: a decision which would affect the future of the denomination. Pastor H.C. Hoeksema could not join the classis in accusing First Church. He had only one choice: to state his objection and that of his elder and to leave the meeting. This episode was the beginning of the split of 1953 in the West. It came about three months after the separation in the East. The trauma of the split which had happened in the eastern part of the denomination in the summer was repeated in the West in September. The tensions, uncertainties, and separations were heart-rending, for the churches, the symbols of refuge for believers, were in chaos.

Only one congregation in the West stayed intact (two families left) and remained loyal to the doctrines of Scripture as interpreted in the Reformed creeds. That was the congregation of Doon, Iowa.

In the immediate aftermath of this traumatic rift, when many members of the western congregations which had split felt anxious about keeping those members who were Protestant Reformed intact as congregations, they looked for immediate help. In the next weeks, either the church or the parlor of the manse in Doon began to be the headquarters for the members who wanted to stay with those who opposed conditional theology.

Almost immediately the congregations of both Hull, Iowa, and Edgerton, Minnesota, split — approximately in half; and both groups in these two congregations needed guidance in the chaotic atmosphere of a split in their congregation. Those who followed the DeWolf faction could consult their pastors, who were all on the side of DeWolf.

The ones who followed Herman Hoeksema and his interpretations of the Scriptures, found only one pastor in the West to whom they could go for help: the pastor of the Doon congregation. It was to the manse in Doon that the members of the split consistories came immediately after the formal split in the West. The week in the first part of September, 1953, immediately after the split, later came to be known as the "classic" week.

Except for Doon, the congregations of Northwest Iowa were split about half and half. On the Monday morning after the split, at nine o'clock, representatives from the congregation of Edgerton stood at the door of Doon's manse, asking for help and advice. Early in the afternoon delegates from the consistory of Hull, Iowa, came for advice. In the evening the consistory of Doon met to try to formulate some advice. Throughout that week, troubled people from various congregations were at the manse morning, afternoon, and evening, trying to solve problems and struggling to understand how to re-organize.

Already immediately after the split in the West, the members of the Hull and Edgerton congregations who stood with the Hoeksema group made an urgent telephone call to the Rev. Herman Hoeksema, asking him and the Rev. G. Ophoff to come immediately to help them. Early in the "classic" week the Reverends Hoeksema and Ophoff arrived in Doon to give advice to the people coming and going, morning, afternoon, and evening.

On Sunday, September 13, the Reverends Ophoff and H. Hoeksema preached in Edgerton. Neither went to preach for the group in Hull because these people had run into some trouble. The consistory of the Hull congregation had decided on the previous Thursday evening (September 10) to postpone indefinitely the adoption of the decisions of Classis West. The representatives of the consistory who were faithful to the Protestant Reformed denomination asked for help in drawing up a letter to their fellow officebearers who were on the DeWolf side of the issue. The letter read as follows:

> Mr. P. DeLeuw, Clerk
> Boyden, Iowa
> Dear Sir:
>   We understand that at your last consistory meeting you decided to postpone indefinitely to decide whether or not to adopt the decision of Classis West in re the suspension of DeWolf and the deposition of the apostate elders of the First Church of Grand Rapids, Michigan. Therefore:
>   1.   Seeing, that according to Art. 31 of the Church Order that decision of Classis is nevertheless settled and binding upon you as long as you do not publicly renounce it:
>   2.   Seeing that by your decision the congregation also falls under the binding decision of Classis West;
>   3.   Considering, moreover, that we, the undersigned, cannot be bound by such a decision for reasons we have explained to you in detail in our former communication to you;
>   4.   We inform you that from September 16, 1953, we will consider ourselves the legal consistory and congregation, and function accordingly until you publicly announce and inform us that you will no longer be responsible for, and consider yourselves bound by the above-mentioned decision of Classis.
>   You will understand, further, that as the legal consistory and congregation of the Hull Protestant Reformed Church we also claim the right to the church property, even though temporarily we must meet separately.
> Respectfully,
The legal consistory and congregation of the
Hull Protestant Reformed Church [115]

---

115.   H. Hoeksema, "What Happened in the West," *Standard Bearer*, Vol. 30, Oct. 1, 1953, p. 7.

The week of the split, the first week in September in the year 1953, was a very hot week; and the people who crowded into the manse in Doon during that week brought fans and cold drinks along with them. These were pre-air-conditioning days.

Suddenly early one afternoon the earnest talking, often by several people at once, turned to utter silence. One of the officebearers, in his nervousness and stress, had fainted. After cold washcloths and more air, the man regained consciousness, had a drink, and went on with the business of the church. This episode, however, illustrates the depth of concern which the troubles had created.

During the stay of the Reverends Ophoff and Hoeksema those people who were faithful to the Protestant Reformed denomination in the congregations of Hull, Iowa, and Edgerton, Minnesota, were re-organized.

Gradually the troubles spread to other congregations in Classis West. The split in the Redlands, California, congregation came in October of 1953, and in the Lynden, Washington, congregation in December of 1953.

In several congregations the great majority of the members sided with the pastors of Classis West. These congregations did not split, although some of their members transferred to other area Protestant Reformed congregations: Oskaloosa, Pella, Rock Valley, Sioux Center, and Orange City, Iowa; Manhattan, Montana; and Bellflower, California.

Although the issues of the split were serious biblical and doctrinal matters and issues of obedience to God's Word, they were also days when feelings ran high, when families were torn apart, when there was slander and bitterness, and when the people were speculating whether they would be able to keep their church properties. Often parents underestimated the tensions which were pressing down on their children, even the younger ones.

One incident in the manse in Doon illustrated a young child's feelings and also his loyalty in these days of upheaval. The incident occurred on the day that the Rev. M. Schipper from Grand Rapids arrived at the manse. Rev. Schipper was a friendly, cheerful, and rather self-assured man. As he strode confidently into the house he put out his hand to the four-year-old child, standing near the door, and said, "Shake hands!"

The young boy spread his legs, put his hands behind his back, and said, "Not until you tell me whose side you're on!"

The visiting pastor was suddenly speechless, deflated because of a young child's loyalty to the beliefs of his father. When the two finally shook hands, the four-year-old furnished the explanation for his initial refusal to shake hands: "You see, this is the hind-quarters of Classis West."

That was humor. There was also joy. Those who clung to the Scriptural truth of God's unconditional grace developed a deeper understanding of God's sovereignty in saving His people. Because of the trouble, they were forced to study in order to understand the doctrine of God's grace in the line of covenant generations. The split had drawn members of the various congregations to come together for in-depth studies of the doctrine of God's sovereignty in saving His people. They delved more deeply into the doctrine of God's grace in the line of His covenant generations. And they listened with joy when it was preached from the pulpit.

※   ※   ※   ※   ※   ※   ※

The split was a reality. People on both sides realized that life went on. So did the polemics. On July 21, 1953, the first issue of a pamphlet-type publication titled *The Reformed Guardian* (published bi-weekly in Grand Rapids) arrived at the homes of members of both factions in the recent church split. It was the new publication of those who agreed with Rev. DeWolf and his followers. The foreword of the first issue announced:

> This is a free publication published periodically for members of the Protestant Reformed Churches.
> In behalf of truth and justice in these days of stress and controversy this little magazine makes

its way into your home through the efforts of THE
REFORMED GUARDIAN ASSOCIATION.
Extra copies for distribution may be had at all
times free upon request....

In this and following issues the author(s) of the *Guardian*
took issue with those on the opposite side of the controversy
for

the gross injustice committed by the brethren
imposing suspension upon the Rev. DeWolf, and
deposition upon eleven of his elders. By this
illegal action a schism of such proportions has
been caused in our churches which, if God does
not graciously prohibit through your defense of
right and justice, will continue unabated, and
shame and disgrace shall be heaped upon the
name of Christ.

It is unnecessary at this time to enter into the
doctrinal dispute which led to these unjust disci-
plinary proceedings. Were a man guilty of the
grossest heresy such proceedings could never be
justified neither tolerated in the Church of Jesus
Christ. That the Rev. DeWolf was not guilty of
heresy is evident from the examination to which
he was submitted by his Consistory, and evident
also from the following apology which he ten-
dered to said body....

Then follows Pastor DeWolf's unauthorized apology. [116]

In each of the issues of the *Reformed Guardian* the
authors continued their polemics; and Editor Hoeksema
published some replies in the *Standard Bearer*. These
polemics were really a review and summation of the issues
leading to the traumatic split in the Protestant Reformed
Churches. And these polemics — though expected and
probably necessary—did not work toward the healing of the
rift. The split was now over. It was time for the churches to

---

116.   H. DeWolf and A. Cammenga, Vol. 1, pp. 7, 8.

go on from there, to develop and to teach the precious doctrines of the Scriptures as interpreted in the Reformed creeds.

The reason for this need of diligence is that the fungus in the garden of Reformed plantings had split the garden in half. Many of the plants had left and now lived in other gardens. Those who remained in the garden of Reformed plantings had been bruised by the struggles with the fungus. It was imperative that these plants strike their roots down firmly and deeply in the fertile soil of God's sovereign grace.

Chapter 14
The Aftermath of the Split

Chaos prevailed in all areas of the split denomination. The Protestant Reformed Churches had suffered a tremendous blow. More than half of the members, and also the pastors, had left them. The following congregations, also mentioned in the previous chapter, had left the denomination and soon ceased to exist: Pella, Oskaloosa, Rock Valley, Sioux Center, and Orange City, Iowa; Manhattan, Montana; and Bellflower, California. Many of the remaining congregations were so decimated and weakened that they could not continue to exist without denominational help. In some of these congregations only small handfuls of members remained.

Finding a solution to the problem of pastors for these small, courageous remnants took immediate priority after the split, especially for the congregations in the West. The only remaining pastor of the Protestant Reformed Churches who lived in the West was Rev. H.C. Hoeksema. He regularly preached three — or four — times on each Sabbath to help the area churches. But the West needed more help. Although the East also had a dearth of preachers, Classis East prepared schedules for the Eastern ministers to give temporary help to the Western congregations.

Adding to the difficulty was the dearth of seminary students in these days of upheaval. Student Herman Hanko was in his second year of seminary in the fall of 1953; and he was the only student available for this emergency. Rather early in the semester, Professors Hoeksema and Ophoff asked him to take a six-week break from his classes and preach in the congregation of Edgerton, Minnesota, which urgently needed help. Student Hanko complained that he had only one sermon as yet, and when he had preached it in class for practice preaching, his professors had agreed that it was not a very good sermon. The professors did not accept his excuse. They offered him some sermon help and sent him west, promising that they would see to it that he kept up on his classroom work — by correspondence. Student Hanko went to Edgerton with a double load: he was a student and a preacher. And he returned to Grand Rapids shortly before mid-term examinations.

The urgent need for pastors was not the only pressing problem in the ravished denomination. The structure of the denomination was in chaos. Due to the split the ecclesiastical bodies and officers — the classes and synod and the denominational clerks and committee members — had to be restructured. Making matters more difficult was the fact that all the archives in Classis West were held by the DeWolf group, who still claimed to be the rightful denomination of the Protestant Reformed Churches. In the East many of the ecclesiastical documents were also in the hands of the opposing group. Later they made an agreement with the DeWolf faction to get photo copies of some of the documents.

The Protestant Reformed denomination was also in financial straits because the pastors and consistories in most of the congregations in Classis West had claimed all the funds for the DeWolf faction. In Classis East the situation was not much better, for the treasurer of the Classis was a member of the DeWolf faction, and he made any funds unavailable.

The church courts were not only in transition *structurally*, but suddenly main issues which had had high priority on the agenda of classis and synod were suddenly no longer important issues. One example was the Declaration of Principles. The Synod of 1953 had decided to recess unto March, 1954, and then re-convene in order to have further discussion and debate on the issue. Now there was no need for the continued synod. The group who had stayed with Herman Hoeksema as leader were agreed on the issues.

Because the congregations in the Protestant Reformed denomination had suffered a tremendous blow, and many had lost pastors, members, or properties — and in some congregations all three — they were staggering to get on an even keel again. They were preoccupied with the immediate need of surviving. Some denominational work came to a standstill. For example, there was no time, money, or man power at this time to take on mission work. All the denomination could do was struggle to survive.

The parental grade schools in the denomination suffered, too. Many pupils whose parents had denied themselves in the struggle for parental grade schools based on Protestant Reformed principles now left the schools; and the teachers who followed the DeWolf faction could not renew their contracts. Suddenly the grade schools were much smaller ... and poorer; for their parental support had been cut in half.

※　※　※　※　※　※　※

In the teaching and preaching in the congregations, the pastors of the Protestant Reformed Churches agreeing with Herman Hoeksema made it clear that if they had to appeal to the secular courts for justice they would be fighting for their *name* and for the *future* of the Protestant Reformed Churches with its distinctive proclamation of the doctrines of the Scriptures. These were the priorities of the denomination. They also wanted to retain their properties pre-empted by the DeWolf group, because they believed that the properties belonged to the groups faithful to the Protestant Reformed denomination. Many of these congregations — and all the congregations in Classis West except Doon, Iowa — were meeting in temporary facilities: schools, homes, or halls; for their property was occupied by the followers of the DeWolf faction. For the second time in the history of the Protestant Reformed Churches (the first was in 1924), the question of the ethics of turning to the secular courts to regain their name and their properties was being examined and debated.

In the *Standard Bearer* of December 15, 1953, Editor Hoeksema wrote an article about this issue. Titled, "The Court Case and I Cor. 6:1-8," he wrote:

The Consistory of the First Protestant Reformed Church of Grand Rapids was finally compelled to appeal to the secular court in order to obtain justice over against those that meant to rob them of their very name.

By doing this, they acted according to the Church Order, Article 28:

"The consistory shall take care, that the churches, for the possession of their property, and the peace and order of their meetings, can claim the protection of the authorities; it should be well understood, however, that for the sake of peace and material possession they may never suffer the royal government of Christ over His church to be in the least infringed upon."

At first, the consistory was of the opinion that I Cor. 6:1-8 was applicable to their case. These verses in part are:

"Dare any of you having a matter against another, go to law before the unjust, and not before the saints?... If then ye have judgments of things pertaining to this life, set them to judge who are least esteemed in the church. I speak to your shame. Is it so that there is not a wise man among you? no one that shall be able to judge between his brethren? But brother goeth to law against brother, and that before unbelievers. Now therefore there is utterly a fault among you, because ye go to law one with another. Why do ye not rather take wrong?..."

But after further consideration of the case, also in the light of the above named passage, the consistory became convinced that the above mentioned passage is not applicable to their case. For this they have the following reasons:

1.   They certainly do no wrong or defraud when they claim their rightful property. And this they certainly do when they claim that the name *First Protestant Reformed Church*, the archives of said church, as well as the buildings belong to them and certainly not to a group of schismatics.

2.   It is not a question of a matter of brother

against brother, but of the First Protestant Reformed Church against a group of schismatics that intend to rob them of everything: their name, the archives, and the buildings. Remember:

The consistory does not appeal to the secular court for any personal matter, for personal gain or filthy lucre but for the well-being of the congregation. They have been called by God to seek the good of the church even, according to the Church Order, in regard to their material possessions. In this case, they would be unfaithful to their office if they did not appeal to secular court....

I conclude, therefore, that, in the present case we do not violate the injunction of Scripture in I Cor. 6:1-8.

Rather would I apply that other injunction of Scripture that is found in Rom. 13:3, 4: "For rulers are not a terror to good works, but to the evil. Wilt thou then not be afraid of the power? do that which is good, and thou shalt have praise of the same: For he is a minister of God to thee for good."

Even Paul appealed to Caesar. [117]

In the same issue of the *Standard Bearer* the Rev. M. Schipper made some end-of-the-year comments as a rebuttal to a polemic written by the Rev. P. VanTuinen in the *Banner* of the Christian Reformed denomination.

Protestant Reformed Split Spreads

Rev. Peter VanTuinen writes under the above heading in his department of the *Banner* of November 6th. We will not quote his entire article, but only give you the thread of thought running through it.

He tells us that there are "unfortunate developments in our somewhat estranged but near relative and close neighbor, the Protestant Reformed Churches, during the past months." The

---

117.   *Standard Bearer,* Vol. 30, pp. 126, 127.

"rift in First Church ... has spread throughout the denomination, and has torn the Church beyond any hope of repair."

"The hopelessness of the split is apparent from the fact that it will be impossible to hold a General Synod which will be composed of delegates representing both sides of the issue." According to the Reverend, because our Synod is composed of two Classes, and because one Classis is opposed to the stand of the other, and deems the other schismatic, no Synod will be possible. And this means that there can be no opportunity to appeal either the doctrinal or church-political matters involved.

He concludes with the following paragraph. "It is obviously not incumbent on an outsider to pass judgment on the merits of two opposing positions. But it is evident that something has gone wrong. The `Protestant Reformed Churches' as a whole has not had opportunity to speak its mind on the dispute. Nor, according to the precedent set in Classis East, will it be able to. One sector of the Church has declared itself to be the Church, thus closing the door to proper synodical action, and virtually cancelling the right of appeal. This looks like an overthrowing of the Church Order's safeguard against the fallibility of minor assemblies (Church Order, Article XXXI)."

In commenting on this article, we recall a statement of one of our ministers made in a speech at the last special meeting of Classis East. He made the statement to the effect that "the Church never splits, and we didn't split either." I shall never forget that remark, and I don't think others who heard it will either. It is true that individuals, and even churches may leave a denomination of churches, but the church never splits. And this is exactly what has happened in the Protestant Reformed Churches. There are those who have separated themselves from us, but the church is still intact. And we will go on without them who have chosen to differ with us until they repent....

One more remark in closing. Rev. VanTuinen does not tell us that the schismatic element in our churches lost the right of appeal and recognition when they became schismatic. This may not be forgotten. Had the Rev. DeWolf and his elders submitted to the decision of the consistory and then appealed, that would have been their prerogative. But this they would not do. They continued their schismatic way. Had Classis West gone the church-political way instead of schismatically jumping the gun, the grievances it had might have come to Synod for disposition. But Classis West separated itself from the communion of the Protestant Reformed Churches, and thus the faithful church must go on without them. Those in the Protestant Reformed Churches that are not schismatic can live under the order of Article 31 of the Church Order. No doubt about that. [118]

The filing of a Bill of Complaint by First Protestant Reformed Church in the secular courts was immediately publicized in the secular press. In the November 2, 1953, issue of the *Grand Rapids Press* the headline read: "Church Files Injunction Suit Against 11 Members, Pastor." The article stated that:

First Protestant Reformed church, Fuller av. and Franklin st., SE, Thursday filed a bill of complaint in circuit court against 12 members of the church, including its pastor, Rev. Hubert DeWolf, seeking an injunction requiring the defendants to turn over to "proper officers of plaintiff" all church property, including real estate.

The congregation was split early in the summer when members disagreed on doctrinal matters. Part of the congregation is holding services every Sunday in the auditorium of Grand Rapids

---

118.   *Ibid.*, p. 142.

Christian High school. It is this group that is the plaintiff in the case.

Plaintiff contends it always has been affiliated with the Protestant Reformed churches and represents the only church entitled to call itself the First Protestant Reformed church of Grand Rapids.

It further contends it has been declared the only First Protestant Reformed church in Grand Rapids by the classis of the church and that its consistory has been declared to be the only legal consistory of the church.

The bill of complaint refers to the defendants as "former members of the consistory of the plaintiff," and states that all, including Mr. DeWolf, have been deposed from office under the discipline of the Protestant Reformed churches and that the deposition was affirmed by Classis-East of the Protestant Reformed church, meeting last Oct. 6-9....

Shortly afterward the *Grand Rapids Press* reported the following:

Church Unit Files Reply
Denies Illegal Seizure in Doctrinal Split

Twelve members of First Protestant Reformed church, including Rev. Hubert DeWolf, have filed a cross-suit in superior court against members who split from the congregation last summer over a doctrinal matter.

The crossbill was filed with an answer to a bill of complaint filed by plaintiff members of the group who left the church. The latter group, led by Rev. Herman Hoeksema, started suit to regain the church property, now being used by members following Mr. DeWolf.

In the answer, Mr. DeWolf and his consistory deny they illegally seized control of the church property at Franklin st. and Fuller ave., SE. and excluded Mr. Hoeksema's group.

The defendants further deny that Mr. DeWolf

ever was suspended as a minister by the Classis East of the Protestant Reformed church. They admit a notice of suspension was served on him, but contend it was not served by legal officers of the church. They further deny that the doctrine Mr. DeWolf has been preaching is contrary to the church order or is heretical.

The split in the congregation occurred last summer following two sermons in which Mr. Hoeksema said Mr. DeWolf preached heretical teachings regarding the salvation of man.

In their crossbill, Mr. DeWolf and his consistory ask the court to rule that they constitute the true First Protestant Reformed church and have rightful use of the church property, to restrain Mr. Hoeksema and his followers from interfering with the use of the church and to restrain Mr. Hoeksema and his followers from using the name First Protestant Reformed church. To support his contention, Mr. DeWolf and his consistory quote the church's articles of association which state that any question of the use and control of the church shall be determined by the majority of the congregation. The defendants contend the majority of the congregation follows Mr. DeWolf.

They further allege that Mr. Hoeksema is a "domineering character" who would not tolerate opposition to his ideas and has attempted to split other congregations of the Protestant Reformed church.

Mr. Hoeksema established the Protestant Reformed church many years ago after the split from the Eastern Avenue Christian Reformed church on doctrinal matters. [119]

It was the Rev. DeWolf who had asked the *Press* to publish this article, a part of his legal crossbill, which was filled with untruths. Three of the lies in it are "that any question of the use and control of the church shall be deter-

---

119.   Undated *Press* clipping.

mined by the majority of the congregation," that "Mr. Hoeksema has attempted to split other congregations of the Protestant Reformed church," and that "he split from the Eastern Avenue Christian Reformed church on doctrinal matters."

The truth was that although Herman Hoeksema was the leader, he was not a dictator. He worked through his consistory and congregation. The last allegation should read that "Herman Hoeksema was *put out* of the Christian Reformed denomination by the Synod of 1924 without being allowed a hearing in its broader courts."

The first part of the Bill of Complaint filed by the consistory of which Herman Hoeksema and Cornelius Hanko were chairmen outlined the legal technicalities of the property and the rules of the Church Order, which governed the *structure* and *procedures* of the denomination: the rules of government in the Protestant Reformed Churches, the properties First Church owned, and the legality of this Bill of Complaint.

The next item in the complaint registered the grounds for this complaint.

> That the defendant, Hubert DeWolf, has, since June 26, 1953, unlawfully pretended to represent the plaintiff church; that he has seized the pulpit in the Church Sanctuary and since June 26, 1953, has preached a doctrine which he represents to be the doctrine of the First Protestant Reformed Church; that the doctrine preached by said defendant, Hubert DeWolf, is contrary to the Church Order of the Protestant Reformed Churches, and the Classis of said Protestant Reformed Churches has found and determined that the preachings of said Hubert DeWolf are heretical; that said Hubert DeWolf now threatens to continue his seizure of the pulpit of a church which was dedicated to the teachings and beliefs of the Protestant Reformed Churches, and plaintiff fears that he will continue to preach in said pulpit unless he is restrained by an injunction of this court from occupying said

pulpit and from interfering with the proper offices of plaintiff in placing in said pulpit a Minister of the Word and Sacraments duly authorized by the Protestant Reformed Churches.

After relating the history and the details of this plea, the plaintiffs, Herman Hoeksema and his consistory, ended their complaint with several requests, among which are:

1. That the defendants may, on oath, full, true, and direct answer make to all the allegations of this bill of complaint.
2. That the defendant, Hubert DeWolf, may be restrained from holding himself out or representing himself to be a Minister of the Gospel of the First Protestant Reformed Church of Grand Rapids, Mich.
3. That all of the defendants may be restrained and enjoined from holding themselves out or representing themselves to be elders of the First Protestant Reformed Church of Grand Rapids, Michigan.
4. That the defendants, severally and collectively, may be enjoined from occupying plaintiff's property at the corner of Fuller Avenue and Franklin Street, Grand Rapids, Michigan.
5. That a mandatory injunction may issue requiring the defendants severally and collectively, to turn over to the proper officers of plaintiff, the possession and control of all of the personal property, bank accounts, books and records of the plaintiff, as well as the real estate, title to which is found by this court to be vested in plaintiff.
6. That the defendants may be restrained and enjoined from using the name FIRST PROTESTANT REFORMED CHURCH and from representing themselves or their associates, as having any official or unofficial connection with said church.... [120]

---

120.   Undated court record.

On December 16, 1953, the group following Rev. DeWolf filed a crossbill, claiming that *they* were the group who deserved the name and property of First Protestant Reformed Church. Portions of this document read:

>   1.   That these defendants represent the true First Protestant Reformed Church of Grand Rapids, Michigan, and that Herman Hoeksema, Cornelius Hanko, and Gerrit Stadt, who signed and executed the bill of complaint in this cause, do not represent the true First Protestant Reformed Church of Grand Rapids, Michigan, and that the other cross defendants herein are persons who pretend to represent First Protestant Reformed Church of Grand Rapids but in fact do not do so as hereinafter stated.
>   2.   Defendants further show that the above named persons, who are individually made cross defendants herein, pretend to be the Consistory representing the First Protestant Reformed Church of Grand Rapids, Michigan, and are properly made cross defendants herein.
>   3.   Defendants further show that cross defendant Herman Hoeksema was formerly a regular ordained Minister in the Christian Reformed Church and was occupying a pulpit in the church known as the East Street Holland Christian Reformed Church in the city of Grand Rapids, Michigan.
>   4.   Defendants further show that the said Herman Hoeksema, while occupying the pulpit in the said East Street Holland Christian Reformed Church, by his acts and conduct and by his refusal to acknowledge the duly constituted authorities of said church and its decrees and pronouncements, caused a schism in said church and a splitting of the membership which attended said church while he was its pastor. That the said Herman Hoeksema and his followers took possession of the property located on Eastern Avenue and insisted that he, said Herman Hoeksema, and

others, were entitled to the use of the church edifice and parsonage, and did for a long period of time following said schism occupy said premises.

Note in Article 4 that the authors of the crossbill seemed to have had regrets about the reformation of 1924, for they criticized Hoeksema for his conduct and convictions — his opposition to common grace and his fighting for sovereign, particular grace. Some of the office bearers of the DeWolf group had been members of Eastern Avenue Church in 1924. They had experienced this rift and had gone along with those who had left the Christian Reformed denomination. Now they seemed to regret the birth of their Protestant Reformed denomination, along with the fact that temporarily they had been allowed to keep possession of the Eastern Ave. Church in 1924.

Articles 9, 10, and 15 state:

> 9. Defendants further show that said cross defendant Herman Hoeksema was the person principally responsible in forming the First Protestant Reformed Church of Grand Rapids, Michigan, and was the person who largely dictated the provisions of the Articles of Association of said church. That at the time of the incorporation of the First Protestant Reformed Church of Grand Rapids, the said Herman Hoeksema wanted to make sure that the congregation of the new church, that is, the First Protestant Reformed Church, should forever control the real estate of said church independent of any decision or action of any other body connected with the said First Protestant Reformed Church such as Classis or Synod, and therefore the said Herman Hoeksema and others who joined in said association the following provision:
> "All matters in question regarding the use, control and right to possession of the real property of said church shall at all times be determined only by a majority vote of the members of the congregation

of said church."

10. Defendants further show that until the time of the recent schism in the First Protestant Reformed Church and the leaving of said church by Herman Hoeksema and the other cross defendants herein, it was always assumed and believed that the possession of the real estate and its control and use was exclusively to be determined only by a majority vote of the members of the congregation of said church.

15. Defendants further show that said Herman Hoeksema, commencing early in his life, has been a domineering character whose word is law and who would not tolerate any opposition to his conclusions or pronouncements, and that in organizing the First Protestant Reformed Church of Grand Rapids he assumed to be the head thereof and to dictate its policies, and would not tolerate any opposition to his own ideas or wishes, became very intolerant, and as time went on he created a feeling of dissension and opposition to him in this church.

The last part of the crossbill gives a brief history of Rev. DeWolf's statements in the two sermons which he preached and which precipitated the breach in the denomination. Then follows a long list of grievances, including accusing the "cross defendants" of the conspiracy to get possession of the property and assets of the First Protestant Reformed Church. The defendants also claimed that

Herman Hoeksema has recently made visits to locations where the churches of Classis West are located and there has attempted to create and in some instances has created schisms in said churches, has attempted to split the congregations and organize a new congregation over which he could have control....

The crossbill further put the total blame on defendant

Hoeksema for causing splits in both classes, and who "is completely wrecking said denomination and by said conspiracy is causing an intolerable condition in said churches."

The document ended by stating that:

> These defendants further show that the cross defendants in carrying out their conspiracy to split the congregation known as The First Protestant Reformed Church, on or about the 8th day of October, 1953, caused to be sent substantially all of the members of the First Protestant Reformed Church ... a certain paper designated as a declaration. [121]

Although there was a brief attempt on the part of both sides to settle their ecclesiastical difficulties out of court, the effort failed. On Tuesday, May 25, 1954, the Superior Court of Grand Rapids was in session to hear the case. The proceedings and the testimony were heard by the Hon. Thaddeus B. Taylor; and the attorneys were Mr. Robert Tubbs for the plaintiffs and Mr. Jay Linsey and Mr. John VanderWal for the defendants. This was the second time in his life that Reverend Hoeksema faced Mr. Linsey as the attorney of the opposition. The first time was in the court trial of 1924, when Mr. Linsey was the counsel for the opposition, the Eastern Avenue Christian Reformed Church.

The proceedings of the court trial of 1954 filled 497 pages. Starting with Mr. Tubbs' examination of Herman Hoeksema, the attorneys of both sides questioned and cross-questioned many witnesses from both sides, entering into doctrinal as well as church political issues.

During the questioning of the DeWolf group by the attorneys, it became evident that this group differed from the Protestant Reformed Churches not only in *doctrine,* but also in the concepts of *church structure* and *government.* In an article in the *Standard Bearer* which he wrote at this time, Editor Hoeksema wrote the following resume:

---

121.   Undated court record.

When the complete record of our case in the Superior Court is published, which I sincerely hope will be done in some future time, it will be revealed that our opponents defended a congregationalistic or independentistic form of church government: the consistory alone has power, classis and synod have no power whatsoever.

I think it will even be shown that they testified that the consistory is the highest court, while classis and synod are the lower and lowest courts respectively.

That was their view.

And to defend and maintain this conception of church polity was, of course, their privilege.

But what is far worse is that they tried to leave the impression with the court that their view is the Reformed conception of church polity. In this they did not succeed, because the judge had before him in court a copy of the Church Order.

And what probably was worse still, they attempted to make the impression with the court that their view is the same as that of the Rev. Ophoff and the undersigned. They tried to show, by all kinds of faulty and partial quotations that the brethren Ophoff and the undersigned had always taught the same church political view as they. [122]

The court case lasted ten days, with some recesses, from May 25, 1954, to June 23, 1954, when the opinion of the Hon. Judge Thaddeus B. Taylor was issued. It was a lengthy and thorough document which favored the group led by Hoeksema. This opinion gave back to the group their name, property, and assets.

An article in the *Grand Rapids Press* described the trial and decision as follows:

---

122.   "Independentism," *Standard Bearer,* Vol. 31, Oct. 15, 1954, p. 124.

Court Orders Church Title Awarded to
Hoeksema Group

Rev. Herman Hoeksema and his consistory are legally entitled to the property and assets of the First Protestant Reformed church at Fuller av. and Franklin st., SE. Superior Judge Thaddeus B. Taylor ruled Thursday.

Mr. Hoeksema and his consistory brought suit in superior court to regain the church which had been taken over June 23, 1953 by Rev. Hubert DeWolfe (sic) and members of the church congregation which followed him in an intrachurch controversy.

Plans to Appeal

John H. VanderWal, attorney for Mr. DeWolfe, said Thursday he would appeal the decision to the state supreme court.

In his 21-page opinion, Judge Taylor wrote that under the church order of the Protestant Reformed denomination, the classis is the ruling body of the denomination and that "this court may not substitute its opinion in lieu of the authorized tribunals of the church....

Must Return Money

The congregation which followed DeWolfe took over the church property and assets, and the congregation which upheld Mr. Hoeksema met elsewhere.

Judge Taylor ruled the classis had acted within its constituted authority, but added, "whether the action of classis was right or wrong is of no concern of this court."

The judge also ruled that if the church under Mr. DeWolfe has "collected or obtained money during the time they have maintained physical possession of said church, they will turn over to plaintiffs all money or assets collected in the period from June 23.

Mr. DeWolfe contended the congregation following Mr. Hoeksema had split from the church, but Judge Taylor ruled differently. He noted that Rev. DeWolfe's group had changed locks on the

church doors and had barred members of the
other part of the congregation from entering.

Needn't Use Force

"One may not be convicted of desertion,"
wrote Judge Taylor, "on the ground that he must
use physical force to establish his claim. The
plaintiffs were not bound to attempt to incite a riot
by attempting to use physical violence in order to
occupy the church property."

Judge Taylor concluded his opinion: "It is not
the intent or purpose of this court to determine
who are the members of this church congregation
and it is not to be considered, or interpreted, as
preventing any person who was a member or
communicant of said church on June 23, 1953,
from participating in the affairs of this church
under the administration of those who have been
declared by the classis to be the legal consistory
and presidents of said church." [123]

In an editorial titled "Repercussions" Editor Hoeksema
commented:

All our readers have, by this time, received
and read the "Opinion" rendered in the case of the
name and property of the First Protestant Reformed Church of Grand Rapids, Michigan, by the
Superior Court of this city.

Personally, although naturally I am glad that
the court rendered a decision in our favor, I was
not surprised about it. The more I thought about
the matter, the more, too, I heard, in court, the
testimony of the opposition corrupting our Reformed Church Polity, which, evidently they never
understood, and the more I heard, in court, the
honorable Judge Taylor insist repeatedly that his
judgment had to be based on the eighty-six articles
of the Church Order, the more I became convinced
that the court's decision had to be in our favor.

---

123.   Undated *Press* clipping.

Editor Hoeksema also reflected that:

> It stands to reason that the case of the First Protestant Reformed Church of Grand Rapids will have its repercussions for virtually all of our churches.
> The entire opposition, both in Classis East and Classis West, will lose the name and the property....

In a post script to his editorial Hoeksema wrote:

> P.S. In the meantime I learned that the opposition has appealed to the supreme court. This means that we will wait another year for the final outcome of the case. [124]

The opposition *did* appeal. On January 6, 1956, just a little over a year after the first verdict, the State of Michigan Supreme Court issued its decree on the appeal. The *Grand Rapids Press* of March 1, 1956, gave the following report:

> **Church Case Edict Upheld**
> **Rev. Hoekstra's (sic) Group**
> **Gets Building, Assets**
> The state supreme court upheld unanimously Thursday a superior court decree awarding property and assets of First Protestant Reformed church at Fuller av. and Franklin st. SE, to Rev. Herman Hoeksema and his consistory.
> The high tribunal found in the briefs no account of funds collected or other information which would allow a ruling on the plea of the First Protestant Reformed church for payment of rental on church property by the congregation of Rev. Hubert DeWolf which has occupied the premises of the church for services since a split on doctrinal grounds with the Hoeksema faction in June, 1953. The supreme court referred the matter of determi-

---

124.   *Standard Bearer,* Vol. 31, Jan. 15, 1955, pp. 172, 173.

nation of damages to the court of trial — superior
court here.

DeWolf Group Appealed

The matter of damages arose on appeal by the
DeWolf faction of a ruling Dec. 22, 1954 by Judge
Thaddeus B. Taylor in superior court that the
Hoeksema faction is entitled to the church property and assets. Judge Taylor also ruled that if the
church has "collected or obtained money during
the time they have maintained physical possession of said church, they will turn over to plaintiffs
(the Hoeksema group) all money or assets collected in the period from June 23, 1953.

Judge Taylor, in making his ruling, noted that
under the church order of the Protestant Reformed denomination, the classis is the ruling
body of the denomination; that DeWolf and other
members of the consistory who supported him in
the dispute had been deposed under discipline of
the Protestant Reformed churches, and that the
deposition was affirmed by Classis-East of the
denomination, meeting Oct. 6-9, 1953.

DeWolf Groups to Vacate

Judge Taylor ruled the classis had acted under
its constituted authority and added "this court
may not substitute its opinion in lieu of the authorized tribunals of the church."

Since the schism, the Hoeksema group has
held church services at Grand Rapids Christian
High school auditorium and the DeWolf group in
the church.

Following the supreme court decision, Mr.
DeWolf announced Friday that his consistory and
congregation is vacating the church and will meet
Sunday, and thereafter in the Calvin college auditorium. Services will be held at 9:30 a.m. and 7
p.m.

In the March 15, 1956, issue of the *Standard Bearer* Editor
Hoeksema titled his editorial "Back in Our Own Church."
The editorial is a reprint of the decision of the State of
Michigan Supreme Court. It is a lengthy document, detail-
ing once more the history of the controversy of 1953, includ-

ing the heretical statements made by the Rev. DeWolf, his refusal to apologize, and the changing of the locks on the doors of the building.

The decision also mentions the several hundred pages of testimony taken by the court stenographer at the trial, along with the precedence of other cases similar to the controversy in the Protestant Reformed Churches.

Editor Hoeksema commented on the decision of the controversial issue — the source of the *authority* in the denomination — as follows:

> The trial judge hearing the case, and relying upon those decisions, concluded that the plaintiff First Protestant Reformed Church under its articles and constitution, and the Church Order, was dedicated to the discipline, rules and usages of the Protestant Christian Reformed Churches of the United States as authorized and declared from time to time by the Classis of said churches. The court concluded that the Church Order became the constitution of the church, to which every member subscribed, and that the court was bound to recognize it as controlling the issues.
>
> We are in accord. We decline to hold, with the defendants, that the Hoeksema Consistory had departed from the doctrines and practices of the Protestant Reformed Churches.... We have further held that the Synod was a proper body to hear, try and determine whether the action of the defendant Reverend DeWolf and his followers was heretical and in conflict with the confession of the church; and that the decision of the Synod, the Classis and the consistory in the matter is final and binding upon the court.... We do not agree with the defendants that there was any substantial infirmity in the steps taken to reach that conclusion, in the instant case. [125]

---

125.   ***Standard Bearer,*** Vol. 32, pp. 270, 271.

The First Church court case was over, and the members of the congregation would soon be worshiping in their own church building once more. The bulletin of Sunday, March 4, 1956, informed the congregation that "Next Sunday, D.V., the Lord's Supper will be celebrated at all services, in our own church. All this week's meetings will be held in the Adams St. School as usual."

The building was theirs again; and although the DeWolf faction had vacated it a week earlier and the congregation could have worshiped in their building on the Sunday of March 4, the consistory thought it wise to keep the building empty for one week, lest some people from the opposing group stayed in the building merely for the sake of "the brick."

On the Sunday of March 11 the members of the First Protestant Reformed Church worshiped in their own property again, and the bulletin announced that the following week "All our church activities will be held in the church."

※　※　※　※　※　※　※

The court case of the Second Protestant Reformed Congregation (later called Southwest) of Grand Rapids took on a different aspect. It was a rather complicated trial, with many behind-the-scene intrigues.

When the congregation split in 1953, approximately half and half, all the officebearers except two deacons stayed with their pastor, Rev. J. Blankespoor, who sided with the DeWolf faction. They also kept the church building. The two deacons, Theodore Engelsma and James Swart as plaintiffs, filed a Bill of Complaint in Kent County Circuit Court, claiming the name *Protestant Reformed* and also the property.

While the court case of Second Church was going on, the writers of the *Reformed Guardian* and their opponents from the *Standard Bearer* tangled about this unique case. The Rev. M. Schipper, who was at this time the pastor of those members of Second Church who had stayed with the Protestant Reformed denomination, wrote an article in the *Stan-*

dard Bearer in which he described the situation.

Another Court Case

Such is the title of an article appearing in the May 10 issue of the *Reformed Guardian* written by the Rev. J. Blankespoor. In the April 10th *Reformed Guardian* Rev. J. Howerzyl also reflected on this case of Second Church, and we promised to give answer to him and the Rev. Blankespoor now.

I am not only interested in what Rev. Blankespoor wrote relative to the history of the case, the events that led up to the pending court trial, but also what he did not write and should have written.

In the introductory part of his article he writes as follows:

"Legal proceedings have been initiated for another trial regarding church properties here in Michigan. This time the Second Prot. Ref. Church is involved. As usual, there are many rumors afloat regarding what happened in our church, also prior to the last actions taken. In order that our people may know what actually transpired we will try to give a brief sketch of our correspondence with those who left us.

"First of all, let me state that we are incorporated differently from all of our other churches. Without entering into details, let is be sufficient to say that our articles very clearly state that the *majority* in a certain situation is entitled to its share of the buildings and in another situation to all of the buildings. [126]

This information about the incorporation of Second Church had a bearing on the court case; for after the court trial was over, the judge stated:

Briefly, the issues are: Is Second Church an "inde-

---

126. "All Around Us," *Standard Bearer,* Vol. 32, July 1, 1956, p. 428.

pendent autonomous" ecclesiastical body, or is it
a part of a presbyterial denomination, or is it a part
of a presbyterial denomination so that it is subject
to the decisions of the judicatories of the denomination?

And if the latter, which of the two
"Consistories" adheres to and is recognized by the
highest judicatory of the denomination which has
passed upon the question? [127]

The rest of the trial was a confused mixture of contradictory witnesses stating their beliefs about the structure of the
denomination. Although the witnesses insisted that the
structure of the denomination was congregational, yet they
emphasized the importance of the synod, the broadest gathering of the churches in the denomination.

Some of the defendants testified that the Hoeksema
group did not attend the continued synod which was held in
the building of First Church, therefore forfeiting their right to
claim the property. The reason for the absence of the
Hoeksema contingent was that the Hoeksema group was
locked out. They were obliged to accept the hospitality of the
members of the Fourth Church who invited them to meet in
its parlors.

In the *Standard Bearer* of December 15, 1956, the Rev. M.
Schipper quoted the Rev. P. VanTuinen's article in the
Banner of November 23, 1956.

> The situation with respect to the church property
> disputes between the two sides in the Protestant
> Reformed Church schism is becoming more com-
> plicated. The newest complication arises from the
> decision of circuit judge Fred N. Searl with respect
> to the property of the Second Protestant Reformed
> Church of Grand Rapids, Michigan. By deciding
> in favor of the group associated with Rev. H.
> DeWolf, Judge Searl brought about a situation

---

127.   State of Michigan Circuit Court for the County of Kent,
p. 2.

with respect to Second Church directly opposed
to that which the Michigan Supreme Court sustained with respect to First Church. The First
Church property was awarded to the Hoeksema
group, and now the Second Church property has
been awarded to the DeWolf group, locally headed
by Rev. John Blankespoor. Both decisions assume
a Presbyterian church polity as basis for the action
taken.

How could this confusing situation arise in
the same city? It appears that the latest decision is
based on a much more complete picture of the
schism than the earlier decision. Judge Searl's
ruling finds the Hoeksema group schismatic in
that it ignored the properly constituted Synod of
the Protestant Reformed Church. In the decision
regarding First Church's property, this broader
question did not enter....

Rev. Schipper answered Rev. VanTuinen as follows:

I have two brief comments to make. In the first
place, it is true what Rev. VanTuinen writes:
"Both decisions assume a Presbyterian church
polity as basis for the action taken." Here was a
case where the chameleon changed his color again.
In the First Church case both before Superior
Court Judge Taylor and the Michigan Supreme
Court the case was won by the Hoeksema group
on the basis of Presbyterian church polity. In spite
of the fact that the DeWolf group tried desperately
to defend the Congregational form of church
polity, under the leadership of the Rev. B. Kok, the
courts would not listen, and decided that the
Protestant Reformed Churches had the Presbyterian form of church government. When the case
of Second Church came before Circuit Judge Searl,
the DeWolf/Blankespoorian group realized they
wouldn't get to first base on their old tactics, so
they initiated their cause by conceding that the
form of government in the Protestant Reformed

Churches was Presbyterial. And then introducing what appeared to be a new phase in the case, the matter of the Synod, they succeeded in impressing the judge with the idea that the highest ruling body in the church had been ignored by the Hoeksema group. The fact of the matter was that neither the case of First Church, nor that of Second Church had ever gotten any higher than the Classical level to the time of the split. This Judge Searl refused to see.

Therefore, in the second place, the case of Second Church is being appealed to the Michigan Supreme Court. There can be no doubt that the latter court not only will be able to "untangle the present confused picture," but will also sustain the Hoeksema group for the same reasons it decided in their favor the first time. [128]

However, the Michigan Supreme Court decided in favor of the defendants of Second Church, Rev. Blankespoor and his consistory. Now there were two opposite opinions in the two trials, with the same problems, in the same denomination. When the DeWolf group learned of this decision favorable to them, they filed another petition, an appeal against the First Church decision, on the basis of having new evidence in the case. They tried to hang a new case on the decision of the Second Church case. The *Grand Rapids Press*, dated March 26, 1958, tells that:

> The new petition asks the court to amend the decree, returning the church properties at Fuller av. and Franklin st., SE, to the DeWolf faction. It also asks that an injunction barring the defendants from using the name Protestant Reformed church be dissolved and a permanent injunction be issued restraining the Hoeksema group from using the name "First Protestant Reformed Church of Grand Rapids," and from claiming its members are part

---

128.   "All Around Us," *Standard Bearer*, Vol. 33, p. 144.

of the Protestant Reformed Church of America.

The answer to the appeal appeared in the January 5, 1960, issue of the *Grand Rapids Press*. It quoted the pertinent paragraph of Judge Taylor's answer to the appeal:

> As to the first action by synod, we regard the language complained of as dictum since the decision in First Church was planted on the action of Classis East reversing the finding of heresy and recommendation of ouster against Mr. DeWolf, nothing contained therein disputes the right of the Hoeksema consistory to continued control of First church property.

⁂ ⁂ ⁂ ⁂ ⁂ ⁂ ⁂

Although these congregations in Grand Rapids had the first court trials in the denomination, and with two opposing decisions, the other congregations in the stricken denomination which had just split were experiencing similar problems. Each of the two opposing groups in the various congregations claimed the right to the denominational name of *Protestant Reformed* and also the rights to the properties. Each congregation whose troubles sent its members to the secular courts had slightly different circumstances and problems.

The problems in the court trial of the South Holland, Illinois, congregation were unique. On the evening of April 16, 1958, five years after the split in the denomination, a group of former members of the congregation, who had left the congregation of South Holland as individuals, came to the consistory with the Rev. B. Kok. Rev. Kok, who sided with the DeWolf group in the controversy, had been pastor of the Holland, Michigan, congregation. Now he had come to South Holland to unite these former members of the South Holland congregation, who had left as individuals, and to organize them into the "Orthodox Protestant Reformed Church of South Holland."

On the night when this group came to the consistory of the South Holland congregation, Rev. Kok came as leader of this group. He claimed that this group was the rightful congregation of the South Holland Protestant Reformed Church. This group also claimed the property rights. Neither the consistory nor the members of the congregation had known that these families had joined as a dissident group.

The consistory did not recognize this group as an organized congregation and would not discuss any issues with them that evening. In a later letter of response the secretary wrote that "the consistory will not allow itself to become involved in a property discussion."

Soon the consistory of the South Holland congregation also learned that Rev. Kok, along with this group, had filed a complaint for his group — as plaintiffs — in the Superior Court of Cook County in Chancery. This congregation, recently organized, and calling themselves the Protestant Reformed Church of South Holland, Illinois, was in court claiming the name and the property of the South Holland Protestant Reformed Church founded soon after the controversy of 1924.

The trial took place in the Hearing Room of Llewellyn A. Wescott, Master in Chancery, at 10:30 o'clock in the forenoon, on Friday, October 23rd, 1959. During the lengthy questioning and cross-questioning of Rev. Kok, the attorneys complained that he kept changing his convictions. A sampling of the exchange of questions and answers will furnish examples of the deviousness of the answers and the tensions which the questions and answers brought to the court room.

When Mr. Moran, attorney for the defendants, asked Rev. Kok what was the highest authority in the local consistory, Kok answered: "We were always taught to emphasize this word *majority* unless it be proved to conflict with the Word of God. That was a matter for individual conscience...."

Mr. Moran questioned him further on this subject:

Mr. Moran: Q. Didn't you state that this was a principle for which you sacrificed and upon which the Protestant Reformed Church was built?

A. The authority of conscience is a principle for which we have sacrificed.

Q. Do you no longer believe in that principle?

A. Not according to the interpretation.

Q. You mean —?

A. Not according to the interpretation of the Presbyterian form of church government.

Q. Do you have a change then in your conviction since you testified in the First Church case?

A. I would say, some.

Q. And that conviction change is different from what you had been taught, as you said?

A. If you want me to go into it in detail....

Q. You testified that was what you had always taught?

A. Yes, that the individual conscience and the conscience of the consistory is the highest point of authority.

Q. And you state that, do you?

A. Not as far as property is concerned, it seems.

In his questioning about the ecclesiastical structure of the denomination, Attorney Moran asked Rev. Kok to describe the structure of the government of the Protestant Reformed Churches, and Kok answered:

Well, it is meant that the local church is incorporated into a classis, and that the classis is the next gathering to which appeals may be made from the lower assemblies or the consistories and the classes.... And if anyone feels he has been wronged by a lower assembly he has a right to appeal to a particular synod and whatsoever is decided by the majority, that is considered to be binding unless it be proved to be contrary to the Word of God....

Q. Now, in that First Protestant Reformed Church case, didn't you testify there that the classis is above the synod and the consistory above the classis?

A. At that time I think I made a quotation from one of Rev. Hoeksema's writings, I think.

Q. You stated that was your opinion?

A. That is what we had been taught.

Q. Would you state then that the synod has not power over the consistory and that the classis has not power over the consistory?

A. Yes....

A little later in the examination, in connection with the doctrinal issues in 1952-53, the attorney asked Rev. Kok:

Q. In 1952 or '53 there was a doctrinal dispute in the First Church of Grand Rapids, is that right?

A. Yes.

Q. And this concerned the preaching of the Rev. DeWolf?

A. Not the preaching of Rev. DeWolf.

Q. What was it?

A. Two statements.

Q. Those statements were made in sermons?

A. Yes, but objections were only against those two statements.

Q. They were doctrinal, were they not?

A. No, I don't think doctrinal.

Q. What were the statements?

A. One was that God promises everyone of you that if you believe you shall be saved, and the other statement was our God made conversion a prerequisite to enter the Kingdom of Heaven.

Q. You say these are not doctrinal statements?

A. Well, yes, I imagine you can make them to be — they are very doctrinal statements, I would say.[129]

In this 300-page record of the court trial in the Superior Court of Cook County, when the Rev. Kok gave vague or

---

129. Court Record, pp. 7, 9, 45, 55, 56, 75, 76.

contradictory answers or complained, "I don't recall," the attorney for the defendant finally asked him, "Now, Reverend, why can't we get a straight answer?" And when Kok changed his story on the witness stand, one of the attorneys exclaimed in exasperation, "Rev. Kok, you can change your stories as easily as you change your clothes." Although it was stricken from the record, it had been said.

The trial dragged on for years, until in April, 1961, the court honored a Consent Decree as the solution of this case. The original Protestant Reformed congregation kept its name, its pastor, and its property. Before the report was issued, the small group of individuals had disbanded. The Rev. Kok had already joined the Christian Reformed Church of Munster, Indiana, and asked for admittance to the ministry of the Christian Reformed Church.

❋ ❋ ❋ ❋ ❋ ❋ ❋

In the court trial of the split congregation of Edgerton, Minnesota, the defendants were those men who supported Rev. DeWolf and his followers, and who also were holding the property. The trial itself was a rather short procedure, ending with District Judge Nelson's decision:

> Nothing is more lamentable than a dispute of this nature. Many of the exhibits herein include vehement protestations of a desire for peace and harmony. Nothing has been shown by either group to indicate any disposition to give an inch in any direction to aid in achieving the peace and harmony which all parties claim is so desireable. This court has nothing to do with the doctrinal differences between the pro and anti DeWolf factions. Nor would it be competent to decide which group is correct in their interpretation of the doctrine of the church.
>
> Suffice it to say, that not much has been shown in this proceeding, and all matters connected with it, to make the court believe that the two groups

desire the peace and harmony which they so vehemently claim they desire. I cannot but believe that the matter could have been decided within the church organization had either group been willing to submit to the action of their own governing bodies as the Church Order requires. The presbyterial form of government, such as the churches of this denomination have, requires, as does any democracy, that the minority submit to the will of the majority.

It is possible that the action of the consistory of the plaintiff church can be reviewed by or possibly reversed by a legal meeting of Classis East or synod, but in the opinion of the court this has not yet been done. Therefore the conclusions of law reached by the court must of necessity be that the defendants are the legal consistory of the Edgerton church and as such entitled to control of the church properties at Edgerton. [130]

The rebuke of Judge Nelson in paragraph one that at times both groups expressed undo antagonism and bitterness was correct. The records of many of the court cases illustrate their polarization. However, in this secular court, Judge Nelson was in error when he stated, "This court has nothing to do with the doctrinal differences between the pro and anti DeWolf factions; for Romans 13:3, 4 has given all judges their mandate: "For rulers are not a terror to good works, but to the evil. Wilt thou then not be afraid of the power? do that which is good, and thou shalt have praise of the same: for he is the minister of God to thee for good."

✳ ✳ ✳ ✳ ✳ ✳ ✳

After the split in the congregation of Hull, Iowa, there was no court trial because both sides opted for an agreement

---

130.   Court record of Minnesota State Supreme Court, March, 1957.

outside of the secular court. With legal help, they agreed to the following:

> Whereas the parties to this action have expressed and declared their desire and intent to resolve and settle all their disputes and differences involved in this cause in an amicable and christian manner, commensurate with the harmony and unity expounded by their respective teachings, and to terminate this costly protracted litigation:
>
> Now therefore, the parties to this action do hereby stipulate and agree as follows:
>
> 1.   All parties shall dismiss with prejudice their respective actions herein; the plaintiff (those of the Hoeksema group, GH) shall dismiss their petition; the defendants shall dismiss their cross petition; and the intervener shall dismiss its petition of intervention and cross petition.
>
> 2.   Each of the parties shall pay their or its own attorneys and no attorney fees shall be taxed as costs in the case. Plaintiff shall satisfy the court costs of record herein....
>
> 3.   The possession of the portion of the real estate on which the church building is located shall be transferred and relinquished to the plaintiffs on July 11, 1964, and the possession of that portion of the premises on which the parsonage is located shall be surrendered on Aug. 1, 1964.... [131]

Six congregations in Classis East stayed intact, but their numbers were decimated: Kalamazoo, Holland, Hope (Walker), Hudsonville, in Michigan, and Randolph in Wisconsin. The small congregation of Grand Haven, Michigan, was also intact, but later it disbanded because of its small size and lack of growth.

The Redlands, California, congregation lost their property to the schismatics after a brief court case. The decision of Judge Jesse W. Curtis, Jr. stated that:

---

131.   Decision of the District Court of the State of Iowa, in and for Sioux County.

The plaintiff group, however, contends that it is in fact the true Church because the consistory and the defendant group had become schismatic and therefore not truly representative of the Church. Whether this is true or not can only be determined by the duly constituted tribunals within the Church and not by this Court or by a group of individual members.

Judgment will, therefore, be for the defendants and against the plaintiff, and defendants' attorneys shall prepare the Findings of Fact, Conclusions of Law and Judgment.

Dated this 14th day of August, 1957. [132]

The small congregation of Lynden, Washington, had no property to lose, because they had been worshiping in a rented hall. But the small congregation was split in half; and for several years after the rift of 1953 the group loyal to the Protestant Reformed Churches was a struggling but courageous group. Rev. H.C. Hoeksema described them this way:

Small but staunch.

Thus I would characterize our little congregation in Lynden, Wash., especially after they were delivered from a group of schismatics who, for some time already, revealed that they were no longer in harmony with the Protestant Reformed truth.

I recently had the privilege of spending a couple of weeks, three Sundays, in their midst, and to me it was, indeed, refreshing to meet them and to discover how they understood and loved the truth as our churches have always embraced it.... [133]

---

132.   Superior Court of the State of California decision.
133.   "Lynden," *Standard Bearer,* Vol. 30, March 15, 1954, p. 271.

The garden of Reformed plantings had been torn apart. The plants no longer bloomed in peace and harmony. Although all the plantings fought for what they claimed to be their places in the garden, they found it impossible to grow and blossom together. More than half of the plantings uprooted themselves and found other gardens.

Chapter 15
More Aftershocks

The Protestant Reformed Churches had suffered a grievous shock in 1953; and the result of the shock had been that congregations and families were torn apart, never to join again in the former communion of saints. The split had been a sad rift which had torn the churches in half.

The members of the denomination may not have fought so hard if they had not been fighting for the very life of their denomination. Yet while the litigation continued, the members of the congregations had lived with a measure of instability, in a "what next?" atmosphere. Their struggles also lent a rather negative outlook to their lives.

Running concurrently with the attempt of the ecclesiastical courts of the Protestant Reformed denomination to retain their name and properties before the courts of the land were also the struggles in the organic area of their church lives — the areas of teaching and of fellowship in the congregations.

Most of the Christian grade schools were in trouble. Many classes had been decimated and had to be combined with other grades. Even though the schools did not need so many teachers anymore, they had lost many staff members in the split and suddenly faced a serious teacher shortage. Because of the urgency of the problem — the existence of the parental Protestant Reformed schools was at stake — several older teachers came out of retirement; and even mothers with families made temporary adjustments so that they could offer their help in this crisis.

In the ecclesiastical area of the denomination the consistories, classes, and synods once again became smaller, and their agendas more simple.

Many of the members of the denomination in the post-split years of the 1950s expressed that they had feelings both of relief and emptiness; they were relieved that the tenseness of the controversy was past and that they were able to discuss the truths of the Scriptures and the doctrines of grace without arguing. On the other hand, many members of families were now in different camps; for most of the ties of friendship and family closeness had been damaged or shattered permanently by the split. At best many of the post-split relationships were impaired and uneasy.

Among those who sat in the pews and those who guided them from the pulpits there remained a bitterness toward the DeWolf group. Many were angry and defensive and often expressed that anger in writing. Especially after the records of the various court trials were made available, the people, and especially the pastors, expressed their resentment because the court records had showed many inconsistencies, distortions of facts, and untruths spoken under oath by the witnesses of the DeWolf group.

As a result, the latter years of the decade of the 1950s and about half of the decade of the 1960s were years of ongoing polemics, often conducted in a spirit of bitterness. Others felt the need of justifying the position of the Protestant Reformed denomination. During these years the pastors were often defensive in their preaching. Due to their tragic experiences, the focus of the preaching of the Word was rather narrow. Some of the pew-sitters commented that somehow in every sermon they heard why *conditions in God's covenant* were wrong.

Gradually, as the trauma of the troubled fifties receded, the pulpits and the church periodicals lessened or stopped their recriminations and started to look around and also ahead with more positive and instructive sermons and magazine articles.

However, during these years of polemics the church papers on both sides of the conflict — the *Standard Bearer* and the *Reformed Guardian* — belabored the recent conflict with both doctrinal and personal elements entering into their polemics. As late as the year 1956 the *Standard Bearer* carried articles with the following captions: "The Apostates of 1953 and the Three Points," "The Court and Church Property," and "The Proper Use of the Term 'Condition.'"

As the denomination of the Protestant Reformed Churches entered the 1960s, many discerning members called it "the decade on dead center" or "the doldrums." The denomination had not as yet broken through its backward look and small boundaries.

In this period of the late fifties to the mid-sixties the future of the Protestant Reformed denomination looked bleak, even numerically: for the majority of the members had gone with the DeWolf group.

However, negativism was only a temporary aspect of the aftermath of the rift of 1953. Gradually a positive and a forward-looking attitude took its place: for the years when the denomination seemed to function on dead center had also been years of reflection. In the preaching and the writings of these years the members and clergy recognized that sins had been committed on both sides. They also learned that the Lord had preserved His remnant: for splits are chastisements from the Lord, a reformation designed to purge the church from false doctrine and to correct and refine His people, His church on earth.

They began to understand that the benefits they reaped from this trial far out-weighed the negative aspects; for the churches — both pastors and laity — emerged stronger. They had experienced through their bitter trials that this split was God-sent, and that it was God's way of working with the denomination: for when a man or a congregation or a denomination gives a defense against false doctrine, even though he knows the results will be trouble and disunity, that man or congregation or denomination also knows that the uprooting of false doctrine and the study of the truth will strengthen and purify the church.

Through the decade of the 1950s the Protestant Reformed Churches had lived alongside of the other group who also called themselves the Protestant Reformed Churches. In the mid-fifties this group had begun to call themselves the

Orthodox Protestant Reformed Churches. While this schismatic group was still fighting in court to get the rights for the name and the properties of the Protestant Reformed denomination, they were also making overtures to the Christian Reformed Church. In 1957 and 1958 they sent out feelers as to their reception into the Christian Reformed Church. The pastors and their congregations did this individually, not as a denomination. But in 1959 the group formally approached the Synod of the Christian Reformed Churches. The account of this endeavor is recorded in part by Editor H. Hoeksema.

Re-Union?

The late Synod of the Christian Reformed Church appears to have been favorably inclined to a re-union of their churches with those of the DeWolf group. In the *Banner* of July 3, 1959, we read:

"With a view to carrying on further discussions with the Protestant Reformed Churches (DeWolf group) it was decided:

"1. To address a communication to the Synod of the Protestant Reformed Churches in order to pave the way for further consideration regarding an eventual unification.

"2. To continue the present committee which will hold itself in readiness to confer with a committee of the Protestant Reformed Churches if further conferences should be desired by them to work out various details necessary for effectuating such a possible reunion."

From this I receive the impression that, apart from some "various details" the reunion may be realized as far as the Christian Reformed Church is concerned....

☞   ☞   ☞   ☞   ☞   ☞   ☞

Also the Rev. Henry Kuiper, in *Torch and Trumpet,* writes very much in favor of such a reunion. He does so on the basis of the fact that the

schismatics have virtually adopted the chief contents of the "Three Points." Writes he:

"A study of the report shows that the committee succeeded in attaining to a large measure of
agreement on the points of doctrine that have been
in dispute for over thirty years. Minor conces-
sions were made by the Christian Reformed contingent in the joint committee. In regard to Point
One of common grace, the Protestant Reformed
members now agree that there is indeed a certain
divine favor or grace which is shown to God's
creatures in general. The term 'creature' naturally
includes all men, even those who die in sin and are
ultimately lost....

"The Protestant Reformed brethren also accept the essence of Point Two, namely, that through
the grace of God there is a restraint of sin in the
hearts and lives of those who are not saved. They
also agree to the Third Point in so far as it teaches
that the unregenerate can perform civic good."

From all this it is evident that the Rev. H.J.
Kuiper agrees with what I wrote on the reports of
the two committees, namely, that the schismatics
adopted the "Three Points" and therefore are not
Protestant Reformed.

Kuiper, however, still has one serious scruple.
It concerns the question whether the offer of the
gospel is, on the part of God, grace for all that hear
the gospel. This must be maintained at all costs.
Yet, the schismatics do not appear ready to accept
this. After Kuiper quotes a few passages from the
Confessions and from Scripture, he writes: "All
such expressions imply that the Lord loves sinners
though he hates their sins. If this is not true, the
offer of the gospel can hardly be called a sincere
offer; it is nothing more than a presentation of the
claims of God and a declaration that those who do
not believe in Christ will perish in their sins. The
gospel goes far beyond such a cold presentation...."

Of course, it is not my purpose, in this connection, to criticize the Rev. Kuiper. I merely present his reactions to the report of the committees. Nevertheless, I cannot refrain from making one remark. It is that he, evidently, must have nothing of the doctrine of reprobation which, after all, was one of the chief questions before the Synod of 1924. The question was whether God loves the reprobate wicked. This question Kuiper answers in the positive: "the Lord loves sinners," all sinners, as is evident, mind you, from the "sincere offer of the gospel," so that God, evidently, means to save them....

But now it seems that the schismatics are not as yet ready to unite with the Christian Reformed Church.

We have no official report on the matter as yet, but according to an oral report of one that was present at their 'synod' there must have been a proposition before the meeting to postpone action on the question of uniting with the Christian Reformed Church until the next "synod." This, according to the reporter, was adopted by a very small majority....

They are not quite ready. [134]

In spite of the wariness of some of the schismatics to unite with the Christian Reformed Church, the DeWolf group went back in 1961, although all the details of the merger were not immediately completed.

The Synod of the Protestant Reformed Churches sent a letter, dated July 12, 1961, to the Rev. J. Howerzyl, the stated clerk of the Orthodox Protestant Reformed Churches. It was a letter of caution and admonition. In part, it reads as follows:

Dear Erring Brethren:
The Synod of the Protestant Reformed Churches, in session June 7 to June 13, 1961, at the First Protestant Reformed Church of Grand Rap-

---

134.   *Standard Bearer,* Vol. 35, Aug. 1, 1959, pp. 436, 437.

ids, Michigan, has decided to address to you and your membership this last admonition and warning to desist from the evil path you have chosen and have continued to follow ever since your acts of schism in 1953. Herewith we also reply to and reject the demand made in the letter of your synod dated January 1961....

We want to assure you that we do not admonish you in a spirit of pride and superiority, but in all humility....

Permit us to point out with fear and trembling that God has been your Judge in the subsequent history. Frequently it was pointed out in the period of the struggle prior to the schism that you were abandoning the historic position of the Protestant Reformed Churches and moving in the direction of the Christian Reformed Churches, which cast us out in 1924....

Since 1953 many of your number, among them several of your ministers also, have defected, either individually or as groups, to the Christian Reformed Churches, and that too, without your dissent....

We earnestly call upon you to repent of all these evils, to desist from them, and by the grace of God to return to the way of the truth in the only possible way, that of upright and open-hearted confession before God and His church. [135]

After the leaders of the schismatic group of congregations made their decision to join the Christian Reformed Churches, many of the members in their congregations followed them, but not all. Scattered members in the various congregations refused to go to the denomination from which the Protestant Reformed Churches had broken in 1924. They were sorry that they had left the Protestant Reformed Churches, and they wanted to come back. Immediately

---

135. "That 'Final Letter,' " *Standard Bearer,* Vol. 37, Sept. 1, 1961, pp. 462, 463 (was signed by Rev. G. VandenBerg, Stated Clerk).

questions about the necessary procedures for taking back
these former members arose. In answer to the question
Editor Hoeksema wrote the article: "How Can the Schismatics Return?"

> ... The answer to this question is briefly: they
> must make confession of whatsoever sins they
> committed.
> What are these sins? They are enumerated in
> a letter sent to them by our Synod as follows:
> 1.   You have for the last five years or more,
> defended and supported those who preached and
> defended the heretical statements, namely, "God
> promises to everyone of you that if you believe
> you will be saved"; and, "Our act of conversion is
> a prerequisite to enter the Kingdom of Heaven."
> These statements are really worse than the Three
> Points of Kalamazoo. Every one feels at once that
> a promise of God is greater and warmer than any
> offer. An offer needs acceptance; but a promise
> depends on nothing but the faithful Godhead for
> its realization.
> 2.   Some of your ministers have gone over to
> the Christian Reformed Church or are in the
> process of returning.
> 3.   The conferences with the Christian Re-
> formed Church show clearly that your leaders are
> willing to compromise the truth not only but
> accept *in toto* the Three Points of Kalamazoo.
> 4.   Because of your initiative we are deprived
> of churches and parsonages which were erected
> and dedicated to the promulgation of the Protes-
> tant Reformed truth.
> 5.   You have withdrawn your children from
> the wonderful system of Prot. Ref. Education; you
> have cancelled the very *Standard Bearer* of the
> truth you loved so much, and you have taken
> away your support from the Reformed Witness
> Hour.
> 6.   You have repudiated the Declaration of
> Principles which contains everything we have

held dear for decades.
These are the sins they who desire to return to
us must confess. [136]

Editor Hoeksema further explained in particular that
those who had left the denomination must not only confess
that they had done wrong, but that this confession be made
to the consistory of the congregation which they had left. He
emphasized the necessity of confessing to the consistory of
the congregation they had left because it was the proper way
and also the only way according to the rules of the Church
Order. Not all the consistories in the denomination agreed.
The Southeast congregation not only wanted to receive into
their fellowship members who had left from another congregation, but they started to receive, without a confession,
former members of the First congregation.

First Church insisted that before these members could
come back into the fellowship of the churches they must
confess their sin of leaving the denomination to the consistory
of the congregation they had left. Some of the grounds which
the consistory of First Church furnished were:

1. That Southeast Church violated Article
84 of the Church Order which reads as follows:
"No church shall in any way lord it over other
churches, no minister over other ministers, no
elder or deacon over other elders or deacons."
2. Southeast consistory's action of receiving
schismatic members of First Church is based on
the erroneous notion that the schismatics simply
left the First Church and formed a new church or
rather continued to function as the legal First
Protestant Reformed Church, while the fact is that
they were guilty of rebellion, of mutiny.
3. The consistory of Southeast church is not
even seeking the welfare of the schismatic members concerned. These know very well that they

---

136.   *Standard Bearer*, Vol. 38, Feb. 1, 1962, p. 198.

have sinned against the consistory and members
of the First Church and that they never repented
of and confessed their sin in the proper way or in
any way at all. They cannot feel at home in the
several meetings held by the members of the
Protestant Reformed Churches. And they cannot
feel in their hearts that the blessing of God rests
upon them. [137]

The consistory of the Southeast congregation did not
listen to the warnings of First Church but accepted, with no
confessions, members who had left First Church in 1953. The
problem was appealed to Classis East.

In an editorial dated April 1, 1962, Editor Hoeksema
quoted an illustration which the advisory committee had
drawn up.

A steals 500.00 dollars from B. A repents of his
misdeed, but he goes to C to make amends. What
will C do when A approaches him? Will he say to
A: "I am very happy that you saw your sin, and I
heartily accept your confession?" Of course he
will not talk this way if he wants to do what is
right, both over against A and B. Rather, he will
say to A: "You stole the money from B, not from
me, so go to B and tell him your fault and reconcile
with him. And only when you do that can you be
a friend of mine, for when you hurt B you also hurt
me." This the committee applies to the case that
was before classis. [138]

For several months during the latter half of the year of
1961, First Church and Southeast sent a series of protests and
answers to one another's consistories arguing the matter of
the Southeast consistory's receiving these people as mem-

---

137.   "How Should the Schismatics Return?" *Standard Bearer*,
Vol. 38, March 1, 1962, p. 244.
138.   "How Should the Schismatics Return?" *Standard Bearer*,
Vol. 38, p. 292.

bers without their confessions to First Church for leaving their congregation. At the annual synod, held at First Church from June 5 to 15 in 1962, after the protests had been read and the synod had had long discussions, the delegates formulated and adopted the following articles:

Article 174
A motion is made to adopt I, B, 4, of Supplement XXI, i.e., "that synod declare that Southeast Church did violate the ethical principle that reconciliation can only be made between the parties involved. Grounds: Matt. 5:23ff., Art. 71, C.O.
Article 179
...That Southeast Consistory rectify this matter by rescinding their decision to receive the Doezema family, and by instructing this family to reconcile with Creston Church before Southeast can receive them with clean papers.[139]

In the summer of 1962 the Rev. R. Veldman, pastor of the Southeast congregation, who did not want to follow the Church Order nor the classis and synod in the matter of taking back those who had left another congregation in the denomination, broke relationships with his congregation and left the denomination. Editor Hoeksema expressed his sorrow that a fellow pastor who had been a faithful minister for many years in the denomination and had fought for purity of doctrine in the trauma of 1953 had left the denomination now. He also lamented the *way* in which Rev. Veldman left. He wrote:

Exit, The Rev. R. Veldman
And now the Rev. R. Veldman apostatized from the Protestant Reformed truth, left our churches, joined the Christian Reformed Church, expressed himself in agreement with the "Three

---

139.   *Acts of Synod* of the Protestant Reformed Churches in America, 1963, pp. 32, 33.

Points" of 1924, and justified the deposition of
faithful ministers of the Word of God by what at
that time were Classes East and West of the
Christian Reformed Church in Grand Rapids. He
did this all without the knowledge of his consistory, while he was still chairman of that consistory
and while he was still preaching from the pulpit of
the Southeast Protestant Reformed Church of
Grand Rapids, Mich.

How is it all possible?

How is it possible from a spiritual viewpoint?...

Does he ever say to the Lord, as he did in the
above mentioned gathering of Classis, according
to reliable reports, that God restrains sin so that
sin does not develop as fast as it would apart from
that restraint? Does he in his prayers confess that,
in all the years he was minister in the Protestant
Reformed Churches, he was in error or he was a
hypocrite in not preaching that God restrains sin,
but now he will faithfully preach it?...

But I can now understand the speech which
the Rev. R. Veldman delivered at Synod and
which is included in the report of the Synodical
Committee which was appointed for this matter
and which reads as follows:

"Synod with sorrow records in its minutes
that in its session of Wednesday morning, June 13,
the Rev. R. Veldman, pastor of the Southeast
Church in Grand Rapids:

"1. Declared himself in basic disagreement
with our churches:

"a. In regard to the decision of Classis
East in re the two literally heretical statements of
Rev. H. DeWolf.

"b. In regard to the suspension of Rev. H.
DeWolf and the deposition of his supporting elders, and related actions of consistory and classis....

"2. That he 'has reached the point of no return' with respect to his own position of disagreement in regard to the decisions of our churches
concerning the schism of 1953...."[140]

140.   *Standard Bearer,* Vol.. 38, Aug. 1, 1962, pp. 437, 438.

Another pastor who was grieved by the exit of the Rev. Veldman was the Rev. C. Hanko, the co-pastor of First Church. A tall, lean, and soft-spoken man, he was a hard worker in his ministry especially in the days of the traumatic rift in the denomination. Although he had a gentle personality, he never compromised the truths nor the guidelines of the Scriptures; and he worked hard with the Rev. Veldman to show him the biblical and proper way to receive those families who had left in 1953. He, too, was saddened by Rev. Veldman's demise.

Shortly after Rev. Veldman had left the denomination in July, 1962, the Rev. Alvin Mulder, a young pastor who was a recent graduate from the seminary and currently serving the Kalamazoo congregation, also left the denomination.

✳ ✳ ✳ ✳ ✳ ✳ ✳

Back in the late 1940s, when the Rev. M. Schipper was the pastor of the South Holland, Illinois, congregation, he began to have contact with three pastors from the Reformed Episcopal Churches. These men had learned about the Protestant Reformed denomination and its teachings by listening to the radio broadcasts sponsored by the South Holland congregation.

After further contact with Pastor Schipper and his congregation, and after the pastors had studied the doctrines and life of the Protestant Reformed denomination, they left their denomination and became members of the Protestant Reformed Churches. In the fall of 1950 the three pastors moved to Grand Rapids to attend the seminary. They graduated in the year 1953, and were made eligible for calls to the ministry in the churches. The Rev. E. Emanuel accepted a call to the Randolph, Wisconsin, congregation. The Rev. J. McCollam went to Holland, Michigan, and the Rev. R.C. Harbach became pastor of the Kalamazoo, Michigan, congregation.

Neither Pastor Emanuel nor McCollam stayed very long in the denomination. Rev. Emanuel left — at least in part —

because he had problems with the doctrine of reprobation. Contrary to the doctrine of the Protestant Reformed Churches, he taught a reprobation which made God the author of sin.

Rev. McCollam ran into trouble — not of his making — in the Holland congregation. The issue of labor unions and the question whether one could be a conscientious objector ballooned far out of proportion in the congregation. The trouble was too much for him, and in August, 1959, he resigned from his office.

Besides his pastorate in Kalamazoo, the Rev. R. Harbach also served the congregation in Lynden, Washington. He did mission work in Houston, Texas, and in British Columbia. While in Canada, he had to leave the mission field because of his failing eyesight; and his handicap forced him to retire. Despite his eye problems, in his retirement years he still was able to do some preaching and writing.

✳   ✳   ✳   ✳   ✳   ✳   ✳

In the early to mid-sixties the emphasis in the denomination started to change. One reason may have been the "changing of the guard." The older pastors were retiring or were close to retirement age, and the names of new, young preachers appeared in the churches.

The emphasis in the preaching was changing, too. It was less polemic and introverted. The pastors expressed more joy as they preached the gospel. Especially in the periodicals the writers looked around them at the ecclesiastical scene of the world and urged their parishioners to look with them.

The pastors and those who sat in the pews understood that if any church can do mission work, the Protestant Reformed Churches can: for they preach the gospel of a sovereign God, Who chooses and saves His people over all the world. Exactly because *God* brings the fruit of conversion to the mission field, the emissaries of the Protestant Reformed Churches can do mission work: and they knew that predestination is not a hard, cruel doctrine, but a doctrine of comfort to take to the mission field. They understood more clearly than ever before that they were only God's instruments, and that the fruit of their efforts was God's work. Therefore a strong belief in predestination exactly qualified their emissaries to do mission work.

In 1962 the radio committee, who were overseers of the Reformed Witness Hour which was still broadcast weekly, had the opportunity to broadcast over Transworld Radio, which was able to reach almost every part of the world. During the course of these broadcasts on Transworld Radio, a pastor in England contacted the Rev. C. Hanko, who was pastor of First Church at that time. He informed Rev. Hanko about the little churches of Jamaica with whom he was acquainted and who could also receive Transworld Radio in their country. He urged Rev. Hanko to investigate.

The Protestant Reformed Churches investigated and the mission committee decided not only to broadcast there but to send emissaries to investigate the field. Soon Jamaica became a mission field. This was the first real mission work the denomination had done. All the rest of the expansion of the denomination had come through church extension work.

The September 1, 1962, issue of the *Standard Bearer* informed the readers that:

> From identical announcements in Hudsonville's and First's bulletins comes this item of denominational interest: "Our last synod decided that there was an urgent need to send a committee to investigate the Island of Jamaica as a possible field for our missionary effort. The Mission Committee acting upon this mandate appointed the brethren H. Zwak (Hudsonville) and H. Meulenberg (First) as a committee to visit this field. The brethren, accompanied by their wives, expect to leave August 13, the Lord willing, and they earnestly covet your prayers on their behalf. [141]

---

141.   John M. Faber, "News From Our Churches," *Standard Bearer*, Vol. 38, p. 480.

The plants in the middle of the garden of Reformed
plantings slowly started to look around at the garden; and
they saw other places and other Reformed plantings in the
garden. Gradually they began to break down the fences of
the little circle in the center of the garden; and they looked
around. Next, they sent visitors to other areas of the garden,
and gardeners with seeds which they could plant in other
regions of the garden. Then they prayed for fruits.

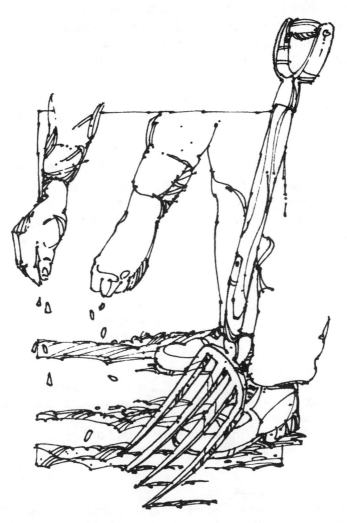

Section 5: BLOSSOMING
Chapter 16
The Awakening of the Sixties

The "changing of the guard" which had taken place among the clergy of the denomination (and was mentioned in the previous chapter) also reached the seminary. In the summer of 1958 the Rev. G.M. Ophoff and his wife vacationed in Canada. On their way home the Reverend felt ill. As his condition worsened, he and his wife found a hospital in Toledo, Ohio. The doctors there diagnosed the problem as a stroke. After he was taken home, he rallied somewhat, but his eyesight was impaired and he was no longer able to carry a full load of teaching in the seminary during the next school year. Two of the local pastors, the Reverends Vos and Schipper, helped out temporarily. Rev. Ophoff's condition gradually worsened, and the Synod of June, 1959, granted him his emeritation. At the same time they expressed a sense of emptiness and great loss. The Rev. Ophoff had been a seminary professor since 1925, besides being a pastor and a loyal defender of the truth of God's Word. In his unique way, often ponderously, he not only had lectured his students and written his own syllabi, but he was also a staunch defender of God's sovereignty.

The news column in the July 1 issue of the *Standard Bearer* expressed the feelings of the members of the denomination at the loss of this staunch warrior.

> Our beloved Rev. G.M. Ophoff, Emeritus Professor, was taken to his heavenly rest Tuesday, June 12, at the age of 71 years. Southwest's bulletin expressed it this way: "After standing in the line of battle for the truth, God has given His servant rest and a wreath of victory." Rev. Ophoff's old-time friend and colleague, Rev. H. Hoeksema,

263

preached the funeral sermon and the Rev. C. Hanko spoke at the graveside. Rev. Hoeksema's text was Psalm 73:24, Asaph's beautiful confession: "Thou shalt guide me with thy counsel, and afterward receive me to glory." Rev. Ophoff will be missed by all of us, but he has left us a legacy in the volumes of the *Standard Bearer*, as over the years he has delved into the nooks and crannies of the Old Testament Scriptures from whence to bring out its treasures, new and old. "Know ye not that there is a prince and a great man fallen today in Israel?" [142]

Suddenly the synod was faced with replacing Rev. Ophoff in the coming fall. A decade earlier the Theological School Committee (similar to a board of trustees) had foreseen this situation and had prepared for it back in the years of the late forties, the years when Homer C. Hoeksema was a seminarian. Before his graduation the ruling committee asked him to consider taking two more years of study after he graduated — this time graduate studies — to prepare himself for a career as a seminary professor when the need for him arose.

Hoeksema had mixed feelings about this offer because his wish was to be in the pastoral ministry. He wanted to preach! Yet he realized that without theological professors there would be no more ministers in the Protestant Reformed denomination. He accepted.

After his graduation from the seminary and his graduate work, in 1949 he had accepted a call to the Doon, Iowa, congregation. He was not yet needed in the seminary, and it was necessary that he have experience in the pastoral ministry. He stayed in Doon for five and a half years and then accepted a call to the South Holland, Illinois, congregation. After four and a half years there, he received the call to the seminary. The news editor reported that "The 1959 Synod is history.... Some of the decisions made are: Rev. G.M. Ophoff was granted his request to be made emeritus

---

142.   J.M. Faber, "News From Our Churches," *Standard Bearer*, Vol. 38, p. 432.

professor; a call was issued to Rev. H.C. Hoeksema to be professor in our seminary." [143]

The next issue of the *Standard Bearer* gave an update:

> Be sure to attend First Church the evening of September fourth! Rev. H.C. Hoeksema will then be installed in the office of Professor of Theology at 8 p.m., D.V. This will be a "first" in the history of our denomination. Let's make it necessary to open the balconies to seat the audience! Rev. G. Vos of Hudsonville, will read the installation form, and Rev. H. Hoeksema will preach the sermon. [144]

Next the editor briefly described the evening:

> Sept. 4, 1959, was indeed a highlight in the history of our denomination. Upon that date a Professor of Theology was formally installed into office for the first time. Rev. H. Hoeksema, Rector of our seminary, preached the sermon which was based on II Timothy 1:1, 2, which reads, "Thou therefore, my son, be strong in the grace that is in Christ Jesus. And the things that thou hast heard of me among many witnesses the same commit thou to faithful men, who shall be able to teach others also...." The entire service was spiritually moving to those in attendance, and impressed us of the necessity of praying for our seminary and professors in order that our churches may remain pure in doctrine through the instruction the ministers receive in that seminary. The situation was an analogy of that which prompted the Apostle Paul to write to Timothy. The professor-elect was Rev. H.C. Hoeksema, son of the Rector who had instructed his son in the doctrine of the church among many witnesses, and who was now being called by God to instruct others also in the same things that he had heard from his father. Rev. G.

143.   J.M. Faber, "News From Our Churches," *Standard Bearer*, Vol. 35, July 1, 1959, p. 432.
144.   J.M. Faber, "News From Our Churches," *Standard Bearer*, Vol. 35, Sept. 1, 1959, p. 480.

Vos, our next senior minister, read the form for installation and heard the responses of the professor-elect, and Professor H.C. Hoeksema closed the service by pronouncing the blessing. The evening of joy was not entirely unmixed with sadness because of the reason behind it all. Professor G.M. Ophoff has been led in ways of illness which necessitated his emeritation. Although our churches will miss his leadership in the future, they also will remain affected by his leadership in the past. Emeritus Professor G.M. Ophoff, God go with you 'til we meet in the Church Triumphant: Professor H.C. Hoeksema, God bless you in the Church Militant! [145]

✳ ✳ ✳ ✳ ✳ ✳ ✳

The next change of the guard took place six years later, in 1965. The change was due to events in the Hoeksema family. In the early 1960s Mrs. Hoeksema, never a robust woman, gradually became weaker. After a short stay in Pine Rest, a Christian psychiatric hospital, the Lord took her — on September 23, 1963. Herman Hoeksema was lonely and ill, and in August, 1964, he suffered another stroke. By March of 1965 his health had failed so far that he also had to have total care at Pine Rest. The News Editor noted that:

> The Manse at First Church is strangely dark and silent nowadays. Rev. H. Hoeksema has been hospitalized at Pine Rest. The need for constant care has necessitated this move. The bulletin reports that the "Dominee" is gradually becoming adjusted to his new surroundings and is responding to care and medication. [146]

Suddenly the denomination needed replacements in two areas: the editorship of the *Standard Bearer* and a professor

145.   J.M. Faber, "News From Our Churches," *Standard Bearer,* Vol. 35, Sept. 15, 1959, p. 500.
146.   J.M. Faber, *Standard Bearer,* Vol. 41, May 1, 1965, p. 360.

in the seminary. Herman Hoeksema's son took over the editorship in the October 1, 1964, issue. The Theological School Committee called the Rev. Herman Hanko, who had graduated from the seminary in 1955, to be the successor of Herman Hoeksema as seminary professor.

The Rev. Hanko, who was at the time pastor of the congregation of Doon, Iowa, accepted the call, moved to Grand Rapids, and began the task of trying to take the place of the experienced and gallant warrior — all in one summer!

On September 2, 1965, the Lord took Herman Hoeksema home. His son wrote the following editorial:

> My copy for this issue was not all ready yet when the tidings came early this morning, September 2, that the Lord had granted my beloved father the desire of his heart, that he would be delivered from this life, which is nothing but a continual death, into the glory of the inheritance incorruptible, and undefiled, and that fadeth never away....
>
> His departure, though painful for and mourned by his dear ones and by all of us who came to know him as pastor, teacher, and friend, was not unexpected. For several months already the Lord had removed him from his active labors in our churches, and particularly in his beloved First Church. Besides, he himself had expressed the wish, when he was losing his ability to communicate a couple of months ago, that "I hope it won't be long." And now the Lord has delivered him. Last Sunday we at First Church prayed that when we could no longer reach him, the Lord might reach him with His Spirit and grace to comfort him. Well, the Lord certainly answered that prayer. He reached him and called him home. [147]

The News Editor described the ceremony which took place just one week after Herman Hoeksema's death. He wrote:

---

147.   "Reverend Herman Hoeksema 1886-1965," *Standard Bearer,* Vol. 41, pp. 484, 485.

Thursday evening, Sept. 9, was another milestone in the history of our churches. At that time Rev. Herman Hanko was installed into the office of Professor of Theology. The Rector of the Seminary, Prof. H.C. Hoeksema, preached the sermon and Rev. G. Lubbers, vice-president of the Theological School Com., read the Form for Installation. The Rector's sermon was an exposition of the words, "And he gave some ... pastors and teachers ... for the edifying of the body of Christ," found in Eph. 4:11, 12.... The Rector stated that Seminary Professors quite really shepherdize the whole denomination because, "as the faculty — so the seminary; as the seminary — so the pastors and teachers; as the pastors and teachers — so the churches. Corrupt the seminary, you corrupt the denomination; and, conversely, maintain the truth in the seminary: so will the churches remain strong in doctrine." The Rector further admonished the new professor that he must vindicate the sound doctrine of the Scriptures, drawing the lines according to the foundation laid by the Apostles. May our entire membership esteem our new Professor for the sake of his office and appreciate him as a gift of Christ to His Church "for the edifying of the body of Christ." [148]

The changing of the guard, however, was not accomplished without difficulty. The controversy which was often his lot in life dogged Herman Hoeksema's footsteps to the grave and even beyond in an unusual, unhappy, and unique way. It was unusual because for once Herman Hoeksema was not an actual participant but rather a bystander in the controversy; unhappy because the influence of the so-called two hundred percenters mentioned previously reared its ugly head for the last time; and unique because the controversy raised issues and problems never before faced by the Protestant Reformed Churches from a judicatory and church political perspective.

148.   J.M. Faber, "News From Our Churches," *Standard Bearer*, Vol. 42, Oct. 1, 1965 p. 18.

Already in his declining days Herman Hoeksema suffered the continual and progressive mental and physical deterioration that always characterizes arteriosclerosis, until family attempts to care for him at home became impossible, and upon medical advice he was hospitalized. The following Sunday Prof. H.C. Hoeksema, filling the vacant pulpit of First Church, read the consistory's announcement of his father's hospitalization. This apparently innocuous event unleashed a sudden and unexpected storm of trouble which began with a handful of people in First Church and eventually enveloped the denomination to the synodical level.

A few individuals evidently could not accept the severe illness of their beloved "dominee" and did not want to see him hospitalized. Never having understood what Hoeksema truly stood for theologically and church politically, many were followers of the *man*, something that Herman Hoeksema himself had always *despised*. Coupled with the hyper-defensiveness and super-critical attitudes which had characterized the late 1950s and early 1960s, this became a dangerous combination. Soon a combination of innuendo and gossip was directed at the Hoeksema children, focusing in a slanderous attack on Prof. Hoeksema. He was accused by the grapevine of trying to neutralize his father in order to take over his leadership position in the denomination.

The consistory of First Church understandably had a difficult time dealing with this problem because gossip and slander in their very nature are hard to trace and even harder to prove.

The individuals involved knew this and used it to their advantage. Even after the gossip was formalized by accusations of public and private sin against Prof. Hoeksema, the ecclesiastical assemblies had difficulty dealing with it. As the accusations and protests against individuals and consistories wound their way by appeal to both classes and ultimately to synod, the cases took up a great deal of the time and effort of the denomination and disturbed its members. The last gasp of these two hundred percenters culminated in the public distribution on behalf of the troublemakers by the Stated

Clerk of Synod of exact mimeographed copies of executive session of Synod.

Although all charges were found to be unwarranted interference in a private family matter and the name of Professor H.C. Hoeksema was vindicated, the various cases consumed a great deal of ecclesiastical energy from 1966 to 1971. The matter was finally terminated when the dissidents left and formed a small independent congregation under the leadership of the former Protestant Reformed minister convicted of schism in the same case.

Through all the twists and turns of the whole sorry episode the Protestant Reformed Churches not only experienced how hard it is for ecclesiastical assemblies to deal objectively with difficult characters and their covert gossip, but they also relearned the truth of James, in chapter 3, verse 5: "Behold how great a matter a little fire kindleth!" And they saw firsthand that seeds sown many years earlier — also in the garden of Reformed plantings — can occasionally bear completely unanticipated fruit, causing the Reformed plantings to droop.

✳   ✳   ✳   ✳   ✳   ✳   ✳

In the decade of the sixties the denomination started to grow numerically. In the year 1960 the denomination, depleted by the split, had only six hundred seventy-two families, which numbered a total membership of two thousand eight hundred twenty-two individuals. This stagnation changed in the latter years of the decade. These were years of enthusiasm and growth, both internal congregational growth and growth through new members from other denominations. The number of congregations did not change in the decade of the sixties, but the membership almost doubled — to four thousand seven hundred fifteen members.

The emphasis of the preaching and the writings began to change in the latter half of the decade. The Protestant Reformed denomination, through leaders in its pulpits and its periodicals were again looking around at the Reformed church world, not only in the United States, but also in Europe; and they commented on it.

In the last two editorials which Editor H. Hoeksema had written in the *Standard Bearer,* he was looking around once more at the Christian Reformed Churches, and particularly at Professor Harold Dekker of Calvin College and Rev. H.J. Kuiper, pastor of Neland Ave. Christian Reformed Church in Grand Rapids. In his article dated July 1, 1964, titled "Dekker, Kuiper, and H.H.," he started with his usual zest by stating:

> Dekker: God loves all men.
>
> Kuiper: God loves all men, but with a qualitative distinction: special love and common love, special grace and common grace.
>
> H.H.: God loves the righteous and hates the wicked; He loves the elect and hates the reprobate.[149]

Editor Hoeksema had predicted for many years that because of the doctrine of common grace adopted by the Christian Reformed Churches, some day someone in the denomination would postulate the theory that God loves all men. Basically, the Rev. Kuiper agreed with Harold Dekker's heresy that God loves all men. Hoeksema quoted Kuiper as follows:

> Likewise Dekker has right along taught that the universal love of God comes to expression in the universal and sincere offer of the gospel, that is to say, in God's command to His church to preach the gospel to all men and His earnest overture of salvation to all to whom the gospel comes. There are those — the Reverend Herman Hoeksema, for instance — who have taken Dekker to task for that position, branding it as "sheer Arminianism." But again Dekker is right. To quote but a few of several portions of Scripture

---

149.   *Standard Bearer,* Vol. 40, pp. 412, 413.

which prove him to be right, in Ezekiel 18:23 and
33:11 God affirms emphatically that he has no
pleasure in the death of the wicked but therein that
the sinner turn from his evil way and live, and II
Peter 3:9 assures us that the Lord is "not willing
that any should perish, but that all should come to
repentance." In harmony with those Scriptural
passages the Canons of Dordt assert: "As many as
are called by the gospel are unfeignedly called.
For God has most earnestly declared in his word
what is acceptable to him; namely, that those who
are called should come unto him (III, IV, 8)."

Hoeksema had a short remark about this heresy: "There
you have it again, the 'Three Points.'"

Hoeksema's last editorial, in which he did not really
finish his comments on the subject of God's love, had concerned the defense of the center of his life and his teaching:
God's sovereign, particular grace.

When Prof. H.C. Hoeksema became editor, his editorials
in the year 1965 were ongoing polemics with Dr. James
Daane, Assistant Editor of *Christianity Today* and Dr. Harry
Boer, Principal and Teacher of the Theological College of
Northern Nigeria, both of whom followed the views of
Harold Dekker. Dr. Daane went one step farther and denied
limited atonement. The ongoing discussions and argumen-
tations in the mid-sixties remind the reader of the terms used
forty years earlier, in 1924.

In the November 15, 1965, issue of the *Standard Bearer*
Editor H.C. Hoeksema said:

We have seen that Dr. James Daane very
bluntly denies that the atonement is limited in its
nature. He denies that our Reformed creeds teach
a doctrine of limited atonement.... Moreover, the
doctor assumes the offensive, and asserts that it is
Prof. Dekker's opponents, and not Dekker, who
are skirting the heretical on the matter of the
nature of the atonement.

However, let us remind ourselves that the
issue is after all very simple.

It is this: Is the atonement by the death of

Christ limited, that is, for the elect alone? Or is it unlimited, general, that is, for all men and every man?

If anyone, Dr. Daane included, wants to phrase the question so that it speaks of the atonement "in its very nature," or "in its design," that is perfectly all right. It really adds nothing of value to the question. Moreover, if the terminology *particular ... general*, rather than *limited ... unlimited* is used, that is also good. The simple fact is that everyone knows, even though the precise term *limited atonement* does not occur in our confessions, that what is commonly called the doctrine of limited atonement is the doctrine that Christ died and atoned only for the elect, not for all men. [150]

In these years of the middle to the late sixties the leaders in the denomination also looked at the theology — or perversion of it — overseas. They commented on the philosophy of many German theologians, and also of those in The Netherlands, especially of the men who staffed the Free University.

In 1965 the *Standard Bearer* took a good look at the errors of the Swiss theologian, Karl Barth, through the pen of the Rev. D.J. Engelsma. In a series of articles he acquainted his readers with Barth's writings and he gave a thorough critique of his errors. He wrote:

In *The Word of God and the Word of Man,* Barth remarks on the so-called formal principle of the Reformation, the principle of the sole authority of the Bible, and, in one statement, shows his deep disagreement with the historic, Reformed estimation of Scripture: The Reformers "had the courage to allow so accidental, contingent, and human a thing as the Bible to become a serious witness of the revelation of God, to allow a book which was in itself profane to become *Holy* Scripture" (in the chapter entitled "Task of the Reformed Churches"). The Bible is accidental and contingent, even profane, that is, secular, worldly. It is these things,

---

150. "The Nature of the Atonement Limited or General?" *Standard Bearer,* Vol. 42, p. 77.

> with all they imply, because the Bible is thor-
> oughly human. Barth loves to speak of "the
> humanity of Scripture," most forcefully when
> opposing the historic, Reformed dogma of an
> inspired, infallible Scripture. We have seen that
> Barth utterly repudiates the "orthodox" doctrine
> of an infallible, inerrant Scripture. We must now
> note with what Barth would replace that doctrine
> in the mind and confession of the Reformed
> Churches. [151]

In his subsequent critique of Barth's writings, Engelsma gave the members of the denomination a refresher course on the doctrine of Scripture.

Besides being alerted to the dangers of non-Scriptural doctrines and practices the denomination took a look at itself and the positive area of its life. In sermons, discussion groups, periodicals, and in the day schools the members were discussing practical issues. These teachings, especially from the pulpits, led to a practical application of Scripture's teachings concerning amusements—movies, dancing, lodge membership—along with issues such as divorce and remarriage and the proper training of covenant children.

In December, 1965, Rev. H. Hanko wrote about "The New Morality." He stated:

> First of all, the new morality advocates that
> the entire law of God is of little or no value to us
> in this modern 20th century. The entire law as
> given in Scripture (including the ten command-
> ments) is to be abandoned as hopelessly out of
> date. It cannot possibly serve as a rule of life and
> conduct. This is not to say that the law of God can
> be burned. We ought to keep some record of it.
> But its importance is something quite different
> from the rule of our life which Scripture insists
> that it is. This law is really only an opinion of what
> some ancient people once thought was good and
> proper to do. Many years ago the Hebrews were

---

151.   "Barth's Doctrine of Scripture," *Standard Bearer,* Vol. 42,
Nov. 15, 1965, pp. 90, 91.

convinced that acceptable conduct could be defined in this law contained in the Scriptures. But this was merely their opinion — one opinion among many. And, while perhaps it was adequate for those days, we err seriously if we think that this law is equally binding upon us in our day....

Hence we find a man like Bishop Robinson who shook the ecclesiastical world with his book *Honest To God* promoting this new morality. He insists, for example, that "there is not a whole list of things which are 'sins' *per se*"; that any conceivable act is right if only the situation is right; that there are "no unbreakable rules" in all the world. And he is also the one who so openly denied every truth of Scripture.

But to return to this new morality and its views: what does this theory put in the place of the law of God as a norm of conduct? The answer to this question is, negatively, that no single act of which man is capable is *of itself* right or wrong. Any given act can be, under the right circumstances, perfectly proper and good....

This brings us to the question: What determines the right circumstances? What proper occasion is there to commit murder or to steal or to fornicate? The answer to this question is very simple: one must *love*. That is all. [152]

Hanko ended by reminding the reader that love is always first of all love of God. For in love we ask in humility, "What wilt thou have me to do?"

Both in the preaching and in the periodicals the pastors and authors went to the Scriptures to get at the *heart* of contemporary issues and to instruct their listeners and readers not only to see the wrong in them, but how to live in positive obedience.

The emerging atmosphere of a positive outlook and development in the denomination showed itself in various enterprises. For example, several years before the forty-fifth

---

152.   *Standard Bearer,* Vol. 42, Dec. 1, 1965, pp. 115-117.

anniversary of the Protestant Reformed Churches was to be celebrated, the library committee of the Theological School Committee started to publicize a plan to raise funds to be used for "The Hoeksema Memorial Library." The idea of this fund was to establish a permanent source to build up a special section of the seminary library devoted to worthwhile dogmatic works.

Another evidence of this forward-looking attitude from the middle to the end of the decade of the 1960s was that the churches in the denomination sponsored public lectures. In the Grand Rapids area the first one was held on October 27, 1965, in the Civic Auditorium in the downtown area. To a large audience of people of various denominations Professor Hoeksema spoke on "Our Reformed Heritage"; and a massed choir from local congregations furnished the music.

The following year on October 31, 1966, the professor spoke again at the Civic Auditorium, this time on the topic "The Children of the Reformation."

Two more lectures followed, this time in the auditorium of First Church. The topic of the first one on March 3, 1967, was "The Creation Period: Literal or Not?" The topic of the second one, held on January 27, 1968, was: "Is the Bible in its Entirety the Divinely Inspired, Infallible Word of God?"

These topics — the Reformed heritage of sovereign predestination and the literal inspiration of the Scriptures — were being denied in the church world of the later years of the 1960s; and the Protestant Reformed Churches brought these issues to the attention of the Reformed community in the Grand Rapids area.

The year 1964 was the fortieth birthday of the Protestant Reformed Churches. The *Standard Bearer* put out a special issue for this anniversary, and the news editor reminisced about the history of those forty years as follows:

> October 1, 1925 — The first news letter appeared in the *Standard Bearer* in the form of a personal letter by the Rev. H. Hoeksema to "My Friend in the West." This was written in the Holland language as was most of the material in

the early issues. This "first" was in the first anniversary number of our magazine. In the same issue was a news account of the organization of a church in Byron Center, Mich., which occured (sic) Sept. 30, 1925.... The dedicatory program scheduled speeches by Rev. Ophoff and Rev. H. Hoeksema. With this issue the S.B. became a bimonthly magazine — doubling the output!

Oct. 15, 1927 — Then came the glad news that our seminary had graduated two students who were also immediately placed in congregations. Rev. W. Verhil was installed by Rev. G.M. Ophoff in Hull, Iowa, Sept. 20, and the next day Rev. H. Hoeksema officiated at the installation of Rev. G. Vos in Sioux Center, Iowa. The two firstlings were "rushed" through their Theological studies because of the dire need for ministers, especially in the West far from student supply.

Oct. 15, 1928 — This year saw the beginning of newsletters written by Rev. G. Vos under the title "Stemmen Uit Westen," which as any S.B. reader in those days knew to be "Voices From the West." That "voice" was a reflection on the comparative youth of our ministers: that our denomination could not even boast of a 50-year old!...

Oct., 1930 — The sixth volume of the S.B. carried the news of the Classis Reports and the preaching schedule of our sixteen ministers and students.   Noteworthy is the fact that Rev. Hoeksema regularly preached three times in his church, a supply being provided for only one of the four services each Sunday.

Oct. 1, 1958 — Finally, under this dateline, this announcement was placed in the S.B.: "The Staff, in its last meeting, decided to institute a new column under the rubric, News From Our Churches. This decision is in response to the popular demand from many of our readers who are desirous of a closer unity between our churches; a unity wherein we can share one another's joys and sorrows; a unity based on one hope, one love, one Lord Jesus Christ. So in this issue you will find an introductory column devoted to church news as it affects each one of us. The Ministers of each congregation and the presidents of consistories of

vacant churches are requested to mail their bulle-
tins and other important news directly to the
editor of this column." And for six years, every
issue (but one) of our *Standard Bearer* has carried
"News From Our Churches." [153]

The latter half of the sixties was not so much a period of
reminiscing or looking back, but rather years of looking
forward and of positive accomplishments. One example of
rallying was the enthusiasm for reviving the parental grade
schools which had been impoverished or closed as a result of
the split of 1953.

The members, particularly the young parents in the
denomination, were interested in establishing and maintaining biblical and Reformed parental schools. Understanding
that according to His promise, He saves *His* children through
the generations of *their* children, these parents took seriously
God's command in Deuteronomy 6:7: "And thou shalt teach
them diligently unto thy children, and shalt talk of them
when thou sittest in thine house, and when thou walkest by
the way, and when thou liest down, and when thou risest
up." As soon as it was possible, the parents in the denomination started committees to make plans for Protestant
Reformed parental schools.

The first grade school in the denomination had been
organized in 1934 in Redlands, California, and met in the
basement of their church. In 1941 the members of the
congregation built a two-room school next to the church, and
the school prospered until 1954, in the aftermath of the split
of 1953. Because they lost members and property, the school
could not survive, and not until the year 1975 were the
members of Redlands able to start over again. Now Hope
Christian School in Redlands is an attractive concrete block
building — with air conditioning! Until recently two teachers plus one part-time teacher have been able to manage the
growing school.

---

153.   J.M. Faber, "News From Our Churches," *Standard Bearer*,
Vol. 41, Oct. 1, 1964, pp. 23, 24.

✳ ✳ ✳ ✳ ✳ ✳ ✳

The first school which was organized and which contin-ued functioning without interruption was Hope Protestant Reformed grade school in Walker, Michigan. It opened in September of 1947 with fifty-two students and two class-rooms and two teachers. Two weeks later both teachers, the Misses Jessie Dykstra and Della VanderVennen, were seri-ously injured in a car accident. Quickly-acquired substitutes taught for several weeks until the injured teachers were able to come back.

In 1951 the newly-organized school society of the Hudsonville congregation joined the Hope school society, and the number of students doubled. Due to this merger of the two societies two classrooms were added. In 1954 students from the Holland, Michigan, congregation also joined the student body at Hope, and attended until the year 1985, when parents in the Hudsonville area established Heritage Protestant Reformed School. Because Hudsonville is closer to Holland than to Hope, Walker, the children of the Holland congregation have attended Heritage since 1985, when the new school opened its doors. By 1970 the Hope school building had again become too small, and six more classrooms were added to accommodate the steady growing number of students. During its first five years Heritage School has become over-crowded, too. As a temporary measure the students are using portable classrooms and as a long-term solution the school board has organized drives to collect money for expansion.

✳ ✳ ✳ ✳ ✳ ✳ ✳

As early as January 28, 1937, a group of men of the southeast side of Grand Rapids met to discuss the possibility of starting a school society. At an April 15 meeting of that year, a society was organized with the purpose of starting a high school. From 1937 to 1941 the feasibility of a high school was debated; and on April 8, 1941, the society for a high

school disbanded because the members realized it was too
ambitious an undertaking; and a re-organized society was
mandated to begin laying plans for a grammar school. In
1942 the steering committee bought a plot of land at the
corner of Adams Street and Fuller Avenue for four thousand
dollars. Because of lack of funds the building progressed
very slowly. But after thirteen years of hard work, on
September 6, 1950, the new school, called Adams Street
Protestant Reformed Grade School, opened its doors to two
hundred thirty-five students and teachers. For the next two
years the school was a busy and growing establishment.
Then the results of the split of 1953, when many families left
the denomination, suddenly gave the school plenty of room.
Through the decade of the sixties the school rallied, but no
expansion was needed until the years 1989-1990. In 1988 the
board of the school approved plans for the renovation and
expansion of the building, which included more library and
classroom space. In a 1990 dedication booklet is a photo of
two third-generations pupils who are attending Adams
School.

* * * * * * *

The town of Edgerton, Minnesota, is a small town,
surrounded by farmland. The Protestant Reformed congregation there is also comparatively small, but growing—with
third generation Protestant Reformed youngsters. In the
early 1950s the small congregation started a two-room school.
Through the years their school has prospered, even though
it has remained small in numbers and in finances. Sometimes the supporters of their school were hard-pressed to
find Protestant Reformed teachers for their little school. In
the decade of the 1980s, with internal third-generation young
pupils, the school is growing and the parents are encouraged
by this internal covenantal growth.

* * * * * * *

The Loveland, Colorado, Protestant Reformed Grade

School opened on September of 1961 with seven students in grades one through five. Their first classrooms were primitive. The students met in an abandoned schoolhouse without running water, and consequently with an outhouse instead of bathrooms. The school used this facility until 1965, when the people of the Loveland congregation built their new church building. The school met in the basement of the church until 1973. Then they left their basement and moved into a new brick-trimmed steel building — their school!

With Mr. Tom DeVries as principal for many years, the school grew. Soon there were two teachers and a part-time kindergarten teacher. At the time of this writing, with Mr. R. Koole as principle, the school has more than forty pupils from kindergarten through grade nine.

* * * * * * *

The parents of the South Holland, Illinois, congregation also started a school in 1961. Through growth in the congregation their original building was expanded twice to accommodate its present one hundred sixty pupils and seven teachers. The school is now an attractive six-room school with a large assembly room.

* * * * * * *

On August 27, 1967, a new three-grade school, dedicated to Protestant Reformed education in the area of Doon, Iowa, opened its doors. The Northwest Iowa Protestant Reformed School started with an enrollment of thirty students. In 1990 the school is prospering with forty-five students and four teachers.

* * * * * * *

About twelve miles away and nine years later the members of the Hull, Iowa, congregation opened their new grade school. From a small beginning the school has grown to seventy-two pupils, four teachers, and two part-time teachers. Twice a year the three schools — Edgerton, Minnesota, and Doon and Hull, Iowa, get together on a rotating basis for a combined chapel, with special activities in the afternoon, a day for both teachers and students to get to know one another better and to enjoy special fellowship.

*   *   *   *   *   *   *

In 1978 the small congregation of Lynden, Washington, tucked in the mountains of the Northwest, started its grade school with grades one through eight, thirty students and two teachers. During the next year they took on a weighty project: they added both kindergarten and grade nine. In succession the next three years they added grades ten, eleven, and twelve. The school instructs its approximately fifty pupils from kindergarten through grade twelve.

*   *   *   *   *   *   *

In the year 1959 a small group representing various Protestant Reformed Churches in the Grand Rapids area met to discuss the possibility of forming a high school, and on September 15 of that year the Society for Protestant Reformed Secondary Education was organized with ninety-five members.

In the early 1960s appointed committees formulated a constitution, bought land in the Hope, Walker area, and hired an architect. On April 20, 1968, a "date stone" ceremony was held, and from then on the new high school building took shape. On September 5 of 1968 the school was ready for students in grades ten and eleven. The next year the twelfth grade was added. The building has been enlarged three times — for a gymnasium and more classroom space. One hundred thirty-nine pupils from the Grand Rapids area studied under ten teachers in Covenant Christian High School in the 1990-1991 school year.

* * * * * * *

On December 7, 1956, the combined school boards of the Adams St., South Holland, and Hope, Walker schools met at Hope School. This meeting was the beginning of the permanent organization of the Federation of Protestant Reformed School Societies. A committee was appointed to draw up a constitution. After all the schools in the denomination had been contacted and had approved of the constitution, the Federation was constituted.

With their meetings held in the Michigan-Illinois areas, the Federation Board makes arrangements for seminars, workshops, teachers' conventions, summer mini-courses, and the financing of these activities. The T.E.D. (Teacher's Education Development) Committee of the Federation Board brings recommendations for publishing educational materials. It is an organization which gives cohesiveness to the denomination's parental schools scattered over the United States. It is also an organ of fellowship, communion, and communication, especially for the teachers and administrators who live and teach in isolated areas of the states.

* * * * * * *

Through the years many of the teachers, especially the younger teachers, have blended their efforts with other young people in the denomination to publish *Beacon Lights*, a youth magazine. Started in 1941, the pioneers of this new young people's magazine published five trial issues. The issues in the second year of publication were expanded to include the rubrics "Current Events," "Soldiers' Correspondence," and "Open Forum," along with the original "Editorials," "Bible Outlines," and "Book Reviews." Since the year 1941 *Beacon Lights* has been published monthly, except for the months of July and September.

* * * * * * *

Back in the year 1955, just two years after the split of 1953, the denominational mission committee called the Rev. George Lubbers, who was at that time pastor of the Creston congregation in northwest Grand Rapids, to be the *first* domestic missionary in the denomination after the split of 1953. He accepted the call and went to Pella, Iowa, the congregation he had served as pastor from the years 1937 to 1944. Although the work in Pella was not strictly home mission work, Rev. Lubbers tried to bring peace to the small congregation, which was suffering the internal problems and polarizations brought about by the trouble of 1953.

Some months later the Rev. Lubbers was contacted by the Rev. Herman Mensch, a minister in the German Reformed denomination, who had his roots in the German Reformed Churches based in South Dakota. Through the contacts and conferences between the two denominations in the late 1940s, Mensch had become interested in the doctrines of the Protestant Reformed Churches. As a result of this contact, he had studied at the Protestant Reformed Seminary and was now a minister in the denomination.

Rev. Mensch alerted Rev. Lubbers to the fact that the members of the German Reformed congregation in Loveland, Colorado, were interested in the doctrines of the Protestant Reformed churches. With the blessing of the mission committee Rev. Lubbers began his work in Loveland. In the summer of 1955 Rev. and Mrs. Lubbers settled into a motel in Loveland for the summer, and Rev. Lubbers not only preached during that summer but held catechism classes and led the society meetings.

During much of the next two years, Rev. Lubbers had to work without his wife's presence. She was needed in Grand Rapids by their school-age children.

The members of the Loveland congregation responded with eagerness to the Scriptural and Reformed preaching and teaching and asked to be organized as a Protestant Reformed congregation. They were not organized, however, until after May 8, 1958. The *Acts of Synod* of 1957 gives the reason: "The reason for the delay in requesting organization lies in the fact that they have a case concerning their property pending in the civil courts. The case came up for trial on the 8th of May, but as yet no verdict has been given."[154]

In June of 1958 the members were organized as a Protestant Reformed congregation. They called the Rev. Henry Kuiper, and he accepted their call. In the fall of that year he became their pastor. The congregation was prospering and they invited the Protestant Reformed young people to hold their August, 1961, convention in the beauty of the Colorado mountains. The Protestant Reformed Federation accepted.

After the convention was over, Pastor Kuiper did not feel very well. In September he noticed a lump in his groin, and his doctor diagnosed it as cancerous. Although the doctor removed the lump, Rev. Kuiper was not able to preach again. In October he had a stroke due to the complications of his cancer, and in November of 1961 the Lord took him home.

Meanwhile, the Rev. Lubbers was called to go to another area of the German Reformed settlements — to the area of Isabel-Leola. The members of both the Isabel-Leola area in South Dakota and in the tiny village of Forbes, North Dakota, had asked for help from the Protestant Reformed missionary. The Rev. Lubbers describes his work as follows:

> We went to Isabel. Here we had visited and preached while my dear friend Herman Mensch was minister there.... The people in Isabel were of the same stock as those in Loveland, also their having been indoctrinated in the Kohlbruggian emphasis of justification in a one-sided sense, neglecting the teaching of sanctification in Christ.... This made our work correctional in nature. We did not carry on a concerted polemics, but taught the people the grand truth of the full counsel of God as formulated by the Reformation fathers of the second generation. The people were comforted under our preaching. The work schedule here too was very busy.... It entailed a bit of weekend driving to serve the needs of two small congregations, one in Forbes and the other in Isabel. If I preached on Sunday morning after

---

154.   Pp. 38, 39.

conducting Sunday School, I would need to drive
175 miles in the afternoon to preach in the evening
service in Forbes Schoolhouse. If I preached in
Forbes in the morning, after Sunday School I
would again preach at 2:30 p.m. After this we
would drive to Isabel and preach there in the
evening. That day we would drive 225 miles —
from Aberdeen to Forbes to Isabel. [155]

At the Synod of 1960 both the Isabel and Forbes congregations were received into the Protestant Reformed denomination.

In the summer of 1962 Rev. Lubbers was called to move
to an entirely different area to do mission work with people
from other kinds of backgrounds. He was called to the
Houston-Belaire, Texas, area. People from wide-spread
areas of this sprawling metropolis came to hear Reformed
preaching. But Rev. Lubbers soon learned that he was
preaching to people who were heavily involved with the
John Birch politicians, who were fighting the "great conspiracy from Washington down to the grass roots of society."
They were anti-semitic in their sympathies. [156]

After several months of work there, Rev. Lubbers was
called back to Michigan. He had sowed seeds in the Houston
area which would germinate some years later. The Southwest congregation in Grand Rapids called Rev. Lubbers to be
their pastor, and from June 8, 1964, to September 1, 1970, he
spent six quiet years in the pastoral ministry.

❊   ❊   ❊   ❊   ❊   ❊   ❊

Even before the emissaries H. Meulenberg and H. Zwak
were sent to investigate the possibility of a mission field in
Jamaica (see page 261), the membership of the denomination
had received and answered an urgent request:

---

155.   Personal papers, p. 2.
156.   *Ibid.*, p. 4.

> First Church's bulletin carried an urgent re-
> quest for summer clothing and shoes from the
> churches in Jamaica who have been correspond-
> ing with Rev. Hanko and receiving our literature
> and who express a keen interest in our doctrine.
> The consistory decided to heed the plea and the
> Deacons boxed and shipped the donations con-
> tributed by the congregation.[157]

The members of the denomination answered the request and gave generously. This was the beginning of the "clothes for Jamaica" drives.

The pastors Elliot, Frame, and Rudduck, along with the lay members of the churches in Jamaica, asked the Protestant Reformed churches to send pastors and teachers. They needed men to give Reformed instruction to the men who were already pastors and also to the students studying for the ministry. The problem was that the churches in the states already had a shortage of ministers. The Rev. J.A. Heys was the first man to go to the town of Lucie to give instruction both to pastors and students; but he had a pastorate in the states and could not stay in Jamaica for long periods at a time. In his absence he sent them correspondence lessons.

Because this was not an ideal way to conduct foreign mission work — the first foreign mission work of the de-nomination — the mission committee asked Rev. Lubbers to go to Jamaica for the months of April and May of the year 1969. This was a preparatory step to a call for Rev. Lubbers to become the first foreign missionary in the denomination. Lubbers went to Jamaica for these two months and reported: "I remember preaching 28 times in these two months. I had been very, very skeptical about the Jamaica field, and I went in that bias to Jamaica. However, I felt very strongly that with vigor and vision something quite positive might accrue from our labors under the blessing of almighty God." [158]

157.   J.M. Faber, "News From Our Churches," *Standard Bearer,*
Vol. 38, Feb. 15, 1962, p. 240.
158.   Personal papers, p. 5.

For four years Rev. and Mrs. Lubbers were busy working in Jamaica. With sporadic help from the Rev. J. Heys and Mark Hoeksema he preached, taught catechism classes, instructed seminary students...and repaired his own car.

In connection with this man-power shortage, Editor H.C. Hoeksema wrote an editorial in the May 1, 1968, issue of the *Standard Bearer* titled "Our Most Basic Immediate Need."

> If anyone were to ask me what is the biggest need and the biggest problem which our churches face and which our coming synod will face, I would reply without a second's hesitation: *our severe man-power shortage.*
>
> Understand, I do not speak of this man-power shortage in the carnal sense. I cannot join in the raucous cry for men that has frequently been raised in the church, as though the cause of God's church is dependent upon men and upon mere numbers of men, and as though possibly men may go lost through the church's failure to send forth sufficient laborers into the fields. Nor, in fact, do I wish this editorial to be understood as a mere plea for *men.* Perhaps it might be better to speak in this connection of the shortage of *servant-power.* For, certainly, what we need is not mere men, but *men of God,* dedicated, faithful, hard-working, well-trained, well-equipped, *servants of the Lord....*
>
> For I am of the conviction that this is indeed our largest problem, that, in fact, it will loom up to trouble our synod at more than one point in its deliberation. I hesitate to use the word "emergency," for I am inclined to shy away from emergency-psychology. But let me then use the word "urgent." For I am convinced that we must take this problem very seriously, probably more seriously than we have taken it heretofore. And we must, by the grace of God and in the confidence of our calling as churches, attempt more concretely to solve it....
>
> Permit me to point up the problem. First of all, there is Jamaica. The situation, I think, is obvious.

Anyone in our Mission Board and anyone who has followed the periodic reports of our Jamaica work must be painfully aware of it. Several years ago already the Lord began to open a door for us on that island of the sea. Our churches responded, not only officially but organically. I think it cannot be gainsaid that our people have "had a heart" for the work in Jamaica, and rightly so. To the best of our limited ability our churches have labored there. From time to time men have been sent there for brief periods and have labored intensively while there. Moreover, even when it was impossible to have laborers on the island, the work has been continued through correspondence and through literature and through tapes, and especially during the last two years through the correspondence courses prepared by Revs. Heys and C. Hanko. And also with respect to the work of benevolence and the problem of the Jamaicans' places of worship, our churches have made valiant attempts to be of assistance. But what is sorely needed is men who can labor at length and on the spot, men who for an extended period can devote all their time and labors to the work there....

All of this points to one thing: we need men on the island of Jamaica, men from our churches, and soon....

All this I write not to complain; for there is no reason to complain. Nor do I write it in the spirit of pessimism. For such pessimism, I believe, is wrong. I write it so that we may all consider the problem, and so that our churches may see the very urgent need that will face our synod at many a turn in its deliberations. They will think and probably say more than once: "If only we had more men...." [159]

---

159. *Standard Bearer,* Vol. 44, pp. 342, 343.

In the garden of Reformed plantings the plants were experiencing an atmosphere of awakening, of sunshine and growth, and of showers of blessings.   These Reformed plantings shared some of their seeds and buds and blossoms with other gardens in this world, and taught them the joys of being Reformed plantings.

Chapter 17
The Outreach of the Seventies

Back in the year 1963 a publication committee had been organized to publish the books written by authors in the denomination. Until this time the Eerdmans Publishing Company had handled all the literature which the churches had put out. Now as the denomination was coming out of the doldrums of dead center, some of the laymen as well as pastors decided that they had come of age and were ready for a new denominational venture.

The *Standard Bearer* of September 1, 1963, announced this new organization. It was to be called The Publications Committee, an arm of the Reformed Free Publishing Association — better known as the R.F.P.A. — which had been publishing the *Standard Bearer* since 1924. This committee pledged its responsibility for publishing the books written by authors in the denomination.

Eerdmans Publishing Company agreed to assign the copyrights of the books they had already published to the R.F.P.A.; and they offered their help if needed.

The first book this organization published was *Reformed Dogmatics,* by Herman Hoeksema, a book he had written in conjunction with his teaching of dogmatics in the seminary. The book was published in November, 1966. From that date on, the R.F.P.A. took over most of the publications within the denomination. Kregel Publications, another Grand Rapids publisher, assisted the R.F.P.A. with the publishing and distribution of their books, beginning with *Reformed Dogmatics* and continuing through the late 1970s. A list of the titles of the publications by the R.F.P.A. is included in the appendix.

The Synod of June, 1968, was a noteworthy synod in more than one area. In Professor Hanko's summarization of the synod, his first paragraph contained startling national news.

> The first day of our Synod was under the cloud of the assassination of Senator Robert Kennedy — a shocking reminder of the evil of our times in which the church is called to live. There was a deep awareness in Synod of the growing apostasy of the church world. And it was with one eye fixed upon current events that Synod felt the urgency of her calling, made her decisions, and looked ahead to the work of the church.[160]

One area of discussion at this synod was the denomination's ecumenical calling. The Reformed Ecumenical Synod had asked that delegates from the Protestant Reformed Churches attend their next meeting in Amsterdam, The Netherlands, in August of that year. Although the Protestant Reformed Churches agreed with the R.E.S.'s doctrinal basis in so far as it referred to the Scriptures and the confessions, they could not subscribe to the statement that:

> It has to be emphasized that only a wholehearted and consistent return to this Scriptural truth, of which the Gospel of Jesus Christ is the core and apex, can bring salvation to mankind and effectuate the so sorely needed renewal of the world.[161]

A committee of the synod drew up the following four observations, which embodied their objections and which the synod adopted:

> Neither Scripture nor the confessions hold forth the hope of such a wholehearted and consistent return to the truth of which this statement speaks.

160.   "Report of the Synod of 1968," *Standard Bearer*, Vol. 44, July, 1968, p. 425.
161.   *Ibid.*, pp. 427, 428.

> Neither Scripture nor the confessions hold forth the expectation of a renewal of the world through such a wholehearted and consistent return.
>
> On the contrary, Scripture and the confessions speak of the renewal of all things through the wonder of grace in our Lord Jesus Christ, and of the calling of the church to be a witness of the light in the midst of the darkness of this present world, and to maintain and proclaim the truth of the gospel in order that the church may be gathered and preserved, with a view to the coming of our Lord and the realization of this renewal of all things.

Then the synod acted on the matter as follows:

> Yet it was believed that we ought not to turn our backs upon the RES because of this. It was therefore decided to ask the RES whether they would accept "observers" from our churches with the reservations to their basis which we make. It would be a wonderful thing if we could participate with the RES in this way.[162]

More important at this synod were the decisions about the curriculum of the seminary. Until this date the seminary had offered only the three-year seminary courses. All preparatory work had to be taken at area colleges. At this time:

> Synod decided on a large expansion of our Seminary program. This has been discussed for a couple of years, and in 1968 Synod was ready to move ahead. The Theological School Committee had, in the past few months, done a tremendous amount of work in this area and had come with a complete report to Synod which was adopted. The plan to go into effect will be the beginnings of a pre-seminary program in which our young men will be taught by our own school in their college

---

162.   *Ibid.*

subjects as well as in the subjects of the regular seminary curriculum. The plan will be put into effect only gradually. While it will, the Lord willing, begin this coming September, it will take more than five years before all the necessary subjects are added. And before the full program will be realized, another professor will have to be added to the Seminary faculty. But this is all for the future. The important matter is that the Synod is looking ahead to the expansion of the Seminary program and is making every effort to provide a complete education for our ministers in our own institutions.

Secondly, with respect to our Seminary, the Synod looked ahead to the need for other quarters. If the above program is to be completely effected, other quarters will have to be provided eventually to have adequate facilities for instructing a number of students. A general plan was approved to proceed in this direction, although also this will take some time. It might be worthwhile to consider the possibility of making this a project to commemorate the 45th anniversary of our churches. More on these programs will appear in a future Seminary Newsletter.[163]

At the Synod of 1970 the Theological School Committee reported, through the pen of Herman Hanko, that the decision to add pre-seminary courses had been implemented. Hanko also reported that he had collaborated with various colleagues and had gained their recognition of courses which the pre-seminary department taught. Hanko explained: "That is, if some of our students who have taken pre-seminary courses in our school want to go on to earn their A.B. degree, there are colleges which, with a minimum of effort, will recognize the subjects taught in the Seminary."[164]

---

163.   *Ibid.*, p. 427.
164.   "Report of the Synod of 1970," *Standard Bearer*, Vol. 46, July, 1970, p. 425.

Behind the scenes the Theological School Committee was looking at possible sites for the new seminary building which they needed. Until this time the seminary classes had still been held underground, in the basement of First Church. Eventually they chose a site on a hill in Grandville, a suburb in the southwest area of greater Grand Rapids. Plans were drawn and work was started. Meanwhile, the number of students grew and the pre-seminary program was added. Now the load was too heavy for Professors Hanko and Hoeksema to carry. The Rev. R. Decker, who was at that time pastor of the South Holland, Illinois, congregation, was called as a third professor. In the September 1, 1973, issue of the *Standard Bearer* the news editor wrote:

> If we were to choose from this page one single news item to be that of the greatest significance for the churches of our denomination, it would probably be this, that Rev. R. Decker, pastor of our South Holland, Illinois congregation, has accepted the call to serve as third professor in our seminary. The possibility of a pre-seminary program in our school during the 1973-1974 school year rested with that decision. The fact that the Lord has provided for the need must certainly be an evidence also of His blessing upon the labors there. [165]

Friday, January 25, 1974, was moving-in day for the professors and the students, and the first classes were held on the following Tuesday. The news editor, Mr. D. Doezema, must have been around, for he commented, "The pleasure and understandable pride of professors and students alike was written over every face. One of the former remarked, 'I hardly know how to act here.' And one of the latter, all in one breath, exclaimed, 'This is really different! It's unbelievable! This is so nice!'" [166]

---

165.   Don Doezema, "News From Our Churches," *Standard Bearer,* Vol. 49, pp. 479, 480.
166.   D. Doezema, "News From Our Churches," *Standard Bearer,* Vol. 50, Feb. 15, 1974, p. 239.

Then came the dedication on the evening of February 15, 1974, in the auditorium of First Church. In an editorial titled "An Historic Evening," Professor Hoeksema wrote:

> The evening of the Dedication Program for our new seminary building will be one long remembered by this writer — and undoubtedly by all who were present. It will go down in the annals of our history as one of the high points, one of those occasions when we reach the exhilarating atmosphere of the mountain tops of faith.
>
> The faculty's letter of appreciation, found elsewhere in this issue, was written before that evening of February 15. But even if it had been written afterward, sufficient descriptive adjectives could not be found to describe the God-centered note that was heard throughout the entire program, the outpouring of love and devotion to the cause of our Reformed faith that seemed to hang in the very atmosphere in First Church's auditorium, the joyous exultation and thanksgiving which made the rafters ring from the songs of that tremendous audience. Not since my student days have I been nervous when I had to ascend a speaker's platform; but when the duty fell to me to close the program, I was afraid I would not be able to speak. I had a great lump in my throat — not from sadness, but from overwhelming joy and gratitude! It was one of those occasions when the impact of "What hath God wrought!" simply overwhelms a person!
>
> Indeed, it was an evening to remember!
>
> But why was it such a memorable occasion?...
>
> It seems to me that it was intrinsically an historic occasion. Historic it was, not only in the sense that it represented a climax, a high point, in our history as Protestant Reformed Churches. Historic it was, not only in the sense that it was one of those occasions which one witnesses, perhaps, once in a lifetime or once in a generation. But it was an historic occasion in the deepest sense in

that the *significance* of the history of our forty-nine years of existence as Protestant Reformed Churches all seemed to be concentrated, condensed, into that one evening. The hopes, the fears, the struggles, the labors, the trials and tribulation and tears — yes, all these! But more than all these, the fact that the Lord our God has preserved us as churches, has kept us faithful to the truth of His Word and of our Reformed Confessions, has given strength for the battle, encouragement at times of discouragement, has raised up men, servants, whenever needed, has given to us a singular place as churches, as witnesses of the truth of His sovereign grace and His everlasting covenant of friendship, and that, too, in an era when all around us is apostasy and decadence — all of this seemed to charge the very atmosphere on that memorable evening. It was present in the ringing notes of Prof. Decker's dedicatory address, "That All the Earth May Know That Jehovah Is God." It was present in the Liturgy of Dedication. It was present in the Psalms of praise and thanksgiving which were raised to Almighty God, the God of our fathers. Yes, it was represented even in the personnel of the evening's program: did you not recognize that fact, the glorious fact, that it was the second and third generation of our Protestant Reformed Churches who led us in the program, and that they stood faithful to the same Reformed faith to which our fathers were dedicated?...

Let us go on! Let us go on with renewed zeal and courage! Let us go on, dedicated anew to the preservation, the development, and the proclamation of the same glorious truths of God's sovereign predestination and everlasting covenant of friendship! [167]

After the students and faculty had settled into their new building, they had the room and materials for more ambi-

---

167.   *Standard Bearer,* Vol. 50, pp. 244, 245.

tious projects. Already in the year 1967 the seminary personnel had published a *Theological Journal* twice a year, in December and May. It was easier to publish it now that they had the proper facilities. Since the December, 1967, *Journal* first came out, these biblical and scholarly treatises have been published. The topics of the articles range over all areas of doctrine and the Christian's life. A sampling includes topics such as:

> "The Genealogy of Jesus According to the Flesh" by D. Engelsma
>
> "The Foolishness of Preaching" by R. Decker
>
> "The Place of Women in the Church" by R. Decker
>
> "Paul: An Outline on His Theology" by H. Hanko
>
> "James Daane's `The Freedom of God'" by H.C. Hoeksema
>
> "The Doctrine of Infant Baptism" by H. Hanko

In the year 1978 a newsletter from the seminary told of another up-dated project:

> If you have read the *Acts* of the last Synod, you probably noticed that Synod decided to microfilm all Synodical archives which are at present in the home of Synod's Stated Clerk. We have asked the Synodical Committee and the Theological Committee to carry out this mandate of Synod for the benefit of our Seminary Library. We hope that two microfilm copies can be made of the archives — one for the churches and one for the School Library. [168]

Back in the 1920s when the Revs. H. Hoeksema and G.M. Ophoff started to train students for the ministry and studied in preparation for their classroom lectures, they compiled copious notes, which they later refined as syllabi for class-

---

168.   The Faculty, "Newsletter," *Standard Bearer,* Vol. 54, Feb. 1, 1978, p. 214.

room instruction. The professors who later took their places followed their practice, and also wrote many syllabi in a variety of areas: interpretation of the Scriptures, church history, practical theology, Old and New Testament history. As a result the students—from the birth of the denomination to the present time — have received a consistent, thorough, and scholarly theological education in an atmosphere of unity.

※　※　※　※　※　※　※

Two new congregations were organized in the decade of the seventies. The first was based in the Grandville-Jenison area, southwest of Grand Rapids. Nineteen families from other Protestant Reformed congregations in the area which were outgrowing their church buildings — Hope, Hudsonville, First, and even Southeast—became the charter members. Organized with the blessing of Classis East on February 23, 1973, they met in the auditorium of the Jenison Christian Junior High School. The new congregation chose the name *Faith Protestant Reformed Church*. They called Candidate M. Joostens as their first pastor, and he accepted the call. By God's grace the new congregation prospered numerically, with new members not only from other congregations, but also from internal growth, adding to the thirty-four young children of the original members. After worshiping in the auditorium of the school for almost six years, the congregation moved into their own new building on 20th Avenue in Jenison in December of 1978.

In the same year in which the Faith congregation had been organized—on September 11, 1973, another Protestant Reformed congregation was organized. This group was the first Protestant Reformed Church on the East coast. Wyckoff (or Prospect Park), New Jersey, was an area with a history of early settlers, where many Reformed people had lived for generations. It was also an area of many Christian Reformed churches. A small group in Wyckoff was not very satisfied in the Christian Reformed denomination. For several years they had been reading and studying the literature put out by the Protestant Reformed Churches.

In March of 1973 when the Rev. D. Engelsma was making contact with Reformed people in the Philadelphia area, these interested people from Wyckoff asked him to come to visit them and discuss the doctrinal stance of the Protestant Reformed Churches. After an evening of discussion, the Rev. Engelsma suggested that the group contact the Mission Committee for help. This committee sent the Rev. R. Decker to help them for a month; and in May of 1973 the group held its first worship service in the home of one of the members.

Through the next month the Mission Committee sent other ministers-on-loan, and on September 11, 1973, with the leadership of the Rev. H. Veldman, the group was organized as the Covenant Protestant Reformed Church of Wyckoff, New Jersey. The Rev. A. denHartog became their first pastor. At this writing the congregation numbers eight families and two individuals. They have formed an evangelism committee for the witness of the gospel in their area.

Two years later the denomination welcomed its first congregation in the Canadian West. At that time the Rev. B. Woudenberg was the pastor of the Lynden, Washington, congregation, which is very near to the border of Canada. The program for the evening of the organization of this group — on September 25, 1975 — gives the history of the group in Edmonton, Canada.

> The origin of the First Protestant Reformed Church at Edmonton, Alberta, Canada, is to be found in a Bible study class which met for about two years under the instruction of Rev. B. Woudenberg of Lynden, Washington, U.S.A.
>
> It was in the spring of 1973 that a number of people in Edmonton became deeply concerned with the growing liberalism of their church life. At that time, Mr. and Mrs. F. Tolsma came to visit in Lynden, and to meet with Rev. Woudenberg who offered to come to Edmonton and do what he could to help them. This he did, and the result was

the organization of a regular Bible study class meeting every two weeks for the following two years. Each time Rev. Woudenberg would fly up by plane from Lynden and lead the class, which studied in detail the five points of Calvinism and the Belgic Confession of Faith.

It was during the summer of 1975, when Rev. Woudenberg was unable to meet for about two months, that the members of the class came to the conclusion that they should seek a more stable form of organization as a congregation among the Protestant Reformed Churches in America. When Rev. Woudenberg returned, they consulted with him and afterward with a committee from his consistory as well as one from the Mission Committee of the Protestant Reformed Churches. It was their advice that the group of believers should send a letter of request to Classis West of their denomination to request such organization. This was done on September 3, 1975, and the Classis authorized them to be organized under the direction of the consistory of Lynden Protestant Reformed Church together with Rev. George Lanting of Loveland, Colorado. The meeting has been set for this evening, September 25, 1975, in the Crestwood Presbyterian Church at Edmonton.[169]

In 1976 the Rev. R. Moore became the congregation's first pastor.

* * * * * * *

The decade of the seventies was also the time of the denominational celebrations of the fiftieth anniversaries of the births both of the *Standard Bearer* and the Protestant Reformed denomination. The anniversary of the *Standard Bearer* would logically come first, for its first issue had been

---

169.   H. Hanko, "Welcome Edmonton," *Standard Bearer,* Vol. 52, Nov. 1, 1975, p. 561.

published on October 1, 1924. However, the cover of the *Standard Bearer* of October 1, 1973 heralded this anniversary. The readers in October of 1973 may have been puzzled. The editorial explains the reason:

> If you took note of the cover of this issue of our *Standard Bearer* when it arrived in your mail, you will already have noticed that there must be something special afoot with our magazine. And indeed there is! Perhaps you have already discovered the nature of this special occasion. For if you inspected the new symbol displayed on the cover, and looked carefully at the reproduction of the very first masthead ever used to identify our magazine, you will have discovered, too, that the occasion is the *beginning* of our fiftieth year of publication.
>
> That in itself means that we have reached a milestone.
>
> Actually, however, we of the Staff and of the Board conceive of matters thus, that we are now, as it were, running the last mile before reaching the more important milestone of the *completion* of our fiftieth year. That, if the Lord will that we reach it, will be the Golden Anniversary of our *Standard Bearer.* And plans are already under way, through a joint committee of the Staff and Board, to observe this fiftieth year in some way in all twenty-one issues of this year, yet so that the observance of this golden anniversary year reaches its climax, its grand finale, upon the completion of the volume-year, the actual Golden Anniversary....
>
> How shall we observe this anniversary year?
>
> By saying from the heart: "Thanks be to our Covenant God!"
>
> And what does that thanksgiving imply concretely?
>
> First of all, it implies that we recount before Him, before one another, before our children, before all the public, His manifold mercies and blessings. The very fact that we have been enabled

to publish for all these years is due only to His grace. He has provided the means, even when at times it seemed impossible to continue. He has provided the men — all through the years — to write, to expound, to defend, to hold fast the heritage once delivered unto us, the heritage of the Reformed faith. He has provided the readers, the loyal supporters, the willing givers. Yes, indeed, He has made all things well! It is of the Lord's mercies that we were not consumed long before we ever reached this anniversary year! Thanks be to God!

But even then we have not touched on the most important element. To reach the fiftieth year of publication is wonderful, but only because as we begin this fiftieth year we do so without any essential change from what we were in the first year of our publication, do so with the same Reformed stance as in 1924!

We have not changed!

Our *Standard Bearer* today bears the standard, the flag, of the truth, even as it did in its very first issue. Yes, there have been many changes: changes of format, changes of personnel, changes of readership. Not only so, but there has indeed been change in the *Standard Bearer* in the sense that we have not stood still. There has been *progress*. There has been *development*. But the progress and development have been a following of the same banner of the truth of God's Word and of our Reformed Confessions which was held high from the very beginning of this venture of faith. This was brought home to me forcibly on a Sunday evening not long ago. After serving as a guest preacher in one of our pulpits, I stopped to chat a few moments with two of the "old-timers," men of the first generation of our churches. One was in his eighties, the other in his seventies. I love to listen to these men; they have insights gained from years of experience.

Somehow the conversation turned to the subject of our churches and their heritage. And these

two men testified as they thought back on the
years: "We have not changed! Our churches are
the same in their doctrine and their preaching as
they were fifty years ago." They were right! And
to hear these elder statesmen of the church say this
was music in my ears! But then another brother
joined in the conversation, a man of my own
generation. And he said: "Yes, but we have not
stood still!" "No," said the two brethren, "we
have not stood still. We have developed, but we
have developed in the line of the truth." And that
was music in my ears, too!

But remember this: that we have not changed
is not due to us. No, it is because the Lord has not
changed. Great has been the faithfulness of our
Covenant God.[170]

After a year of celebrating the fiftieth anniversary of the
Standard Bearer, the denomination began to make plans for
the fiftieth anniversary of the denomination, which was to be
celebrated in conjunction with the annual Young People's
Convention, scheduled to be held in the Grand Rapids area
that year. The news editor, reporting on this memorable
event, started with a bit of whimsy:

Did you know that Rev. Kuiper has a vanity
plate? Well, we wouldn't really call it vanity, but,
with a view to this year's celebration, he did
request and receive a car license plate which reads
PRC-50.

An estimated 1900 of our people already know
about that, for it was announced over the public
address system at Douglas Walker Park on the
afternoon of August 6. It hardly seems necessary,
therefore, to report on the activities of that memorable week, because most of you experienced
them personally. At the Wednesday afternoon
program, in fact, it was found, when Mr. Ed
Ophoff read the role of Protestant Reformed

---

170.   H.C. Hoeksema, *Standard Bearer,* Vol. 50, pp. 4-6.

churches, that every single one of our congregations was represented there. But it was too wonderful an occasion to let it pass unnoticed in the *Standard Bearer* news column. So we'll have a few words about it....

Ed Ophoff led in some spirited outdoor singing — accompanied by organ and piano perched on the back of an old International, and by cicadas overhead. One of the songs, we should note, was "Happy Birthday," sung in honor of Rev. Lubbers' 66th, as he stood waving his straw hat to the friendly gathering....

All in all, the events of the week constituted what the writer of Southwest's bulletin called a "thrilling experience." Perhaps it was summed up best by Prof. Hanko, in the final address. Permit me to conclude with his remarks.

"It was for me a very moving experience. This was especially true of the Field Day yesterday; and I'm sure that this was the experience of you all. It was one of those days you almost wish would never end. And yet, in a sense of course, it *will* not end. Because what impressed me more than anything else yesterday was the spirit of unity that prevailed among us. And I'm sure that, after this evening we return to our homes and to our congregations, this unity that we experienced so richly yesterday and throughout the convention, will continue with us. This convention, therefore, and the activities connected with it, as we commemorate together the 50th anniversary of our churches, are in their own way evidence of God's covenant faithfulness to us. We must have felt that very keenly. God gave to us in this week tokens, memorable tokens that will linger with us, of His great faithfulness to us.[171]

✳ ✳ ✳ ✳ ✳ ✳ ✳

171. D. Doezema, "News From Our Churches," *Standard Bearer,* Vol. 51, Sept. 1, 1975, pp. 479, 480.

In this year of celebration, other Reformed groups were watching the Protestant Reformed Churches with interest.

On December 19, 1974, the staff of Calvin Seminary invited Professor H.C. Hoeksema to address the student body with a talk about the fiftieth anniversary of the Protestant Reformed denomination. He accepted and titled his speech "After Fifty Years." This speech is included in the appendix.

Also in this year the churches were continuing their interest in the ecclesiastical scene around them. The September, 1969, issue of the *Standard Bearer* introduced its readers to the theology of Dr. Klaas Runia from the Reformed Theological College in Geelong, Australia. The *Banner* of the Christian Reformed Church had published an article about Dr. Runia's theology with the caption "The Joy of Systematic Theology."

Dr. Runia, a native of The Netherlands, who had studied at the University of Kampen, had criticized Herman Hoeksema's explanation of God's immutability—His changelessness — as Hoeksema had defined it:

> God *is that He is* in all the infinite and constant fullness of His Being. He does not grow older, does not increase or decrease in Being or power, is from eternity to eternity the same in all His virtues, in His mind and will, His love and life, the absolute fullness and Self-sufficient God.[172]

In his writings Dr. Runia plainly showed that he believed in a God Who changes; and when Editor H.C. Hoeksema editorially charged Runia with heresy, he quoted one of Runia's statements: "God does change His attitude toward His people." Runia defended himself by calling his own thinking "a dynamic relational way of theologizing, which gives God's people great joy."

---

172.   H.C. Hoeksema, "Topsy-Turvy Joy from 'Down Under,' " *Standard Bearer*, Vol. 45, Sept. 1, 1969, p. 462.

Taking his cue from this statement of Dr. Runia, Editor Hoeksema titled his series of articles on the topic of God's Being: "Topsy-Turvy Joy from Down Under."

This exchange of doctrinal differences was not so important in itself. It was the resulting contacts with the Reformed Churches of New Zealand — and later with churches in Australia — which this exchange of doctrinal positions triggered that were important.

The Reformed Churches of New Zealand received their pastors from the Reformed Theological College in Geelong, Australia, but they were not satisfied with these pastors. They were Reformed in name, but not in their preaching. The Reformed churches in New Zealand were troubled but had no immediate solution to their problem. Then, in the providence of God, someone who was not a member of the Reformed Churches of New Zealand, but who subscribed to the *Standard Bearer* showed the article about Dr. Runia to Mr. William VanRij, a member of the Christ Church Orthodox Presbyterian congregation. Mr. VanRij was also president of an organization called "The Presbyterian and Reformed Fellowship," whose purpose was to defend the Reformed faith against liberal tendencies and false doctrines.

Mr. VanRij wrote to the *Standard Bearer* and told the editor about the doctrinal trouble in New Zealand; and a correspondence was started. In the winter of 1971, when Mr. VanRij went on a business trip to the states, he stayed in Grand Rapids over a weekend and met many members of the Protestant Reformed denomination. This was the beginning of the contact between the Protestant Reformed Churches and the Reformed Churches of New Zealand.

In the early months of 1971 two elders, Mr. B. VanHerk and Mr. J. Koppe from the Reformed congregation of Wainuiomata (Wellington) on the North Island and Mr. W. VanRij from the Christ Church congregation on the South Island were suspended for refusing to apologize for writing against the heresy of Dr. Klaas Runia. The VanHerk and Koppe families started worship services in their home, using recordings of Protestant Reformed services. Slowly, as meetings were held and services were announced, various groupings formed and grew. They adopted the name "The Christian Fellowship." But they needed help and leadership.

The churches in New Zealand also had contact with the Reformed and Presbyterian churches in Australasia; and these churches, too, were distressed by the liberal pastors who had been trained in Geelong. These men from Geelong also became *their* pastors. The members in several of the congregations were looking for biblical and Reformed pastors.

The members of the churches both in New Zealand and Australia found one source of understanding and help: the Committee for Contact with Other Churches from the Protestant Reformed denomination. They started correspondence with the Contact Committee, giving the details of their problems with the unreformed men who became their pastors.

But correspondence with strangers who have different backgrounds and customs and who live on the other side of the world, even though they are people of like faith, has its difficulties. The Contact Committee made plans to send two representatives from the Protestant Reformed Churches in the summer of 1975, which would be the winter season down under. They asked the Professors H. Hanko and H.C. Hoeksema to be the emissaries, but Professor Hanko could not see his way clear to go at that time to make this extended trip. Then the committee asked his father, the retired Rev. C. Hanko, to take his place, and Rev. Hanko accepted.

The trip had been scheduled for the months of June and July, and the two representatives followed the itinery drawn up by the Contact Committee. The committee instructed the two men that the *purpose* of their visit, in their lectures, preaching, and fellowship was to promote and discuss the Reformed faith as taught in the Scriptures. During the months of June and July the two men followed the heavy schedules which the various area people had added to the original schedule drawn up for them, with too much crowded into too few minutes. They visited, lectured, and preached — sometimes simultaneously in two different congregations.

Fourteen installments in the *Standard Bearer*, in the issues of late 1975 and early 1976, published the details of the visits to the "down under" countries, and also those north of the equator. These articles enlarged on the visits in the countries which the Revs. Hanko and Hoeksema visited. Everywhere they were enthusiastically received. They worked hard, made many contacts, visited in countless different homes, and slept very little.

The itinerary had been planned for a visit to New Zealand first. From there the men crossed the Tasman Sea and visited Tasmania, the island province of Australia. Then they flew north to mainland Australia, visiting many congregations in the coastal area and also visiting the Reformed Theological College in Geelong, where they were welcomed with chilly reserve. Then, flying north from Sydney, they crossed the equator and landed in Jakarta, a city of filth and poverty, in Indonesia. Both men were scheduled to preach in the Spiritual Life Church on Sunday. They knew they would encounter the language barrier, for Indonesia is a sort of melting pot: Chinese, Malaysian, and Dutch mingle with the Indonesians. The members in this church claimed that their knowledge of the Scriptures had originally come through the work of the apostle Thomas, who had preached in the East. The Indonesians, of course, had no knowledge of John Calvin or the Reformed faith.

On the morning of the sabbath day, Professor Hoeksema preached in the English language at the 7 a.m. service, and his sermon was translated by Mr. Cornelis Kuswanto. After a break for refreshments, at 10 a.m. the Rev. Hanko preached in the Dutch language. One of the older men in the congregation, who had been influenced by the Dutch immigrants in Indonesia and had learned their language, translated his sermon, sentence by sentence, into the Indonesian language. It may have been the first time these Indonesians heard a Reformed sermon.

The last stop of the tour, and in some ways the most important contact of the tour, was Singapore, a hot, crowded, but very beautiful, clean, and orderly city. It was the most "foreign" of the cities on the tour partly because of the conglomeration of races. Beside Malaysians, Chinese, and Indians, people from all over the world joined this melting pot. Another foreign element in the city was the idolatrous atmosphere. Idol temples dedicated to Hinduism, Taoism, and Buddism crowded the city. There was also a very little bit of Christianity: a few Christian churches, among which were the New Life Church and a Bible college.

The request for the representatives from the Protestant Reformed Churches to visit Singapore had come from Ong Keng Ho, who had been educated in New Zealand, and had attended the Presbyterian Church in Christ Church. He had planned the meetings in Singapore and suggested topics for the lectures: "The True Church" and "The Believers and the Church." These lectures were widely publicized, and mostly young people — from all kinds of backgrounds — attended these lectures, about a hundred at each lecture.

Editor Hoeksema ended his report about Singapore with mixed feelings: "We left with the conviction that we had spoken the truth of the Word of God, and that seeds were sown. Whether there will be positive fruit of any kind in the future remains to be seen. Through Ong we do have an outlet for some of our literature in that area."[173]

What neither Editor Hoeksema nor the Protestant Reformed denomination as a whole — nor the young Singaporeans — anticipated was that in a few years the Lord would send fruit on this visit in the form of close contact between the Protestant Reformed Churches in America and the eager group in Singapore, which would become a sister church in the next decade.

This tour in the East was by no means the only foreign contact of the denomination in the seventies. Mr. H.

---

173.   "Our Australasian Tour 13," *Standard Bearer,* Vol. 52, May 1, 1976, p. 846.

VanderWal, business manager of the *Standard Bearer* and a friendly man, cultivated and received letters from faraway places. The *Standard Bearer* of February 15, 1972, gives a small sampling of the area of contact the churches had made in this decade.

> From California — "Besides the *Standard Bearer* and the tapes, I have been able to obtain some of your Seminary Notes, and I must say that I know of no other organization that makes available material of such depth."
>
> From England — "Literature received so far has been greatly appreciated, particularly the *Standard Bearer* magazine."
>
> From New Zealand — "Your *Standard Bearer* is very much appreciated, particularly for its sound Reformed position."
>
> From Belfast, Northern Ireland — "Do you publish a catalogue of your publications? We have at the moment works by Hoeksema (*Behold He Cometh, The Triple Knowledge*) which are excellent things, and should be pleased to know of any further of your publications."
>
> From Australia — "I am a bookseller, specializing in Reformed literature, and have been asked for a set of *The Triple Knowledge*—Herman Hoeksema, by a customer. I have read a few copies of the *Standard Bearer* myself and enjoyed them, so I am happy to forward his request to you. If it is possible I should like a catalogue of all the books and booklets you print, with the published prices."
>
> From Paris, France — "I have already read some of Rev. Hoeksema's books. A few months ago I bought the one — on the Book of Revelation. I am interested in almost every one of the books listed in your folder."[174]

---

174.   D. Doezema, "News From Our Churches," *Standard Bearer*, Vol. 48, p. 240.

The garden of Reformed plantings was glad and thankful that their seedlings were being spread to many areas of the earth, transported by emissaries, by books, by tapes, by sermons, and by letters, as an encouragement to the new plantings in faraway places. The garden of Reformed plantings was encouraged by these connections and eager to enter the decade of the eighties.

Chapter 18
The Development of the Eighties

The group of young people living in Singapore, most of them young adults between eighteen and twenty-five years old, who were interested in the doctrines of the Reformed Churches, had had an interesting background. All of them had in common the goal of getting a better understanding of the Scriptures. In a loose association called the G.L.T.D., the Gospel Letters and Tracts Department, they met to study the Scriptures with the various leaders. The Acts of Synod of 1978 gives this background.

> 1. The GLTD had its beginnings about ten years ago as the Monk's Hill Bible Club. This Bible Club was a Bible study group formed by a number of new converts who were attending the Monk's Hill Secondary School. Of this original group only one member remains today in the GLTD, Lau Chin Kwee, who is really the leader of the GLTD.
>
> In time, however, the members of the Bible Club turned their attention more and more to evangelism and the distribution of tracts. In harmony with this they changed their name to the GLTD.
>
> Although the GLTD has always been an independent society, many of its members had been members of the New Life Bible Presbyterian Church in Singapore. About two years ago, however, most of the members of the GLTD withdrew their membership from the Life Church because of certain practices; e.g., Life Church hired a Hindu and a Roman Catholic to teach in their school. Consequently, most of the members of the GLTD are not affiliated with any church.
>
> At about the same time that the GLTD broke

off from Life Church, they received a Baptist missionary pastor. Actually this missionary pastor was one of the original members of the GLTD who had gone to the U.S. to train for the ministry in Faith Seminary, a Baptist institution. His baptist teachings, however, especially his view on baptism, were not received by the GLTD. The result was that about a year ago he left to labor elsewhere....

The GLTD has two kinds of members: constituted and non-constituted members.

a.   To be a constituted member one must have received the sacrament of baptism and have satisfied the leadership "as to their Christian faith, knowledge, and manner of life." This membership allows one to speak and vote at all congregational meetings and to be nominated as a leader. There are 74 such members.

b.   Non-constituted members are those who show interest in the Christian faith and attend functions of the GLTD on a regular basis....

2.   With one exception the members of the GLTD are all single individuals. The one exception is a man without children whose wife is a Hindu....

3.   All of the members without exception are converts from paganism. The oldest member, Lau Chin Kwee, has been a Christian for 10 years; but some have known Christ for 2 years or less. Most of the members have been brought to the Christian faith through the evangelism of the GLTD itself.

4.   There are two very striking and unusual things that ought to be noted here. The first is that individuals and especially young individuals have been gathered, not families. With but a few exceptions, the various members of the GLTD are the only members of their families that have been brought to the faith.... The second unusual thing to be noted here is the fact that converts have been gained apart from the preaching of the Word....

As to the organic life of the GLTD:

The GLTD for all practical purposes is operating as a church with a full-orbed "church life." As is to be expected the exact structure that their organic life assumes is by and large determined by the circumstances in which they find themselves. One overriding factor seems to be their difficulty in meeting as a group. Most of the members have no transportation. In addition, they all come from pagan homes where parents discourage participation in the activities of the GLTD and even persecute them if these activities make them absent from the home too much....

The GLTD knows how to suffer for Christ's sake.... We were told of many who were beaten and locked in their rooms by their parents when they first came to the Christian faith. In almost all cases parents became more tolerant when they saw the transformation which the grace of God worked in the lives of their children. In spite of all this, the members retain a deep respect for the authority of their parents. The members of the GLTD also in other things seem willing to forsake and sacrifice all things earthly and material for the sake of God and His cause.[175]

However, for almost three years after the emissaries had visited Singapore there had been no contact between this group of young people and the Protestant Reformed Churches, and most of the people in the denomination knew very little about the situation in Singapore. Then in late 1977 Mr. Johnson See Choon Hock, originally a member of this group of Singaporeans and who had gone to Scotland to study, wrote a letter to Professor H.C. Hoeksema with many questions about infant baptism. Johnson, remembering his earlier teaching in Singapore by the Baptist missionary from Faith Seminary, was uncertain about Scripture's doctrine of baptism. So he asked for help from Prof. Hoeksema. The two started a correspondence on the subject; and gradually

---

175.   Reported by Rev. James Slopsema and Mr. Dewey Engelsma, pp. 125, 137.

Hoeksema learned that the members of the GLTD did not have a clear nor a Reformed view of the sacrament of baptism. Johnson was very concerned about it. He was due to go back to Singapore soon, and the professor suggested that he go home by way of the states. Johnson eagerly agreed, and the two men set up an itinerary. Because Johnson's plane was scheduled to land in New York City and because the Rev. A. denHartog was pastor of Covenant Protestant Reformed Church in Wyckoff, New Jersey, they arranged that Pastor denHartog would be at the airport to meet Johnson. He stayed for a visit with the denHartogs, and a friendship started which would soon influence the history of Singapore and end in great joy for the young people there.

When Johnson visited the Grand Rapids area and told the Contact Committee about the doctrinal turmoil in Singapore, the committee advised that the Singaporeans bring their troubles to the Foreign Mission Committee, a synodical committee based in Northwest Iowa, whose minister members were the Reverends M. Kamps, J. Slopsema, and M. Hoeksema.

After correspondence and careful deliberation, the Foreign Mission Committee decided that it was premature to send a missionary to Singapore. Instead they suggested sending two emissaries for a six-to-eight week investigation; and also that these two men take books, catechism materials, and tapes put out by the Protestant Reformed denomination. These suggestions were adopted by the Synod of 1978, and the Rev. James Slopsema and Mr. Dewey Engelsma from the Hope, Walker congregation went to Singapore.

After these two men gave their report to the Foreign Mission Committee, the committee suggested that it was now time for Doon, Iowa, the calling church, to call a missionary to Singapore. They called the Rev. A. denHartog on August 15, 1979. Rev. denHartog, who through his friendship with Johnson was closer to Singapore than other ministers in the denomination were, accepted the call, and was installed as missionary on January 25, 1980. Soon he and his family moved to Singapore.

Before Rev. denHartog went to Singapore, the group there had changed their name slightly. The Foreign Mission Committee had suggested that they call themselves "The Gospel Light and Truth *Society*," for their purpose was primarily the distribution of biblical literature. From then on they were the GLTS instead of the GLTD.

One of the problems which faced the Synod of 1980 was the proper time for the organization of this group into a congregation. The Rev. G. VanBaren reported as follows:

> One of the problems which arose in the work of Singapore was connected with the question of organization of the group of young people there into a Reformed church. The young people there desire to be Reformed in confession and walk, but since they have only recently begun the study of our three forms of unity (Heidelberg Catechism, Belgic Confession, and Canons of Dordt), they thought it not proper for them to be organized on the basis of these three creeds. They preferred to organize on the basis of a simplified statement of Reformed truths. The Doon consistory and the Foreign Mission Committee demurred. These bodies decided that Rev. denHartog could help to organize — but only on the basis of our Reformed Confessions. The Synod was deeply impressed by the conscientiousness of these young people and their hesitancy of accepting anything before they could properly understand it. However, Synod also supported Doon and the F.M.C. in their decision, pointing out that a Reformed church should properly be organized on the basis of Reformed creeds. The decision further reminded the young people of Singapore that this decision ought not to be understood as reason for a long postponement of organization. Synod stated, "If the Reformed truth is held commonly among the members, and if they are ready to be organized as a Church holding to Reformed Faith, as the GLTS confesses in their request for organization of 16 March 1980, it seems to the Synod that the GLTS

can soon see that the Reformed Faith is expressed in the Reformed Creeds, so that they can intelligently adopt these creeds as their basis...." The Synod was very encouraged by the desire of this group to be truly Reformed, and in its decision sincerely wanted to direct these young people in the proper manner of organization in order that their Reformed character may continue to flourish. Synod conveyed its greetings also to the Rev. denHartog and family, the Engelsmas, and the young people of the GLTS in Singapore.

Rev. VanBaren also shared the news that:

> One of the young men of the GLTS also requested permission for entrance into our seminary for a two-year period. That request was granted and Synod appointed the F.M.C. the task of raising $4,000 annually for his support through voluntary contributions.[176]

This student was Mr. Lau Chin Kwee, who came to live in the states with his wife Foong Ngee. Mr. Lau attended the seminary for the next two years. After he graduated, was ordained, and the group in Singapore had been organized as a congregation, they chose the name Evangelical Reformed Church of Singapore (or the E.R.C.S.).

In 1983 Jaikishin Mahtani, a Singaporean whose background was in India, came to the states with his Chinese wife Esther to study for three years at the Protestant Reformed Seminary. While they lived in the states, the Lord gave them twins, Jonathan and David, boys who will have dual citizenship for the rest of their lives.

After Student Mahtani graduated from the seminary and went back to Singapore with his family, he knew that he would find that the E.R.C.S. had grown, not only in knowledge, but also numerically; for many members of the congre-

---

176.   "Synod of 1980," *Standard Bearer*, Vol. 56, July 1, 1980, pp. 441, 442.

gation had found mates within their group. They courted, married, and soon there were babies — the second generation — to be baptized. Mr. Mahtani learned, too, that after seven years in Singapore Pastor denHartog had accepted a call to Randolph, Wisconsin, back in the United States.

*   *   *   *   *   *   *

Earlier, when Pastors denHartog and Lau were the pastors in Singapore, the congregation was getting too large and too busy; and in 1983 the group started a second worship center in the area of Toa Payoh in Singapore. The pastors alternated their preaching services. Now that Pastor denHartog was leaving, the two native Singaporean pastors would be the leaders in these two groups. After Pastor denHartog was settled in Randolph, Wisconsin, he reflected on Singapore:

> This is no doubt a very significant stage for the ERCS. They will now have to continue on their own. We believe they can by the grace of God. The church there continues to have a great task before it.... Most of our readers know that a good beginning has been made in the ERCS of starting a second congregation. By the time we left Singapore more than fifty brethren from the first congregation had indicated their desire and intention to be part of the second congregation. The organism of the church is already in existence. Worship services are being held regularly at a beautiful facility obtained in the Lord's providence at the Singapore American School....
>
> Brother Jaikishin Mahtani, who was trained in our seminary for three years, has now become Pastor Mahtani. We were very happy to witness that he is a faithful minister of the Word of God.... He has been received very well by the members of the church and he is working very hard.[177]

---

177.   "Reflections on Our Departure from Singapore," *Standard Bearer*, Vol. 63, March 1, 1987, pp. 254, 255.

In 1988 the group in Toa Payoh was organized. This second congregation took the name *Covenant Evangelical Reformed Church of Singapore,* or C.E.R.C.S. The congregation whose pastor was Rev. Lau added the letter *F* for *First* Evangelical Reformed Church of Singapore, or F.E.R.C.S.

❊　❊　❊　❊　❊　❊　❊

Since the visits of the emissaries to New Zealand in 1975, the correspondence had continued. Their request to the Protestant Reformed Churches, this time by the group in Christ Church in the south island, was: "May we call one of your ministers as our pastor?"

The Protestant Reformed denomination, through a synodical decision said it was possible only if New Zealand would establish a sister-relationship with the Protestant Reformed Churches. Unless or until this relationship was established, the denomination had only the option of giving New Zealand a minister-on-loan for a specified period. The congregation in Christ Church, which belonged to the denomination of the Orthodox Presbyterian Churches of New Zealand, accepted the latter offer. The following letter, dated December, 1977, tells the outcome of this correspondence.

> Dear Friend and Brother:
>
> This time I thought I would write you in public and ask the *Standard Bearer* to bear my letter to you. After all, he travels — in part, at least — by air; and therefore my letter should reach you rather promptly. This public letter has the advantage that since you and I are both rather busy at present, we can, so to speak, kill two birds with one stone. Our American friends can read this letter over my shoulder as I write you, and your and my New Zealand friends can read over your shoulder when you receive my missive.... It certainly is good that we may share positive news after a rather lengthy period of disappointment and discouragement. I refer, of course, to the fact that, the Lord willing, Rev. Ronald VanOverloop and his wife and four children will soon be coming

to Christ Church, and that he plans to labor in your
midst for some eight months....

As of this writing, I am informed that Rev.
VanOverloop and family are planning to leave
Grand Rapids on the seventeenth of December,
provided their visas arrive on time. At that rate,
they may even arrive before you receive my letter.

Your brother in the Lord,

H.C. Hoeksema[178]

In 1978 the good news for the New Zealanders in Christ
Church was that after Rev. VanOverloop's time was up, on
October 13 a replacement for the VanOverloops was coming.
Rev. and Mrs. Heys planned to board a plane for New
Zealand to help the members of the Orthodox Presbyterian
Church in Christ Church for another eight months. After
their stay for another eight months, and with no immediate
replacement available for New Zealand, troubles began to
plague this congregation. Many members became disen-
chanted with the contact with the Protestant Reformed
Churches. They thought that the preaching of the Reformed
truth would impede numerical growth; and they gradually
withdrew themselves from contact with the Protestant Reformed Churches. While Rev. Heys was in New Zealand, he
had also been working in the north island of New Zealand
with two small groups: the fellowships of Palmerston North
and of Wellington. These people, originally from the Reformed Churches of New Zealand, were eager for the Scriptural and Reformed preaching of God's Word.

After Rev. Heys reported to the Synod of 1984, the synod
passed a motion "to authorize the Mission Committee to
request any of our churches to send their pastor or minister
emeritus to labor in Wellington, N.Z."[179]

By the year 1986 the group in Wellington asked the synod

---

178.   "To My Friend in New Zealand," *Standard Bearer*, Vol. 54,
Dec. 15, 1977, pp. 126, 127.
179.   *Acts of Synod* of the Protestant Reformed Churches in
America, 1984, p. 18.

to grant them a sister-church relationship, which they did, on the grounds that "this congregation is thoroughly Reformed, subscribing to the Three Forms of Unity, adopting our Church Order and all our Liturgy, insisting on regular Heidelberg Catechism preaching, and limiting all congregational singing to the singing of the Psalms as versified in our Psalter.[180]

In 1987 the congregation of Wellington called the Rev. R. Miersma to be their pastor. He accepted, and at this writing is still their pastor.

*   *   *   *   *   *   *

During the time when the Protestant Reformed Churches were having correspondence with the folk in New Zealand, down under, a small group of people in Northern Ireland, on the other side of the globe, were reading Protestant Reformed literature sent by the Evangelism Committee of the South Holland, Illinois, congregation. At that time the Rev. George Hutton was pastor of the Bible Presbyterian Church in the town of Larne. In May, 1983, the Contact Committee received its first letter from Larne.

After a year of correspondence, by the time of the meeting of the Synod of 1984, the group in Larne invited emissaries from the Protestant Reformed Churches to visit their country. The synod asked the Reverends H. Hanko and D. Engelsma to go in October to preach and to lecture.

Meanwhile, a group of people from the Protestant Reformed Churches financed the project of sending a school teacher, Mr. Deane Wassink, to Covenant Christian School in Newtownabbey, North Ireland, for the 1984-1985 school year.

The members of the Bible Presbyterian Church reciprocated in the year 1986 by sending their pastor and a deacon to the states. These men were invited to be guests at Classis

---

180.   *Acts of Synod* of the Protestant Reformed Churches in America, 1986, p. 29.

West, held in South Holland, and the pastor was guest preacher in congregations in the Michigan and Illinois areas. Then rather suddenly the session of the B.P.C., with its pastor, George Hutton, broke its sister-church relationship with the Protestant Reformed Churches in October of 1987. They joined the Free Presbyterian Church of Scotland. Not all the members of this congregation went along with those who left. The remaining group, calling itself the Covenant Reformed Fellowship, turned to the Protestant Reformed Churches for help. The denomination sent the Rev. M. Kamps and D. Engelsma in September, 1988, who reported that for doctrinal reasons these people of the Covenant Reformed Fellowship could not in good conscience join the Free Presbyterian Churches of Scotland, and that they had come to love the Reformed faith as taught in the Protestant Reformed Churches. In 1990 the Hudsonville congregation was appointed as the calling church, responsible for calling a missionary to Larne.[181]

*   *   *   *   *   *   *

Through the decade of the seventies the mission work in Jamaica had lagged. Part of the reason was that the denomination was not able to furnish a continuity of missionaries because they did not have the men to send. The other part was that there were internal problems in Jamaica. In 1984 the Rev. W. Bruinsma was called to be missionary to Jamaica and he accepted the call. He describes his stay as follows:

> I started my labors in Jamaica in October of 1984. When I arrived, three of the seven churches we had left were in upheaval for one reason or another. My first task in Jamaica, therefore, was to restore peace and order to the churches there. Stability was necessary if I were going to conduct any systematic instruction of the churches.

---

181.   *Acts of Synod* of the Protestant Reformed Churches in America, 1990, pp. 46, 47.

This stability was finally gained after about two years of labor. It took this long to earn the trust of the people along with that of the leaders. This was accomplished first of all by holding numerous meetings with the ministers and leaders of our Jamaican churches. By means of these meetings I learned what their desires were for their churches, and they, in turn, learned from me what were our desires for them. Where our desires were in conflict we discussed (vehemently argued, is better) until our differences were worked out.

I also tried to concentrate my labors in two churches at a time. Since Waterworks church was without a leader I spent most of my time working with this congregation. Concentrated labors were also performed in Beeston Spring church, Belmont church, and in our congregation in Cave Mountain. My labors consisted in preaching twice on the Lord's day, usually in those congregations where I was concentrating my labors, although I did have a schedule worked out in order that I might visit the other churches also. I also taught two Bible study groups, catechism classes in two churches at a time (until which time the programs could run efficiently on their own), and a class on dating and marriage.

As time progressed monthly meetings with the leaders and ministers were held during which meetings we discussed the offices of the church and how, in a practical way, the ministers and leaders could promote solid Christian marriages and families in their churches. In addition to this the ministers and I met every other week in order to instruct them in preaching, doctrine, church history, and church polity. These classes proved to be of extreme value not only from an instructional point of view, but also in establishing a sense of common purpose and direction. (I wish they could have continued on a regular basis after I left, but ... such was not the will of God.)

Besides the many spiritual labors there were

also the labors of a more practical nature. One such labor was the incorporation of the denomination there as well as the securing of the church properties. This took all the years of labor there to accomplish. Another necessary labor was improvement on the church buildings. The churches needed electricity and a decent place to worship. This too was, for the most part, accomplished by the time I left.

The worst trial my family and I were called by God to endure was that of Hurricane Gilbert which ripped its way down the center of the island leaving devastation in its wake. Our house and many of the houses of our members were damaged and some of the homes destroyed. We were without electricity for a month and without running water for six months. But God uses all things for the good of His people, and this was true of Hurricane Gilbert too. Spiritually, God's people were drawn closer to the Lord. The saints in Jamaica experienced as never before the love and concern of our denomination toward them. This served to draw them all the closer to us. God certainly was good.

In July of 1989 my family and I left the island to come and labor in Holland, Michigan.[182]

* * * * * * *

Although the denomination had reached out to foreign countries with its literature, its radio broadcasts, and its pastors and missionaries, these were not their only spheres of work.

In the year 1978 a small group of four families in the Birmingham, Alabama, area contacted the Mission Committee of the Protestant Reformed Churches. They asked for more information about the denomination and if possible a pastor to visit them. The synod of that year recorded that:

---

182.   Personal papers.

a.   Prof. H. Hanko and Rev. C. Hanko were sent
to Birmingham to investigate a possible field of
labor there in June of 1977.
b.   Rev. J. Kortering labored in Birmingham and
upon his advice and the concurrence of the four
families involved, no other emissary was sent.
c.   Presently we are sending this small group
taped lessons on the Essentials of Reformed Doctrine.[183]

When during the next year the group asked for a full-
time missionary, the synod asked the Mission Committee to
call a full-time missionary to Birmingham. The Rev. Ronald
VanOverloop received and accepted the call.   Pastor
VanOverloop settled in and started a radio broadcast in the
area. During the next two years, although the pastor worked
diligently, the group did not grow. In 1983 the radio broadcast was discontinued. Despite all the efforts, the group did
not become a viable congregation. At the Synod of 1984 the
Mission Committee brought the following advice and the
synod adopted it.

That Synod approve the recommendation of
the South Holland Council and the Mission Committee to close the Birmingham field. Grounds:
1.   There does not seem to be a possibility of
establishing a congregation in the foreseeable future.
a.   There are no men qualified at present to
be officebearers.
b.   Of the group now meeting, only one family and several women could be members of a
Protestant Reformed congregation.
2.   No evidence has been given in the material submitted by the missionary or the Mission
Committee that suggests new contacts for further
labor.[184]

---

183.   *Acts of Synod* of the Protestant Reformed Churches in
America, 1978, p. 61.
184.   *Ibid.,* 1985, p. 13.

* * * * * * *

The congregations already established in the states had grown spiritually and numerically. It was time that some of these congregations organize daughter churches. The members in the Hudsonville congregation were having trouble finding seats at the worship services — if they did not come early. To ease the crowding, members of the congregation asked permission of the denomination to organize a daughter congregation in the Byron Center area. Many members of Hudsonville lived in that area. They were given permission, and on October 20, 1983, a group which included members from other congregations in the area was organized. Temporarily they met in the Byron Center Christian Junior High School. They called Candidate B. Gritters as their first pastor. After five years, on October 16, 1988, the congregation moved into its own new church building. One week later the Southwest congregation, which had outgrown its building, dedicated its new church building in Grandville.

The crowding of the congregations in the southwest area was still a problem, this time mainly in the Hope, Walker congregation. A group asked to be organized as a daughter church of Hope; and some members from area congregations joined them. Temporarily they met in the Grandville Public High School auditorium. Through the years many families joined this nucleus, and on February 9, 1984, the group was organized as Grandville Protestant Reformed Church. For six years they worshiped in the Grandville auditorium — until March 11, 1990, when the congregation met for the first time in its new sanctuary. On March 27, 1990, they formally dedicated their building.

Through the decades of the 1960s and '70s the inner city in some of the southeast areas of Grand Rapids had gradually deteriorated. This included the area of Fuller Avenue and Franklin Street, where First Church stood. As the vandalism to the building increased and it also began to be necessary that the parking lot be patrolled during the services, the congregation made the decision, for the sake of safety, to leave this historic building and area. They built a new sanctuary on Michigan Avenue on the northeast side of Grand Rapids and in 1985 began to worship there.

❋   ❋   ❋   ❋   ❋   ❋   ❋

After Rev. Lubbers had left his work in Houston, Texas in 1964 because he could not at that time find interest in the Reformed faith there, the denomination heard very little from that group — until a decade later. Then a small nucleus from the original group again asked for help from the Protestant Reformed Churches. In 1975 Rev. R. Harbach was sent to Houston by the Mission Committee to investigate and to work there. A year later, on February 20, 1977, the Rev. VanOverloop went to Houston to assist in the organization of this group as Trinity Protestant Reformed Church of Houston, Texas. Their first pastor was Rev. W. Bekkering. At the time of this writing the Rev. R. Hanko is its pastor.

Near the end of the year 1978 Professor Decker answered a call for help from a group of people interested in the Reformed faith in Bradenton, Florida. Through the decade of the 1980s, with some fill-in help from other pastors in the denomination, the retired Rev. C. Hanko has been living in Bradenton for most of each year as a pastor and teacher to this as yet unorganized group.

In 1980 the book *The Voice of Our Fathers,* an exposition of the Canons of Dordt, written by Homer C. Hoeksema, was published. It was a thorough and rather lengthy treatment of the Canons. In June of 1981 Professor Hoeksema had a letter from a man of whom he had never heard. This Mr. VanBrakel wrote him that he had read the book and that *The Voice of Our Fathers* was a worthy companion to Hoeksema's father's work, **Reformed Dogmatics.** The professor answered the letter and these two men started to correspond, for Mr. VanBrakel lived in BlueBell, also called Norristown, a small community in the city of Philadelphia.

After other families in the area showed interest in the

Reformed faith, Candidate Kenneth Hanko was sent to preach for the group; and in June, 1984, BlueBell was declared a mission field with Pastor Hanko as their minister. In January of 1989 the group was organized as a congregation. They took the name of Norristown Protestant Reformed Church, and they meet in a Christian school.

✳   ✳   ✳   ✳   ✳   ✳   ✳

On the far northwest of the continent of America, far away in miles from Norristown, Pennsylvania, is Lacombe, Alberta, Canada. The Rev. T. Miersma reported the organization of a new Protestant Reformed congregation there.

On May 12, 1987, the evening of a beautiful Alberta spring day, the Immanuel Protestant Reformed Church of Lacombe, Alberta, Canada was organized. The new congregation was formed by eight families and one individual, a total of thirty-two souls. The service was held at St. Cyprian's Anglican Church where the new congregation will also meet regularly and was conducted by Rev. Thomas Miersma, Pastor of the First Protestant Reformed Church of Edmonton and by Rev. Dale Kuiper, Pastor of the Hope Protestant Reformed Church of Isabel, South Dakota. Some eighty souls, ranging in age from one month to seventy-plus years, gathered to attend the organizational service. In addition to the Lacombe families those present came primarily from the Edmonton congregation of which the Lacombe families have been members.

Lacombe is a Central Alberta community centered in grain and hog farming, and is about the size of Hudsonville, Michigan. It is located about halfway between Alberta's two major cities, Edmonton to the north, and Calgary to the south, and is also located within a two-to-three hour drive of the great Canadian Rockies. Over half of the men in the new congregation are involved in some aspect of farming, with the remainder in the building trades. One of the young wives is a teacher in the Lacombe Christian School.

The organization of Immanuel Protestant Reformed Church is a very special occasion in the history of our churches, not only because it adds another congregation to our denomination as a whole, but also because it is the second Protestant Reformed Church to be organized in Canada (since the early 1950s, which churches later fell away). It is a special event also for our Edmonton congregation which, though losing a third of its members, will now have a nearby sister congregation. Nearby is of course a relative term, as they are separated by a distance of some ninety miles, but prior to this, Edmonton's nearest neighboring congregation was Lynden, Washington, approximately 750 miles distant.

It is also significant in that it is the second congregation to come into existence in Canada through the church extension work of a local congregation. Our Edmonton church itself was organized a little less than twelve years ago, as part of the church extension work of our Lynden congregation. The organization of Lacombe is the fruit of similar church extension work on the part of Edmonton and also of the commitment of the Lacombe families who have all been members of Edmonton for differing periods of time.

The history of Immanuel Protestant Reformed Church goes back over eight years to some contacts which were made by members of the Edmonton church with two families and some single individuals from Lacombe. These began attending services in Edmonton, and catechism classes and a Bible study class in Lacombe were begun and conducted by Rev. Moore, then pastor of Edmonton.... Catechism classes and Bible Study were held every other week.... The next year, the catechism classes and Bible Study were changed to a weekly schedule, and the Bible Study began meeting in a rented Lutheran church, rather than in the homes of members, as it had previously.

The group continued in this manner through 1985, when the consistory of Edmonton determined to start holding regular evening worship services in Lacombe on the second and fourth Sunday evenings each month....

In the fall of 1986 the Lord brought another family into the group from the Lacombe area. This family had learned of our churches in part from relatives in Ontario who had some contact through the mail with the church extension work of our South Holland congregation. This increased the number and size of the catechism classes in Lacombe, and the Young People's Society not only grew but began to meet regularly once a month in Lacombe. It became increasingly clear that the Lord was blessing the labor in Lacombe and that it was time to move forward towards organization....

Thus it was with the approval of Classis West that Lacombe was given permission to organize. It was with much joy that the families and friends gathered to hold the service on May 13 and the Immanuel Protestant Reformed Church was organized.[185]

✳ ✳ ✳ ✳ ✳ ✳ ✳

Classis West, meeting in Loveland, Colorado, on September 7, 1988, reported that:

The most enjoyable part of Classis' work was that of receiving and granting the request of the South Holland congregation for the organization of a new congregation in Lynwood, Illinois. Twenty-four families and seven individuals from the South Holland congregation requested this organization and Classis, with the concurrence of

---

185.   "New Congregation Organized in Canada," *Standard Bearer*, Vol. 63, Aug. 1, 1987, pp. 452-454.

the delegates from Classis East, advised South
Holland to proceed with this matter.   Rev.
VanOverloop was appointed their moderator and
was also appointed moderator of South Holland
during their vacancy.[186]

The congregation chose the name *Peace Protestant Reformed Church*. Their first pastor is the Rev. S. Houck, and
they are meeting in the chapel of Illiana Christian High
School in Lansing, Illinois. They chose to build their parsonage first, one mile from Lansing.

Earlier, in the summer of 1984, the Rev. Ronald
VanOverloop was called to work with a group of people who
were interested in the Reformed faith in the Northwest
Chicago area. This group had gathered as the fruit of church
extension work done by the South Holland congregation;
and a mission station was established. Four years later the
news editor wrote:

> Our Northwest Chicago Mission has some
> very encouraging new interest. Four new families
> are attending regularly. Pastor VanOverloop also
> writes that the group in the N.W. Chicago Mission
> invited local residents to a series of special wor-
> ship services during the month of April. One of
> these "special" services was conducted by Rev.
> Key, pastor of the Southeast PRC in Grand Rapids,
> Michigan. Pastor Key was asked specifically to
> preach on a text which confronts the subject of
> Creation vs. Evolution.[187]

In April of 1989, the editor noted that:

> Classis West in its meeting on March 1 ap-
> proved of the organization of the mission station

---

186.   Ben Wigger, "News From Our Churches," *Standard Bearer*,
Vol. 65, April 15, 1989, p. 335.
187.   B. Wigger, "News From Our Churches," *Standard Bearer*,
Vol. 64, May 15, 1988, p. 383.

at Northwest Chicago. This group consists of 13 families and has taken the name Bethel PRC. Organization is tentatively set for March 29.[188]

And Rev. Engelsma described the organizational service as follows:

> The worship service held on the northwest side of Chicago on the evening of March 29, 1989, to organize the Bethel Protestant Reformed Church, was a joyful event — a highlight in the church-life of those who participated. In the goodness of God, believers and their children enjoyed the fruit of the organization of a Protestant Reformed church upon the mission work of the church — the wise, diligent work of Missionary Ronald VanOverloop; the zealous, unstinting labor of the South Holland PRC; and the full cooperation of the denomination in money, prayers, and in supervision through the Mission Committee.
>
> We rejoice with the saints of Bethel!...
>
> Now you join your two sisters in Lynwood and South Holland as cities of God, shining with the light of truth and holiness in the spiritual and moral darkness of a great city of man and in the doctrinal and ethical gloom of churches whose candlesticks are being removed from their places.
>
> May you yourselves enjoy fellowship with God and with each other in the light (a "house of God" — a real "Bethel"!); and may your light so shine before men, that they may see your good works, and glorify your father which is in heaven.[189]

Missionary R. VanOverloop accepted the call to be pastor

---

188.   B. Wigger, "News From Our Churches," *Standard Bearer*, Vol. 65, April 15, 1989, p. 365.
189.   David Engelsma, "Editorially Speaking...," *Standard Bearer*, Vol. 65, May 15, 1989, p. 365.

of the Bethel congregation. He reported that the congregation has continued to experience God's blessings in a positive
way in many different respects:

> We continue to grow. We have every reason to
> believe that another individual will be joining
> us.... That will bring our totals to: sixteen families
> and four individuals, consisting of forty confess-
> ing members and thirty-five baptized members.
> An interesting and unique characteristic of the
> congregation is that the members live widely
> scattered to the north, south, and west.[190]

✳ ✳ ✳ ✳ ✳ ✳ ✳

Another congregation in the denomination which is very
joyful as the year 1991 arrives is Hope, Walker, Pastor
VanOverloop's former charge. It is not a new congregation.
This congregation has existed since 1916, with its first years
in the Christian Reformed denomination. In October, 1991,
the congregation plans to celebrate seventy-five years of
blessings, most of them in the Protestant Reformed denomination. One of the anniversary projects is a $300,000 remod-
elling project — a larger narthex, rest rooms, air conditioning, improved lighting, an elevator, new windows, and
lower-level classrooms. As a special celebration this congregation plans to host the 1991 Synod of the Protestant Reformed Churches.

✳ ✳ ✳ ✳ ✳ ✳ ✳

More than a decade earlier the Theological School Committee, with the advice of the professors, decided to expand
the seminary studies from a three-year to a four-year course.
The 1979 Acts of Synod published a rationale for this program.

---

190.   Private correspondence.

a/ The four-year program would reduce the student's normal load to an average of 16 semester hours per term. The present seminary curriculum consists of 110 semester hours which requires the student to register for an average of 18+ hours per semester. This represents an extremely heavy load which the proposal would correct.

b/ The four-year program would allow for the addition of elective courses. This possibility does not now exist — all courses are required.

c/ The four-year program would leave room for the implementation of a supervised field work/ internship program. Presently the student loads are too heavy to allow for little, if any, field or internship work.

d/ The four-year program would allow for the possibility of students engaging in topical seminar courses or in independent study courses.[191]

* * * * * * *

The School Committee, along with the professors, had learned from experience about the trauma of the emergency replacements of both Professors Ophoff and Hoeksema. Through those experiences they determined that there must be a plan for an orderly changing of the guard *before* a professor is ready to retire. They did not want to go through a frantic preparation for teaching such as Professors Herman Hanko and H.C. Hoeksema had experienced some two decades earlier.

The Theological School Committee, with the professors, adopted a policy which would ease the retiree out of office and would gradually initiate his replacement. The policy stated that a professor will retire at the age of sixty-five, with the option of teaching until he is seventy. A conference and check-up would be scheduled for each of the five years, to

---

191.   Pp. 134, 135.

determine whether the incumbent professor was still willing and able to teach.

The Synod of 1988 noted that Professor Hoeksema had reached the age of sixty-five years. With the stipulation that Hoeksema would continue his work in the seminary for a five-year period, the synod voted for his replacement. They synod voted for the Rev. D. Engelsma, who would start to prepare himself to teach Hoeksema's subjects. Engelsma accepted the appointment.

However, at this same synod Committee 2 came with the following proposal: "We recommend that Synod approve the proposal of the Contact Committee that the Contact Committee send Prof. H.C. Hoeksema to the Burnie, Tasmania congregation for twelve months."[192]

Professor Hoeksema had some prior knowledge of this request. In the spring of 1988 he had been approached by the committee and asked whether he was willing to go to Tasmania. After a time of consideration he agreed that if the synod asked him, he was prepared to go. This, however, created an immediate gap in the teaching staff of the seminary. The Theological School Committee had already been facing this possible situation. They noted that the student load for the coming school year was not heavy. Professors Hanko and Decker agreed that they were able to shoulder the work load with a minimum of help from professor-elect Engelsma. And the new professor agreed that while he was also doing graduate work to prepare himself for his new position he would still be able to shoulder some of the work load.

Rev. Engelsma had been given one more duty: to take the place of Prof. H.C. Hoeksema as editor of the *Standard Bearer*. Also at this time Professor Decker became the magazine's managing editor.

When the September 15, 1988, issue of the *Standard Bearer*, the last issue of the volume year, came out, Professor

---

192.   *Acts of Synod* of the Protestant Reformed Churches in America, 1988, p. 32.

and Mrs. Hoeksema were already in Tasmania. They had left on August 16.

The editorial in this issue was Editor Hoeksema's farewell. Titled "Farewell!" it said:

> Since this is the last issue of the current volume-year, this is also my final word as Editor and Managing Editor of the *Standard Bearer*, in harmony with the plans approved by the Staff and announced a year ago. In harmony with those plans, Professor-elect David Engelsma and Prof. R. Decker will take over as Editor-in-Chief and Managing Editor, respectively.
>
> More than one person asked me orally whether I did not fee a certain amount of regret about my pending retirement. I told them this story. After our annual Staff meeting in June, the last over which I presided, I walked across from the seminary to my home, and said to my wife, "Just think! We made a lot of decisions at our meeting about the next volume-year, and I don't have to do anything about them!" I felt as though a heavy burden had been lifted from my shoulders. I suppose that is a bit difficult for anyone to understand, unless he has spent as many years as I have in meeting deadlines of preparing an issue and getting material to the printer for 21 issues per year.
>
> More important than my personal relief and the fact that now I hope to have the time to attend to other writings is my satisfaction that provision has been made for a smooth and orderly transition for our magazine and that two capable men have consented to take over the work.
>
> To my fellow Staff members I say thanks for your help and support over the years.
>
> To my successors I wish the Lord's blessing and pledge my support in continuing the testimony of the *Standard Bearer*.
>
> To my readers I say, "Thank you for your patient bearing with me through the years."

For the coming volume-year I have asked for
a leave of absence from the Staff, though I have
promised to write some informative articles from
Tasmania, Australia, for which land my wife and
I will soon be departing, D.V.

May the Lord continue to bless our *Standard
Bearer.*[193]

At the time that this editorial appeared in print, Professor
Hoeksema was settled in the city of Burnie, on the northwest
coast of Tasmania.

Tasmania is one of the five provinces of Australia, a
heart-shaped island two hundred miles south of the mainland, and about fifteen hundred miles west of the islands of
New Zealand. It is a beautiful, temperate, lush, and moun-
tainous province, with British and Scottish overtones. Shortly
after the Hoeksemas arrived in Tasmania, Professor and
Mrs. Hanko followed them. The reason was that the Synod
of the Evangelical Presbyterian Church met in August, and
the Protestant Reformed Churches had sent these two delegates, Hanko and Hoeksema, as representatives to this
synod. In an article to the churches in the United States,
Professor Hoeksema wrote that:

> These churches have a Presbyterian heritage.
> Yes, that is true in a way; but one might almost call
> it an *adopted* Presbyterian heritage.
>
> You see, these churches have no Presbyterian
> roots historically. The first generation of EPC
> members (and that includes their ministers) did
> not come out of Presbyterianism. On the contrary,
> in some instances they came from nothing ecclesi-
> astically; in other cases they came from the Salva-
> tion Army, from Methodism. And they found
> their way into Arminian crusade-type evange-
> lism. Not a few were students at the World
> Evangelical Crusade College in Launceston. And

---

193.   H.C. Hoeksema, *Standard Bearer,* Vol. 64, p. 486.

then there came about a remarkable change. Through various circumstances they became disillusioned with this rank Arminianism (with some Pentecostal overtones). And through study they came first to a five-point Calvinist position, but remained Baptistic. But in process of time they embraced the Reformed position as set forth in the Westminster creeds. And one of the most remarkable aspects of this theological pilgrimage is that, when they arrived at the Reformed position, they came all the way, so that they repudiated the error of common grace and a general well-meant offer of the gospel. Thus they were constituted in the early 1960s with just a few congregations, first under the name of Reformed Evangelical Church and later as the Evangelical Presbyterian Church. And they were an ecclesiastically very lonely little group of churches....

After furnishing a few more details about this denomination, Prof. Hoeksema wrote:

All of which brings me to the Synod meeting (3 pastors and five elders) at which Prof. Hanko and I represented our churches. We were very cordially received; Prof. Hanko addressed the Synod in behalf of our churches; and on numerous occasions we were asked for our opinion and advice on various matters....

Generally there is credal agreement; there is a full agreement on the doctrines of sovereign and particular grace (and the rejection of the well-meant offer); there is agreement on the Christian's antithetical calling; there is agreement with respect to the truth of God's everlasting covenant of grace. There are also areas of disagreement as to church government, as to purity of worship, as to the question of divorce and remarriage, as to the so-called establishment principle, as to the Westminster position on the covenant of works. All of these areas were spelled out. The committee of ministers prepared a written report to their synod, where matters were again discussed carefully, and we agreed on certain proposed areas of cooperation and further contact. These are:

    1)   The establishment of a relationship which would be less than a full sister-church relation.

    2)   Future help, upon their request, with ministerial supply.

    3)   An exchange of articles in our publications....

    4)   Possible exchange of pulpits.

    5)   Trying to establish some kind of forum to discuss and explore our differences.[194]

During his year in Tasmania, Professor Hoeksema preached twice each Sunday — morning and afternoon — in the E.P.C. of Burnie. Then one of the young men in the congregation drove him one hundred miles to Launceston on two-lane roads which either curved or went up and down, but not straight. He preached the evening service in the Launceston E.P.C. congregation. Although these people practiced purity of worship in their services — no musical accompaniment, along with no observance of the church year (Advent, Christmas, Lent, Easter) — the people of the denomination welcomed Hoeksema's Reformed preaching.

It was the custom in the three Tasmania congregations — Burnie, Launceston, and Winneleah — to have an Easter camp in one of the beautiful mountain resorts on the Easter weekend from Friday through Monday. Almost every member attended. Professor Hoeksema was asked to be the speaker. His duties were to give four lectures on a specific topic, conduct a question hour, and to preach on Sunday.

After the Easter camp was over, the professor complained about not feeling well. He thought he had been over-extended through the weekend. In mid-April he saw one of the doctors in Burnie, and then a specialist in the larger city

---

194.   "Some Impressions From 'Down Under' (2)," *Standard Bearer,* Vol. 65, March 1, 1989, pp. 259, 260.

of Launceston, where he was diagnosed as having a rapidly developing small-cell cancer. That week he and his wife left for home in the states.

In the September 15, 1989, issue, the last issue of the volume year, the editorial assistant, Mr. D. Doezema wrote:

> A year ago the cover of our *Standard Bearer* carried a picture of Prof. Homer Hoeksema, along with a tribute which read, in part, as follows: "HCH, we thank you for your work as editor these past 24 years.... Because both the gifts of the servants of Christ's church and the exercise of those gifts are God's gracious enrichment of His church by the Holy Spirit of Jesus Christ, we thank God for His goodness to us through your work."
>
> That was the first issue of the current volume year. Who would have thought, at that time, that the last would carry an "in Memoriam" to our beloved professor? It seemed, after all, that Prof. Hoeksema's "retirement" was but a vista to opportunity for new exercise of those gifts, for the enrichment of the church militant. There was, as Prof. Hanko points out in his "In Memoriam," so much work just waiting to be done; and, being freed at last from the press of his many responsibilities, not only at the seminary but also for the *Standard Bearer*, Prof. Hoeksema would at last have time to devote to those unfinished projects.
>
> But... such was not to be. For the Lord called him home — before he had opportunity to make progress on even one of those projects. Hardly the way *we* would have planned it. Our perspective however is not that of the wise Master-Builder. With that, we must be content. And we are — especially as we have our attention directed, not to man, but to our God, Who is our Guide, even unto death. Such was the exhortation of Prof. Decker at the Memorial Service of Prof. Hoeksema, in Hudsonville Church, on July 20.[195]

195.   "In This Issue...," *Standard Bearer*, Vol. 65, p. 482.

Now the second "changing of the guard" had taken place: Professor Decker became rector at the seminary and Professor Engelsma took Hoeksema's place in the classroom and in the editorial department of the *Standard Bearer.*

As the activities and students multiplied at the seminary, in July of 1988 Mr. D. Doezema became not only registrar, but business manager and coordinator and solver of problems. A year later Mrs. D. Doezema — Judi — took over the secretarial and office work, making life on top of seminary hill run more smoothly.

✳   ✳   ✳   ✳   ✳   ✳   ✳

Starting in the decade of the 1970s and continuing through the decade of the 1980s, without open controversy, the Protestant Reformed denomination, particularly through the mouthpiece of the *Standard Bearer,* had commented on many issues, doctrinal and ethical, in the church world. The leaders were particularly concerned about the churches in the Reformed tradition who were departing from their Reformed moorings.

The denomination noted that in the early 1970s in The Netherlands there was a spirit of "re-thinking and reevaluating" the Scriptures and the Confessions. One of the first men to deny a cardinal Scriptural doctrine was Dr. H. Wiersinga, an instructor in the Free University of Amsterdam. In his doctrinal dissertation he had denied the doctrine of Jesus' substitutionary atonement. The consistory of the Reformed Church of Amsterdam, where Dr. Wiersinga was a member, made the following statement:

> The consistory of the Gereformeerde Kerk of Amsterdam (central) has expressed: "That the view of the doctrine of atonement set forth in his dissertation by Dr. H. Wiersinga deserves to be taken up as a theological-scientific contribution to the discussion about the atonement, in which he exerts himself to do full justice to all the Scriptural

givens. That thereby he comes in conflict with certain expressions which are established in the confessions may, in the present stage of consideration, consequently not be blamed on him as unfaithfulness to the confessions, but deserves to be noted as a legitimate testing of the confession of the church by Holy Scripture. The merits of this testing deserve to be more closely investigated on the scientific level....

In his comments, Editor Hoeksema said:

We may notice, in the first place, that the subterfuge by which Wiersinga's heresy is defended and protected ecclesiastically is the calling of the church to test the confessions by the test of Holy Scripture. But, you ask, is this not correct? Is it not true that we may not put our confessions on a level with Scripture, but must test them by Scripture? The answer to this question is, in the first place, that it is indeed true that Scripture is our only infallible rule of faith and that our confessions are subordinate standards. This does not mean, however, that we live in the church with continual question marks behind our confessions. On the contrary, we subscribe to our confessions as being the expression of the truth of Scripture.

But it has long been the slogan in the Dutch churches that there must be academic freedom, that there must be the proper climate for the development of theology. It is under this same banner that all the representatives of the new theology are shielded. The Free University — but not it only — has been a hotbed of this kind of theological ferment and revolution. Meanwhile, heresy is allowed to gnaw like cancer at the very vitals of the church and of the faith.[196]

---

196. "Developments in the *Gereformeerde Kerken*," **Standard Bearer**, Vol. 48, April 15, 1972, p. 317, 318.

Through the decade of the seventies and eighties many nominally Reformed churches, particularly the Reformed Churches in The Netherlands, were also teaching a fallible Bible, written by men about God. At their Synod of 1972, the Reformed Churches in The Netherlands adopted their infamous Report 44, a document concerning the re-interpretation of the Scriptures, and consequently of the origin of the world. Their reasons for this new interpretation were that the Scriptures were time-bound and culturally oriented, and must be re-interpreted with *new hermeneutics* — for modern-day believers. These "new hermeneutics" taught God's people the differences between the *packaging* and the *gospel* in the Scriptures, they said.

Many of the authors in the Protestant Reformed denomination wrote rebuttals against this new heresy and at the same time instructed their Reformed readers in the truth of the Scriptures. The instruction was particularly important because this heresy denied the six-day creation record in Genesis 1.

In two extensive articles, the Rev. M. Kamps witnessed against this new hermeneutic. The following are a few excerpts:

> There is a view of Scripture among ministers and professors in the Reformed community which effectively *precludes* maintaining the readability and intelligibility of the Bible as the perspicuous, inspired Word of God....
>
> What is this view of Scripture? Above all, its proponents assure us that they, too, believe in the infallibility and, of course, in the inspiration of Scriptures. But they tell us that the truth of inspiration and infallibility is to be extended only as far as the "message" of Scripture is concerned. About spiritual things the Bible speaks infallibly, i.e., about sin, the wrath of God, salvation, and redemption through Christ's cross. The message is the important thing and it has been infallibly recorded. But that is all that may be considered to

be infallible. About much of which the Scriptures speak we ought not claim infallibility, for this would be foolish in the light of the facts of science and the evidence that historical research has provided us. We must not be obstinate! Rather we must remember the infallible message of God's love for poor sinners comes to us in the vehicle of human words and through fallible human thought structures. These fallible human thought structures can be easily discerned and explained. We are simply to lift the infallible message of God's love out of the vehicle....

Rev. Kamps' rebuttal was:

Remember, to reject one part of Scripture in disbelief is to stand principally over against the whole of Scripture in unbelief.

There is an inseparable relationship between faith in Scripture as God's authoritative Word of self-revelation and divine inspiration. To say that the Bible is God's Word is to presuppose that human writers were infallibly inspired by God to record His revelation. Thus we must maintain the historic position of the Church of Christ concerning graphic, plenary, verbal, and organic inspiration. Many will mock us for our faith; many will taunt us with charges of worshipping a book, Bibliolatry; but they do so to their own spiritual destruction.... [197]

When Dr. VanTil, a professor at Calvin College wrote his book, *The Fourth Day* in 1986, the *Christian Renewal* magazine criticized its content because of its naturalistic evolutionism. With the title "Why Evolution?" Editor Hoeksema commented on this review.

---

197.   "Is the Bible the Word of God (2)," *Standard Bearer,* Vol. 52, March 15, 1976, pp. 784-786.

It is true that *Christian Renewal,* a rather interesting "conservative" paper under the editorship of John Hultink, dealt with this subject at length in more than one issue and also succeeded in ruffling the feathers of some Calvin College professors....

Frankly, I am rather surprised by the fact that there is any fuss whatsoever made about the teaching of evolution at Calvin College. Why? Because, in my opinion, complaining about evolutionism at Calvin College is like beating a dead horse.

The evolution issue at Calvin College (and in the Christian Reformed Church officially) is a dead issue. It was settled long ago. Evolutionism had been accepted — if not by positive decision, then by default. I suppose from time to time some hackles are raised when a book such as that of Dr. VanTil is published or when a college professor expresses himself in the columns of the *Banner.* And I can sympathize with people who are disturbed by it. But the issue as such is dead. It would not be possible, I daresay, to eradicate evolutionism from Calvin College....

However, just because books like that of Dr. VanTil continue to come from the press, and just because the doctrine of creation and the Creator is wrested and denied, and just because our people in general, but our young people in particular, and more specifically some of our young people who attend institutions of higher learning, are exposed to evolutionistic teachings and to various attempts to debunk the clear teachings of Scripture, I wish to re-emphasize certain truths concerning Scripture and creation....[198]

A further departure from the Scriptures in the Christian Reformed Church was more serious — if there are degrees in heresies. If the Christian Reformed denomination had been able to deny that the creation narrative of Genesis 1 was literally true, they had already opened the door for further doubts about the authority of God's Word. The next heresy

---

198.   *Standard Bearer,* Vol. 63, Feb. 1, 1987, pp. 197, 198.

was based on the statement of the first point of common grace formulated by the Christian Reformed denomination in 1924, "which deals with the general offer of the gospel." Professor Harold Dekker from Calvin College, who contributed to the *Reformed Journal*, the voice of the liberals in the Christian Reformed Church, was the proponent of this statement: "God so loves ... all men."

For years the Professors Dekker and Hoeksema had debated editorially; and in these two decades, the 70s and the 80s, the Reformed readers of the *Standard Bearer* had a refresher course both on the *errors* which were posed against the doctrine of salvation by sovereign, particular grace and the *beauties* of believing it.

※　※　※　※　※　※　※

Through the decade of the 1980s the Christian Reformed Church had instructed committees of their classes and synods to study the "headship principle" in the Scriptures. This was a prelude to the decision of whether or not women could share the ecclesiastical offices. After yearly reports from these committees about their studies and conclusions on this subject, and using the "new hermeneutics," the Synod of the Christian Reformed Church in 1990 opened all the offices in their church to women, to be effective after the Synod of 1992. Editor D. Engelsma wrote:

> How deep the division is between the Protestant Reformed Churches and the Christian Reformed Church became painfully evident this June with the decision of the synod of the CRC opening the offices of minister and elder to women.
> The decision was to "permit churches to use their discretion in utilizing the gifts of women members in all the offices of the church."
> It was a major decision.
> The CRC broke with the long tradition of Reformed churches going back to Calvin that reserved the special offices in the church for quali-

fied men. Indeed, this has been the tradition in the church from the earliest post-apostolic church. She did this even though she herself acknowledged that she had no clear, compelling biblical basis for breaking with her own, and the catholic church's tradition. The grounds for the decision to open the offices to women do not include a single biblical reference.

By the decision, the denomination rebels against the sovereign Lordship of the Head of the church with regard to the spiritual policy by which the true church must be governed.... The will of Christ for the government of His church is that the church be ruled by bishops, whose qualifications include that they are men (I Tim. 3:1-7; cf. also Titus 1:5-9). He forbids women to teach or to exercise dominion over the man at church, requiring the female members of the congregation to learn there in silence with all subjection (I Tim. 2:11ff.)....

The possibility of the decision to open the office of women is a view of Holy Scripture different from the creedally Reformed, indeed Protestant, view of Scripture as the inspired Word of God. The CRC decision on women in office expressed a view of Scripture that can reject the authority of explicit apostolic commands for church and home on the ground that the commands reflect the limitations of the time and culture in which the apostle gave them....

Put simply, the issue, women in office, is not whatsoever the issue of male and female, but the issue of the doctrine of Holy Scripture and therefore the issue of the headship of the Lord Jesus in and over His church.

A synod that can open the preaching and ruling offices to women in the face of the plain prohibition of the Bible can also decide anything at all that a determined group in the church fights for over a period of years. Scripture no longer functions in the church as the infallible rule of faith and life (Belgic Confession, Art. 7).[199]

---

199. "Feminism Entrenched in the CRC," *Standard Bearer,* Vol. 66, Sept. 1, 1990, pp. 461, 462.

* * * * * * *

To give its readers variety and at the same time solid instruction, each year the *Standard Bearer* has published three special issues on varied topics and with special themes. A sampling is: "Our Seminary," "Our Christian Schools," "Missions," "The Reformed Publications of the Denomination," "The Doctrine of the Church," "Regeneration," "The Antithesis," and "The Office of Believers." These issues have been some of the favorites for the readers in the denomination.

* * * * * * *

In the summer of 1990, from Tuesday, June 12, through Thursday, June 14, local delegates, local visitors, foreign delegates, and foreign visitors attended an International Conference, the first one sponsored by the Protestant Reformed Churches, through its appointed committee. The conference was held in the First Protestant Reformed Church in Grand Rapids. The topics chosen for this conference were as widely varied as were the homelands and cultures of the speakers and delegates. The Rev. C. Terpstra, pastor of the South Holland, Illinois, congregation, was the keynote speaker. His topic, on Tuesday morning, was "The Holy Spirit — His Work in the Economy of Salvation."

In the afternoon the Rev. C. Coleborn from Brisbane, Australia, spoke on "The Holy Spirit and the Error of Pentecostalism." In the evening of this first conference day both the Revs. R. Miersma and P. Burley described their work in the Protestant Reformed Church in New Zealand and in the Evangelical Presbyterian Church of Australia.

On the morning of the second day of the conference Professor R. Decker addressed the conference on the topic of "The Holy Spirit and the Call to Mission Work and the Spread of the Gospel."

The Rev. J. Mahtani from Singapore, a convert from this mission work, followed with a speech in the afternoon on the topic: "A Reformed Theological Seminary in the Pacific Area." The Rev. P. Rawson of Measbro Dyke Church, Barnsley, South Yorkshire, England, who was at the conference as a result of the church extension work of the Protestant Reformed denomination, spoke about "The Work of the Church in Barnsley." And in the evening the Rev. Lau Chin Kwee, from Singapore, addressed his audience on the subject: "The Acceptance of Baptism from Other Churches."

On the last day of the conference Rev. R. Miersma, pastor of the Protestant Reformed Church of New Zealand congregation, spoke in the morning on "The Promotion of a More Meaningful Sister-Church Relationship." Rev. Mahtani, in his second opportunity to speak, told about "The Work of the Evangelical Reformed Church in Singapore." And at the evening banquet the Rev. P. Rawson also spoke for the second time, this time on "The Beauty of Christian Fellowship."

This is the way Mr. D. Doezema summed up his reactions to the conference:

> ...All too easy it is for churches and denominations to be near-sighted in their perspective, to be so engrossed in contending for the faith in their own little corner of the vineyard that, though they hold in their doctrine to the truth of the catholicity of the church, they nevertheless forget it in their life. A conference such as was held in Grand Rapids a couple of weeks ago, is a sure cure for that. Very quickly it becomes clear that the same Spirit Who works powerfully for the defense of the faith and the development of the truth of the Word of God in one group has done the same among other pockets of believers here and there throughout the world. One cannot help but be humbled by that, when he sits across the table from an Australian pastor who can give eloquent testimony to his church's experience of the same kind of struggles that characterize the history of one's own church. And, in listening to a Singaporean speak of the beginnings of a possible mission labor in India, and of the need for a

Reformed Theological Seminary in Asia, we cannot but be convicted of our need for and dependence on each other.

There's no way, of course, that the mere printing of speeches can convey the spirit which prevailed at that three-day conference. The latter is caught only by actual attendance, where one is able to hear the discussions which follow the speeches and to enjoy the fellowship during coffee breaks....[200]

* * * * * * *

In the last issue of the *Standard Bearer* of the year 1990 Professor R. Decker's special article had an eye-catching title: "What's Happening at 4949 Ivanrest?" In his article he explained that:

> 4949 Ivanrest Avenue in Grandville, Michigan, is of course the address of the Protestant Reformed Theological Seminary. What happens here is that men receive instruction in the various disciplines of the theological curriculum designed to prepare them to serve the Protestant Reformed Churches as ministers and missionaries of the Gospel of God's sovereign grace in Jesus Christ. Here the professors teach their classes in the mornings and spend the rest of the day reading and studying, preparing for those classes and various other lectures and preaching assignments in area churches.... Here too the professors complete their writing assignments for the *Standard Bearer* and the *Protestant Reformed Theological Journal.* The students attend the classes and make use of the library to do their research and write the assigned papers.
>
> One would expect that these activities would happen on a seminary campus. What many of our readers may not know is that a great many other things happen at 4949 Ivanrest. The Staff of the

---

200.   "In This Issue...," *Standard Bearer,* Vol. 66, July 1, 1990, p. 410.

Standard Bearer conducts its annual meeting here in the spring of the year. At this meeting the next volume year of the *Standard Bearer* is planned. The Editorial Committee of the *Standard Bearer* meets here during the course of the year as need occasions. The *Standard Bearer* is typeset and mailed from 4949 Ivanrest by Mr. and Mrs. Don Doezema and Mr. and Mrs. John Veldman. The Committee for Contact With Other Churches meets monthly here. The Mission Committee and its various sub-committees all meet here. The Book Publishing Committee of the RFPA also meets in this building.

As important as all these activities may be for the defense and proclamation of the gospel of Jesus Christ, the most important activity at this address is the instruction of men for the ministry of the gospel....

Finally, we covet the prayers of God's people. Pray that God will give the professors grace to "stand fast and hold the traditions they have been taught" (II Thess. 2:15). Pray that God will give the students grace to "give attendance to reading, to exhortation, to doctrine" (I Tim. 4:13). In this way only will the Reformed Faith as God has so graciously given it to our Protestant Reformed Churches be preserved among us to the glory of God. [201]

Now this history of the Protestant Reformed Churches, through the year 1990, ends where it started — with seeds. Almost five hundred years ago, after diligent study of the Scriptures, and by God's grace, the reformers of the early sixteenth century planted the seeds of the Reformed truth in God's garden of Reformed plantings. Through all the following years God's people and their children planted and re-planted Reformed seeds in their garden. They cultivated their plantings as they watched God's sunshine and rain fall on their garden of Reformed plantings and made their garden prosper.

---

201.   Vol. 67, Dec. 15, 1990, p. 132.

They saw some plantings wither and die. Other Reformed plantings were uprooted. The garden of Reformed plantings was even invaded and the plantings were split. But the Lord, the sovereign Gardener, never let His garden of Reformed plantings be completely destroyed. He always preserved for His plantings a *seminary*, a "seed place," where the seeds could take root and be nourished and taught so that when they were planted in the garden of Reformed plantings they would grow and flourish in truth and beauty in their garden of Reformed plantings, remembering the promise of their Lord, the heavenly Gardener, Who promised: "The Lord shall guide thee continually, and satisfy thy soul in drought, and make fat thy bones; and thou shalt be like *a watered garden*, and like a spring of water, whose waters fail not" (Is. 58:11).

Act of Agreement

"Whereas the Synod of 1924, assembled in Kalamazoo, Mich., adopted three points of doctrine which, according to our most sacred conviction, are in direct conflict with our Reformed Confessions and principles;

"2. Whereas, by the actions of Classis Grand Rapids East and Classis Grand Rapids West, we are denied the right to discuss and interpret said three points of doctrine of said Synod;

"3. Whereas, by the actions of said Classes, the pastors, elders, and deacons of Kalamazoo I, Hope, and Eastern Avenue, together with their congregations are actually expelled from the fellowship of the Christian Reformed Churches;

"4. Whereas it follows necessarily from the action of said Classes, that said office-bearers and their congregations cannot simply submit themselves to the action of said Classes until such time as Synod shall have considered their appeal, which they made in a legal way to Synod, but were forced by circumstances to continue to function in their respective offices as pastors, elders, and deacons of their respective congregations;

"5. Whereas they are informed and know positively, that hundreds of our people outside of our own congregations share our convictions and with us cannot acquiesce in the actions of Classes and Synod, neither from a doctrinal nor from a Church-political viewpoint.

"6. Whereas the above mentioned matters concern us as appealing churches in common, and demand our cooperation and united action;

"Therefore, be it resolved by the Combined Consistories

355

of Kalamazoo I, Hope, and Eastern Avenue, assembled
March 6, 1925 in the Eastern Avenue Church:

"a. That we adopt as our common basis the Three
Forms of Unity and the Church Order of the Reformed
Churches;

"b. That at the same time we stand on the basis of our
appeal and intend to address our appeal to the Synod of 1926;

"c. That we unite as Consistories for the following
purposes: (1) To unitedly bring our appeal from the actions
of Classes Grand Rapids East and West to the Synod of 1926.
(2) To decide on such matters as have reference to the
interests of our congregations in common. (3) To decide in all
matters that pertain to the furnishing of information and
advice to others, outside of our own congregations.

"d. That whatever shall be decided by said combined
Consistories by a majority-vote, shall be considered firm and
binding."

In view of the considerable difference in number of the
various consistories, it was decided, that in case of friction
and upon the request of any consistory, besides the majority
vote of the members present, also a majority of at least two
separate consistories would be necessary to reach a decision.

The name that was adopted was, like the organization,
temporary: *Protesting Christian Reformed Churches.*

Even before 1926, and before they decided upon a permanent form of organization, the Protesting churches grew in
number.

The very meeting of the sixth of March, that had adopted
the *Act of Agreement,* reached another decision of far-reaching importance. They agreed on a plan of action with respect
to propaganda for their views regarding the "Three Points"
outside of their own circle.

This action by the combined consistories was occasioned
by several invitations from different parts of the Christian
Reformed Church to deliver lectures on the controversy that
had led to the deposition of so many office-bearers. Requests
of this nature had been received from Iowa, Wisconsin, and

Illinois. The consistories decided to delegate the Reverend H. Hoeksema in order that he might inform those that evinced interest in the cause about the things that had taken place relative to the origin of the Protesting churches; that he might explain to the people the significance of the "Three Points" adopted by the Synod of Kalamazoo, 1924; that he might inform those interested about the organization of the expelled churches as outlined in the *Act of Agreement;* and that he might serve and aid those that should declare their intention to join us on the basis of the *Act of Agreement* and to be organized as Protesting Christian Reformed Churches. An official copy of these decisions was given the Reverend H. Hoeksema and he was given power to act according to circumstances as he should find them.

From that time until the present the *Protesting Christian Reformed Churches,* and after 1926 the *Protestant Reformed Churches,* have enjoyed a steady growth.

The Lord God has been with them.

Always He has pointed out to them new fields of labor through the means of requests that were received from various Christian Reformed communities to lecture and to preach for them.

And churches were soon organized in different parts of the country.

We shall not weary the reader with a detailed account of the organization of these different congregations. A general sketch of the work and its result may suffice.

The very first field of labor the Lord pointed out to the brethren was Sioux County, Iowa, a community where several Christian Reformed Churches are found. There the brethren and their stand were well-known to many. And the call came from Hull, Iowa: "Come over and help us!" Soon after the meeting of the combined consistories on March 6, 1925, the Reverend H. Hoeksema responded to that call. He was accompanied by W. Verhil, now one of our pastors, who went along to labor in the interest of the *Standard Bearer.* The reception the brethren received will never be forgotten. Those were the days of keen interest and marked enthusi-

asm. Meetings were held in the Town Hall of Hull, on week-
days and on Sunday, and always the Hall would be filled to
capacity. Similar meetings were held in the Town Hall of
Sioux Center and in that of Doon; and later in Rock Valley.
On Sunday services were held in the same halls. During the
week it was always the "Three Points" that were the topic of
discussion; on Sunday the Word was preached. At the end
of three weeks of labor a Protesting church was organized in
Hull consisting of almost forty families; and, besides, many
more had heard the truth. The brethren felt that the Lord had
prospered and comforted them, and that their labors were
abundantly blessed above all expectations. And they went
home rejoicing, because the Lord had opened a door for them
and prepared a field for the defense of the truth of His
sovereign grace.

   Soon after the organization of the church in Hull, work
was begun in Chicago and vicinity as well as in Waupun,
Wisconsin.

   In Waupun a Protesting church was organized as early as
May 1925. The brethren there, however, soon revealed that
they were of a different spirit than the Protesting churches.
There was an influence of sickly mysticism that soon prevailed and led to the destruction of the congregation. They
soon seceded; and their secession cannot be considered a loss
to the Protestant Reformed Churches.

   The labor in Chicago and vicinity gradually became
concentrated in Lansing, Illinois. There a small but healthy
group of Reformed Christians soon were organized into a
Protesting Christian Reformed Church. The church is now
the flourishing Protestant Reformed Church of South Holland, Illinois.

   Still later, a faithful group in Oak Lawn, Illinois, requested to be organized as a Protesting church, which request was granted and executed. It still is known as the
Protestant Reformed Church of Oak Lawn.

   In the meantime Grand Rapids and vicinity were not
neglected. In Byron Center, Michigan, Roosevelt Park,
Grand Rapids, and Hudsonville, Michigan, churches were

organized. In 1929 the brethren in Holland, Michigan, that had agreed with the stand of the Protestant Reformed Churches from the beginning, took courage and became organized as a church. Creston Church was added to the group of Protestant Reformed Churches in Grand Rapids; Doon, Sioux Center, Rock Valley, and later Pella, Oskaloosa, and Orange City joined the ranks in Iowa. Also from California came the call! Redlands took the lead. A church sprang into existence there with nearly forty families as charter members. Los Angeles followed suit. Bellflower was organized in 1935. And when the Reverend H. Danhof refused to join the final and permanent organization of the Protestant Reformed Churches, a small group left him and is today the Protestant Reformed Church of Kalamazoo.

There is, therefore, abundant reason for joy and gratitude, because the Lord was with the brethren that were cast out, prepared the field of labor for them and caused the Word that was preached to find a place in the hearts of many.

To Him alone be the glory!

One more matter of great importance was decided by the combined consistories at that meeting of March 6, 1925.

The consistories clearly realized from the beginning the need of a trained ministry.

If the Lord would bless their labors, kindle in the hearts of others a new love for the Reformed truth, and churches would be organized, these churches would have to be shepherded. There would, therefore, be need of ministers of the Word of God. There were at that time only three ministers and one candidate, but these were needed in the congregations they served. R. Danhof, a brother of the candidate would soon graduate from the Theological School of the Christian Reformed Churches, and by his attitude gave every reason to believe that he would join the movement of the Protesting churches, as, in fact, he also did, for a time. There were also several ministers in the Christian Reformed Churches, that had left the impression of being convinced of the error of the "Three Points" and had given abundant reason to expect that they would join the ranks of the expelled group; but everyone of these proved to be a disappointment. The consistories, therefore, confronted the task of preparing young men for the ministry of the Word. They felt the need of a theological school. And they took immediate steps to establish such an institution. The school was opened as early as June, 1925. There were eight students. The Reverends H. Danhof, G.M. Ophoff, and H. Hoeksema were appointed instructors. It was decided to offer only such courses as were immediately most necessary to prepare young men for the ministry of the Word. Instruction was given in four languages, Dutch, English, Hebrew and Greek; in Old and New Testament Exegesis; in Dogmatics, and Homiletics.

Other subjects were gradually added to the curriculum.

The school has proved to be a great blessing for the Protestant Reformed Churches.

Sixteen young men have thus far been prepared for the ministry and are serving different churches in that important office.

Looking back upon that meeting of the combined consistories on March 6, 1925, we must thankfully acknowledge that the Lord gave them wisdom clearly to discern what would be to the well-being of the churches; and He directed them and inspired them with the courage of faith to decide upon some very important measures, in spite of the fact that it appeared well-nigh impossible for that small group to execute them.

And the Lord richly blessed their efforts.

At the time of this writing they may set up their stone of remembrance, bearing the inscription, as an expression of gratitude and hope for the future:

EBEN-HAEZER!

A Brief Declaration of Principles of the Protestant Reformed Churches

Preamble

Declaration of Principles, to be used only by the Mission Committee and the Missionaries for the organization of prospective churches on the basis of Scripture and the Confessions as these have always been maintained in the Protestant Reformed Churches and as these are now further explained in regard to certain principles — see Article 285.

The Protestant Reformed Churches stand on the basis of Scripture as the infallible Word of God and of the Three Forms of Unity. Moreover, they accept the Liturgical Forms used in the public worship of our churches, such as: Form for the Administration of Baptism, etc. (cf. Article 225).

On the basis of this Word of God and these confessions:

I.   They repudiate the errors of the Three Points adopted by the Synod of the Christian Reformed Church of Kalamazoo, 1924, which maintain:

A. That there is a grace of God to all men, including the reprobate, manifest in the common gifts to all men.

B. That the promise of the gospel is a gracious offer of salvation on the part of God to all that externally hear the gospel.

C. That the natural man through the influence of common grace can do good in this world.

D. Over against this they maintain:

1. That the grace of God is always particular, i.e., only for the elect, never for the reprobate.

2. That the preaching (cf. Arts. 227, 232) of the gospel is not a gracious offer of salvation on the part of God to all men, nor a conditional offer to all that are born in the

historical dispensation of the covenant, that is, to all that are baptized, but an oath of God that He will infallibly lead all the elect unto salvation and eternal glory through faith.

3. That the unregenerate man is totally incapable of doing any good, wholly depraved, and therefore can only sin.

> For proof we refer to Canons I, 6-8; II, 5; II, B, 6; Heidelberg Catechism, III, 8; XXXIII, 91; Netherlands Confession, Art. 14; Canons III, IV, 1-4.****
> The Canons in II, 5 speak of the preaching of the promise. It presents the promise, not as general, but as particular, i.e., as for believers, and, therefore, for the elect. This *preaching* of the particular promise is promiscuous to all that hear the gospel with the *command,* not a condition, to repent and believe (cf. page 105-106; Suppl. II; I, 1; II, 2).

II. They teach on the basis of the same confessions:

A. That election, which is the unconditional and unchangeable decree of God to redeem in Christ a certain number of persons, is the sole cause and fountain of all our salvation, whence flow all the gifts of grace, including faith. This is the plain teaching of our confession in the Canons of Dordrecht, I, A, 6, 7.

"Article 6. That some receive the gift of faith from God, and others do not receive it proceeds from God's eternal decree, `For known unto God are all his works from the beginning of the world,' Acts 15:18. `Who worketh all things after the counsel of his will,' Ephesians 1:11. According to which decree, he graciously softens the hearts of the elect, however obstinate, and inclines them to believe, while he leaves the non-elect in his just judgment to their own wickedness and obduracy. And herein is especially displayed the profound, the merciful, and at the same time the righteous discrimination between men, equally involved in ruin; or that decree of election and reprobation, revealed in the Word of God, which though men of perverse, impure and unstable minds wrest to their own destruction, yet to holy and pious souls affords unspeakable consolation."

"Article 7. Election is the unchangeable purpose of God,

whereby, before the foundation of the world, he hath out of mere grace, according to the sovereign good pleasure of his own will, chosen, from the whole human race, which had fallen through their own fault, from their primitive state of rectitude, into sin and destruction, a certain number of persons to redemption in Christ, whom he from eternity appointed the Mediator and Head of the elect, and the fountain of salvation."

"This elect number, though by nature neither better nor more deserving than others, but with them involved in the common misery, God hath decreed to give to Christ, to be saved by Him, and effectually to call and draw them to his communion by his Word and Spirit, to bestow upon them true faith, justification and sanctification and having powerfully preserved them in the fellowship of his Son, finally, to glorify them for the demonstration of his mercy, and for the praise of his glorious grace; as it is written, `According as he hath chosen us in him, before the foundation of the world, that we should be holy, and without blame before him in love; having predestinated us unto the adoption of children by Jesus Christ to himself, according to the good pleasure of his will, to the praise of the glory of his grace, wherein he hath made us accepted in the beloved,' Ephesians 1:4, 5, 6. And elsewhere: `Whom he did predestinate, them he also called, and whom he called, them he also justified, and whom he justified, them he also glorified,' Romans 8:30."

And in the Heidelberg Catechism, Lord's Day XXI, Q. and A. 54, we read:

"What believest thou concerning the holy catholic church of Christ?

"That the Son of God from the beginning to the end of the world, gathers, defends and preserves to himself by his Spirit and Word, out of the whole human race, a church chosen to everlasting life, agreeing in true faith; and that I am and forever shall remain, a living member thereof."

This is also evident from the doctrinal part of the Form for the Administration of Baptism, where we read:

"For when we are baptized in the name of the Father, God

the Father witnesseth and sealeth unto us, that he doth make an eternal covenant of grace with us, and adopts us for his children and heirs, and therefore will provide us with every good thing, and avert all evil or turn it to our profit. And when we are baptized in the name of the Son, the Son sealeth unto us, that he doth wash us in his blood from all our sins, incorporating us into the fellowship of his death and resurrection, so that we are freed from all our sins, and accounted righteous before God. In like manner, when we are baptized in the name of the Holy Ghost the Holy Ghost assures us, by this holy sacrament, that he will dwell in us, and sanctify us to be members of Christ, applying unto us, that which we have in Christ, namely, the washing away of our sins, and the daily renewing of our lives, till we shall finally be presented without spot or wrinkle among the assembly of the elect in life eternal."

B. That Christ died only for the elect and that the saving efficacy of the death of Christ extends to them only. This is evident from the Canons of Dordrecht, II, A, 8:

"For this was the sovereign counsel and most gracious will and purpose of God the Father, that the quickening and saving efficacy of the most precious death of his Son should extend to all the elect, for bestowing upon them alone the gift of justifying faith, thereby to bring them infallibly to salvation: that is, it was the will of God, that Christ by the blood of the cross, whereby he confirmed the new covenant, should effectually redeem out of every people, tribe, nation, and language, all those, and those only, who were from eternity chosen to salvation, and given to him by the Father; that he should confer upon them faith, which together with all the other saving gifts of the Holy Spirit, he purchased for them by his death; should purge them from all sin, both original and actual, whether committed before or after believing; and having faithfully preserved them even to the end, should at last bring them free from every spot or blemish to the enjoyment of glory in his own presence forever."

This article very clearly teaches:

1. That all the covenant blessings are for the

elect alone.

2. That God's promise is unconditionally for them only: for God cannot promise what was not objectively merited by Christ.

3. That the promise of God bestows the objective right of salvation not upon all the children that are born under the historical dispensation of the covenant, that is, not upon all that are baptized, but only upon the spiritual seed.

This is also evident from other parts of our confession, as, for instance:

Heidelberg Catechism, Q. 65: "Since then we are made partakers of Christ and all his benefits by faith only, whence doth this faith proceed? From the Holy Ghost, who works faith in our hearts by the preaching of the gospel, and confirms it by the use of the sacraments."

And in Q. 66: "What are the sacraments? The sacraments are holy visible signs and seals, appointed of God for this end, that by the use thereof, he may the more fully declare and seal to us the promise of the gospel, viz., that he grants us freely the remission of sin, and life eternal, for the sake of that one sacrifice of Christ, accomplished on the cross."

If we compare with these statements from the Heidelberger what was taught concerning the saving efficacy of the death of Christ in Canons II, A, 8, it is evident that the promise of the gospel which is sealed by the sacraments concerns only the believers, that is, the elect.

This is also evident from Heidelberg Catechism, Q. 74: "Are infants also to be baptized? Yes: for since they, as well as the adult, are included in the covenant and church of God; and since redemption from sin by the blood of Christ, and the Holy Ghost, the author of faith, is promised to them no less than to the adult; they must therefore by baptism, as a sign of the covenant, be also admitted into the Christian church; and be distinguished from the children of unbelievers as was done in the old covenant or testament by circumcision, instead of which baptism is instituted in the new covenant."

That in this question and answer of the Heidelberger not all the children that are baptized, but only the spiritual children, that is, the elect, are meant is evident. For:

  1. Little infants surely cannot fulfill any conditions. And if the promise of God is for them, the promise is infallible and unconditional, and therefore for the elect.

  2. According to Canons II, A, 8, which we quoted above, the saving efficacy of the death of Christ is for the elect alone.

  3. According to this answer of the Heidelberg Catechism, the Holy Ghost, the author of faith, is promised to the little children no less than to the adult. And God surely fulfills His promise. Hence, that promise is surely only for the elect.

The same is taught in the Netherlands Confession, Articles 33-35. In Article 33 we read:

"We believe, that our gracious God, on account of our weakness and infirmities hath ordained the sacraments for us, thereby to seal unto us his promises, and to be pledges of the good will and grace of God toward us, and also to nourish and strengthen our faith; which he hath joined to the Word of the gospel, the better to present to our senses, both that which he signifies to us by his Word, and that which he inwardly works in our hearts, thereby assuring and confirming in us the salvation which he imparts to us. For they are visible signs and seals of an inward and invisible thing, by means whereof God worketh in us by the power of the Holy Ghost. Therefore the signs are not in vain or insignificant, so as to deceive us. For Jesus Christ is the true object presented by them, without whom they would be of no moment."

And from Article 34, which speaks of Holy Baptism, we quote: "We believe and confess that Jesus Christ, who is the end of the law, hath made an end, by the shedding of his blood, of all other sheddings of blood which men could or would make as a propitiation or satisfaction for sin: and that he, having abolished circumcision, which was done with blood, hath instituted the sacrament of baptism instead thereof; by which we are received into the church of God, and separated from all other people and strange relations, that we may wholly belong to him, whose ensign and banner we bear: and which serves as a testimony to us, that he will forever be our gracious God and Father. Therefore he has commanded all those, who are his, to be baptized with pure water, 'in the name of the Father, and the Son, and of the Holy Ghost'; thereby signifying to us, that as water washeth away the filth of the body, when poured upon it, and is seen on the body of the baptized, when sprinkled upon him; so doth the blood of Christ, by the power of the Holy Ghost, internally sprinkle the soul, cleanse it from its sins, and regenerate us from children of wrath, unto children of God. Not that this is effected by the external water, but by the sprinkling of the precious blood of the Son of God; who is our Red Sea, through which we must pass, to escape the tyranny of Pharaoh, that is, the devil, and to enter into the spiritual land of Canaan. Therefore the minsters, on their part, administer the sacrament, and that which is visible, but our Lord giveth that which is signified by the sacrament, namely, the gifts and invisible grace; washing, cleansing and purging our souls of all filth and unrighteousness; renewing our hearts, and filling them with all comfort;; giving unto us a true assurance of his fatherly goodness; putting on us the new man, and putting off the old man with all his deeds."

That all this, washing and cleansing and purging our souls of all filth and unrighteousness, the renewal of our hearts, is only the fruit of the saving efficacy of the death of Christ and therefore is only for the elect is very evident. The same is true of what we read in the same article concerning the baptism of infants: "And indeed Christ shed his blood no less for the washing of the children of the faithful, than for the adult persons; and therefore they ought to receive the sign and sacrament of that, which Christ hath done for them; as the Lord commanded in the law, that they should be made partakers of the sacrament of Christ's suffering and death, shortly after they were born, by offering for them a lamb, which was a sacrament of Jesus Christ. Moreover, what circumcision was to the Jews, that baptism is to our children. And for this reason Paul calls baptism the circumcision of Christ." If, according to Article 8 of the Second Head of

Doctrine, A, in the Canons, the saving efficacy of the death of Christ extends only to the elect it follows that when in this article of the Netherlands Confession it is stated that "Christ shed his blood no less for the washing of the children of the faithful than for the adult persons" also here the reference is only to the elect children.

Moreover, that the promise of the gospel which God signifies and seals in the sacraments is not for all is also abundantly evident from Article 35 of the same Netherlands Confession, which speaks of the Holy Supper of our Lord Jesus Christ. For there we read: "We believe and confess, that our Savior Jesus Christ did ordain and institute the sacrament of the holy supper, to nourish and support those whom he hath already regenerated, and incorporated into his family, which is his Church."

In the same article we read: "Further, though the sacraments are connected with the thing signified, nevertheless both are not received by all men: the ungodly indeed receives the sacrament to his condemnation, but he doth not receive the truth of the sacrament. As Judas, and Simon the sorcerer, both indeed received the sacrament, but not Christ, who was signified by it, of whom believers only are made partakers."

It follows from this that both the sacraments, as well as the preaching of the gospel, are a savour of death unto death for the reprobate, as well as a savour of life unto life for the elect. Hence, the promise of God, preached by the gospel, signified and sealed in both the sacraments, is not for all, but for the elect only.

And that the election of God, and consequently the efficacy of the death of Christ and the promise of the gospel, is not conditional is evident abundantly from the following articles of the Canons.

Canons I, A, 10: "The good pleasure of God is the sole cause of this gracious election; which doth not consist herein, that out of all possible qualities and actions of men God has chosen some as a condition of salvation; but that he was pleased out of the common mass of sinners to adopt some certain persons as a peculiar people to himself, as it is written, 'For the children being not yet born neither having done any good or evil,' etc., it was said (namely to Rebecca): 'the elder shall serve the younger; as it is written, Jacob have I loved, but Esau have I hated.' — Rom. 9:11, 12, 13. 'And as many as were ordained to eternal life believed.' Acts 13:48."

In Canons I, B, 2, the errors are repudiated of those who teach: "That there are various kinds of election of God unto eternal life: the one general and indefinite, the other particular and definite; and that the latter in turn is either incomplete, revocable, non-decisive and conditional, or complete, irrevocable, decisive, and absolute."

And in the same chapter of Canons B, 3, the errors are repudiated of those who teach: "That the good pleasure and purpose of God, of which Scripture makes mention in the doctrine of election, does not consist in this, that God chose certain persons rather than others, but in this that he chose out of all possible conditions (among which are also the works of the law), or out of the whole order of things, the act of faith which from its very nature is undeserving, as well as its incomplete obedience, as a condition of salvation, and that he would graciously consider this in itself as a complete obedience and count it worthy of the reward of eternal life."

Again, in the same chapter of Canons, B, 5, the errors are rejected of those who teach that "faith, the obedience of faith, holiness, godliness and perseverance are not fruits of the unchangeable election unto glory, but are conditions, which, being required beforehand, were foreseen as being met by those who will be fully elected, and are causes without which the unchangeable election to glory does not occur."

Finally, we refer to the statement of the Baptism Form: "And although our young children do not understand these things, we may not therefore exclude them from baptism, for as they are without their knowledge, partakers of the condemnation in Adam, so are they again received unto grace in Christ." That here none other than the elect children of the covenant are meant and that they are unconditionally, without their knowledge, received unto grace in Christ in the same way as they are under the condemnation of Adam, is very evident.

C. That faith is not a prerequisite or condition unto salvation, but a gift of God, and a God-given instrument whereby we appropriate the salvation in Christ. This is plainly taught in the following parts of our confessions.

Heidelberg Catechism, Q. 20: "Are all men then, as they perished in Adam, saved by Christ? No; only those who are ingrafted into him, and receive all his benefits, by a true faith."

Netherlands Confession, Art. 22: "We believe that, to attain the true knowledge of this great mystery, the Holy Ghost kindleth in our hearts an upright faith, which embraces Jesus Christ, with all his merits, appropriates him, and seeks nothing more besides him. For it must needs follow, either that all things, which are requisite to our salvation, are not in Jesus Christ, or if all things are in him, that then those who possess Jesus Christ through faith, have complete salvation in him. Therefore, for any to assert, that Christ is not sufficient, but that something more is required besides him, would be too gross a blasphemy: for hence it would follow, that Christ was but half a Savior. Therefore we justly say with Paul, that we are justified by faith alone, or by faith without works. However, to speak more clearly, we do not mean, that faith itself justifies us, for it is only an instrument with which we embrace Christ our Righteousness. But Jesus Christ, imputing to us all his merits, and so many holy works which he has done for us, and in our stead, is our Righteousness. And faith is an instrument that keeps us in communion with him in all his benefits, which, when become ours, are more than sufficient to acquit us of our sins."

Confer also Netherlands Confession, Articles 33-35, quoted above.

Again, confer Canons of Dordrecht II, A, 8, quoted above.

In Canons III, IV, A, 10 we read: "But that others who are called by the gospel, obey the call, and are converted, is not to be ascribed to the proper exercise of free will, whereby one distinguishes himself above others, equally furnished with grace sufficient for faith and conversions, as the proud heresy of Pelagius maintains; but it must be wholly ascribed to God, who as he has chosen his own from eternity in Christ, so he confers upon them faith and repentance, rescues them from the power of darkness, and translates them into the kingdom of his own Son, that they may show forth the praises of him, who hath called them out of darkness into his marvelous light; and may glory not in themselves, but in the Lord according to the testimony of the apostles in various places."

Again, in the same chapter of Canons, Article 14, we read: "Faith is therefore to be considered as the gift of God, not on account of its being offered by God to man, to be accepted or rejected at his pleasure; but because it is in reality conferred, breathed, and infused into him; or even because God bestows the power or ability to believe, and then expects that man should by the exercise of his own free will, consent to the terms of salvation, and actually believe in Christ, but because he who works in man both to will and to do, and indeed all things in all, produces both the will to believe, and the act of believing also."

III. Seeing then that this is the clear teaching of our confession,

    A. We repudiate:

        1. The teaching:

            a. That the promise of the covenant is conditional and for all that are baptized.

            b. That we may presuppose that all the children that are baptized are regenerated, for we know on the basis of Scripture, as well as in the light of all history and experience, that the contrary is true.

For proof we refer to: Canons I, 6-8; doctrinal part of Baptism Form; the Thanksgiving after baptism. Refers only to the elect; cannot presuppose that it is for all (cf. p. 105-106; Suppl. II, I, 2).

        2. That the teaching that the promise of the covenant is an objective bequest on the part of God giving to

every baptized child the right to Christ and all the blessings of salvation.

    B. And we maintain:

       1. That God surely and infallibly fulfills His promise to the elect.

       2. The sure promise of God which He realizes in us as rational and moral creatures not only makes it impossible that we should not bring forth fruits of thankfulness but also confronts us with the obligation of love, to walk in a new and holy life, and constantly to watch unto prayer.

All those who are not thus disposed, who do not repent but walk in sin, are the objects of His just wrath and excluded from the Kingdom of Heaven.

    Grounds:

    1. Baptism Form, Part 3.

    2. Form for the Lord's Supper, Third Part beginning with "All those" up to "But this is not designed."

    3. Heidelberg Catechism, Q. 64, 84, 116; Canons III, IV, 12, 16, 17; II,IV, B, 9; V, 14; Belgic Confession, Art. 24. (cf. Art. 273).

That the preaching comes to all, and that God seriously commands to faith and repentance, and to all those who come and believe He promises life and peace (cf. Art. 273, and page 106, Art. 21).

For proof we refer to: Heidelberg Catechism (Lord's Day 24); Netherlands Confession, Art. 24; Canons III, IV, Art. 16 (cf. page 105, 106; Suppl. II, III).

    3. That the ground of infant baptism is the command of God and the fact that according to Scripture He establishes His covenant in the line of continued generations.

    IV. Besides, the Protestant Reformed Churches:

Believe and maintain the autonomy of the local church.

For proof we refer to Netherland Confession, Article 31; Church Order, Article 36: only the consistory has authority over the local congregation; Article 84; Form for the Installation of Elders and Deacons: called by the congregation and therefore by God (cf. Article 274, and page 105-106; Suppl. II, I, 3).

Letter to Members of First Protestant Reformed Church 1953

Beloved Congregation:

What a blessed and joyful sabbath we had last Sunday when, as the First Protestant Reformed Church, we worshipped in the auditorium of the Christian High School! What a relief that, once more, we might listen to the pure Protestant Reformed truth without fear of its being corrupted by the heresy of a general promise of God to all that hear, and of our fulfilling conditions before we can enter into the kingdom of God! With us there was joy and peace and love and true fellowship of the saints because the Spirit of Christ that, of late, was grieved and that rejoices in the truth, was with us and dwelled in us. Indeed, the Lord is greatly blessing us. O, we confess we are not worthy. To our God alone be all the glory!

In the meantime, it is a cause of deep sorrow to us that so many of you, that follow the legally deposed consistory members, cannot share our joy in the Lord.

Brethren and sisters that are thus deceived, will you, please, give us your attention a moment, and prayerfully consider the following?

1. Do you still love the Protestant Reformed truth? Then come to us. Be not deceived by those who say that the difference between those that are deposed and us is a mere matter of words. It is a matter of the whole Protestant Reformed truth. The Protestant Reformed truth is that the promise of God is unconditional and for the elect alone: the error which they preach and support is that the promise is general and conditional. Protestant Reformed truth is that God translates us into His kingdom unconditionally; the

error they preach and sustain is that our act of conversion is a condition for our entering into the kingdom of God.

2. Be not deceived by those who claim that it is a question of personalities. If it were, why do they not definitely state those so-called personalities black on white so that we may know and remove them in the proper way?

3. Be not deceived!! If you persist in following the deposed consistory members the inevitable outcome will be that you will place yourselves outside of the communion of the Protestant Reformed Churches. We realize that the Rev. DeWolf and the deposed consistory members try to make you believe that the consistory meeting at which they were suspended and deposed was illegal. Nothing can be farther from the truth. Consider once more the facts:

A. At a legal consistory meeting, June 1, it was decided to adopt the advice of the classis and to act accordingly. This meant that if the Rev. DeWolf did not apologize, nor the elders that supported him, they were already declared worthy of suspension and deposition. This decision was never rescinded. Here the matter was principally decided.

B. At a legal meeting of the consistory, June 22, the elders that are now deposed:

a. Voted against a motion to place the Rev. DeWolf before the question of retraction and apology according to the decision of classis.

b. Voted against the motion to place the elders that supported the Rev. DeWolf before the question of their own apology.

This entire action on their part was thoroughly illegal because:

(1) It was against the decision of June 1 (see above) which was never rescinded.

(2) It was against the decision of classis.

(3) It is contrary to the Church Order: no person may vote in his own case.

C. Hence the meeting of June 23 at which the Rev. DeWolf was suspended and the eleven elders were deposed was certainly legal:

a. They did not have to be informed of that meeting for they could not possibly have voted.

b. They could not plead their case again, as they had so often done in consistory meetings, for it was finished by the decision of classis.

c. At the meeting of June 22 they plainly and definitely expressed that they did not want to apologize, nor have the Rev. DeWolf to apologize.

D. But what definitely closes the door is the following:

a. They never protested against their own suspension and deposition at any legal consistory meeting.

b. They refused to submit to discipline and violated the oath of office.

c. They have lost their right of appeal.

d. They separated themselves from the communion of Protestant Reformed Churches.

4. The consistory warns every one of you, whether you attend our services in the Christian High, or whether thus far you have attended the illegal meetings held in the church building, that you do not attend the illegally called congregational meeting, summoned by the deposed officebearers. We assure you that the next classis will surely declare all their acts illegal. They cannot preach the Word, they cannot administer the Lord's Supper, they cannot baptize infants, and they certainly cannot call a congregational meeting. The only body that can do all this is your consistory, represented by the signatures below this letter. Hence, have nothing whatever to do with their illegal actions!

Brethren and sisters, we invite you to worship with us as before and enjoy the fellowship of the saints. Next Sunday morning, Rev. Hoeksema will conduct the services, next Sunday afternoon and evening Rev. Hanko will preach, the Lord willing.

Your consistory,
Rev. H. Hoeksema, Pres.
Rev. C. Hanko, Pres.
G. Stadt, Clerk

excerpts from
The Reunion of the Christian Reformed and Protestant Reformed Churches

Is it demanded, possible, desirable?

The immediate occasion of this meeting of certain leaders of the Christian and Protestant Reformed Churches was, no doubt, the visit of Dr. K. Schilder among us. Now and then, also before the coming of the professor at Kampen, the sentiment was expressed that the difference between both churches was not sufficiently important or fundamental to justify their separate existence. Never, however, did this lead to any definite action. It was Dr. Schilder who in his lectures among us not only expressed the idea, but also urged, that both groups should seek one another anew, should try to arrange a conference at which the points, which had caused their division, would be discussed, and, if possible, once more live together under one ecclesiastical roof. At the conference which we, as Protestant Reformed ministers, held with the professor, one of the first questions which he laid before us was whether we would be found willing and prepared to attend such a colloquy. And as I wrote in the *Standard Bearer,* the hope was expressed in more than one quarter in The Netherlands that one of the fruits of Dr. Schilder's trip might be that such a reunion would be effected. Therefore, I think the conclusion wholly justifiable that it was especially upon his urging that certain of the Christian Reformed brethren ventured to call a meeting like this together. And personally I desire to express my appreciation and gratefulness for the invitation which we received to attend this gathering....

And then I would begin with that concerning which we undoubtedly all agree. First of all, we certainly all agree on this, that the Church of Christ is one. It is one body, one in its Head, Christ Jesus our Lord, one in the Spirit, united in the bond of peace through the one faith, even as there is one God and Father, Who is above all and in all. This unity must also be realized and manifested as much as possible in the Church upon earth. Therefore it is the sacred and solemn calling of all believers to seek that true unity with all that is in them. That which as Church of Christ belongs together must not be separated, much less live in a relation of enmity. All schism must be avoided. And whoever causes that that which is truly one and belongs together is torn asunder, shall bear the judgment. We agree with Calvin who teaches us that the Church is therefore called general or "Catholic," because one cannot contrive two or three churches without dividing Christ, which is not possible (*Institutes*, chap. 1, 2). And we would subscribe to the word of Bavinck: "As Christians we cannot humble ourselves enough because of the schism and discord which has existed in the church of Christ through the ages; it is a sin against God, in conflict with the prayer of Christ, and caused by the darkness of our mind and the uncharitableness of our heart" (*Dogm.*, IV, 344).

Yet it will not do to urge a union of whatever upon earth calls itself with the name of church. Although it is understandable that men, prompted by a fervent desire for an erroneously conceived unity of the Church oftentimes permitted themselves to be misled to seek the realization of such a unity by power or artificial means, or by syncretism and denial of principle, yet we may not cooperate with such movements. The division within the Church upon earth is simply a fact....

Now I come to the question which faces this gathering, be it not in an official sense: Is it required that the breach be healed? Is it possible? And is it desirable?

...If we ever are to unite, a discussion of the truth, of the question of common grace and of the three points, is first of all demanded. And there are, in my opinion, but two possibilities which we in the abstract, may mutually agree to be possibilities. In the first place, the possibility is conceivable that the Christian Reformed brethren convince us that we erred in 1924 when we refused to subscribe to the three points; and to do this we offer to give them by means of this discussion ample opportunity. On the other hand the possibility exists that we convince them that the three points are unreformed, that the synod of 1924 never should have adopted them, that they therefore must be retracted unconditionally. And unto that end they, the Christian Reformed brethren should give us equally full opportunity. If they succeed in convincing us we will acknowledge that we erred and that we must unite with them upon the basis of the three points. If we succeed in convincing them, they must acknowledge that they erred in 1924, then the three points will presently be recalled, and then they will stand with us upon the same confessional basis. Only in this manner may we proceed. Any other way is the way of compromise, which I will continue to refuse.

In the rest of this essay I now offer you an introduction, from our viewpoint, to the discussion of our doctrinal differences, submitting this introduction, of course, to your free discussion and criticism. I would consider it advisable if also one of the Christian Reformed brethren would present such an introduction. This makes the discussion definite. Besides, then we also have something black on white, so that any misunderstanding will be avoided which might arise concerning that which is discussed by us. And, finally, thereby it will be easier for our people to remain informed concerning the course and the results of our discussion. In this introduction I offer you our view of what is called common grace. I will first speak about the so-called common grace in general, then about the three points, and conclude by submitting twenty propositions for discussion.

The problem of so-called common grace concerns the question of God's attitude over against the influence upon the whole of created things in their mutual connection and their development in time, in connection with and in harmony with God's counsel in general, predestination with election and reprobation, the realization of God's eternal covenant, grace and sin, favor and wrath, nature and grace, creation and redemption, Adam and Christ, and it inquires into the place and calling of God's people in and over against the present world. Viewed thus it is a question of great importance with respect to both, doctrine and life.

And then we proceed from the Scriptural idea, that all creatures are one. God did not create in the beginning an aggregate of creatures, loose, independent of one another, but a world, a cosmos, a harmonic, organic whole. God is *one*. The world is also one. In the midst of the earthy creation stood man. God had formed him after His own image, so that in a creaturely sense he resembled God, in true knowledge, righteousness, and holiness. This man stood at the head of creation, as king over the earthly world. And he stood in God's covenant of friendship from the beginning....

But the image of God turned about into its reverse. His light became darkness, his knowledge changed into the lie, his righteousness became unrighteousness and his holiness became impurity and rebellion in all his willing and inclinations. His love changed into enmity against God. Sin is not merely a defect or lack, but *privatio actuosa*. And the servant and covenant-friend of the Lord became a friend and covenant-ally of the devil. Also thus, however, the Lord continues to sustain and govern creation by His providential power. And the entire organic existence of things remained essentially unaffected. If now in this state of things no further change is brought about, then the final result of history will be that the completed spiritual-ethical fruit of the life of creation is the opposite of that which it should be according to God's creation ordinance.

All this, although effected through the wilful disobedience of the first man, took place, however, according to the counsel and the will of God. Accidents, from the viewpoint of God, never occur.... Therefore, God, immediately at the fall of man, maintains His covenant, in spite of Satan and sin, but that covenant now as eternally firmly established in

Christ. Through the realization of that Covenant immediately at the fall the friendship with Satan in the heart of man is brought to nought, and through the operation of grace enmity is wrought in the heart of man against Satan. Here, however, we face the decree of predestination. For not all the children of Adam have been predestined to enter into the eternal covenant of God's friendship. Grace follows the line of election. Only the kernel is affected by grace, the shell or bolster is rejected. It is exactly through this that the antithesis is realized in the midst of the world. Fact is, also now the creatures in the natural sense continue to exist in organic connection. Also grace, even as sin, does not bring about an essential change in the temporal existence of things. Out of one blood God created the entire human race. From a mere natural viewpoint all men are one. And man ever continues to stand in organic connection with the cosmos, in the midst whereof he moves and develops. There is, therefore, no dualism. Nature and grace are no contrasts. And even now we may remark that grace can never become the cause for man, who becomes partaker of it, to go out of the world. To be sure, the antithesis of sin and grace is called into being by the breach of sin and the entrance of grace, the latter developing along the line of election. All things continue to exist and develop according to their own nature, sustained by God's almighty power, in natural affinity. But amidst this temporal existence of things there arises and develops the spiritual-ethical antithesis of sin and grace, of light and darkness, of the love of God and enmity against Him, of life and death, of heaven and hell. And through all this God does all His good pleasure and He leads all things to their eternal destiny, the eternal separation of chaff and wheat, the eternal realization of the Covenant of His friendship.

Grace is, therefore, never common.

It will now not be difficult for the brethren to understand that it was impossible for us to subscribe to the three points, or also to promise that we, privately or publicly, would never teach anything which would conflict with those points. Such a promise would forever silence our mouth and cause our pen to become dry. Although it is indeed our conviction that the synod of 1924 saw the trees of the three points, but not the words of common grace, yet it is beyond all doubt that it in those points really adopted the entire common grace view of Dr. Kuyper. Nevertheless we also desire to express our objections against those three points in particular.

The first points speaks of a favorable inclination in God towards all creatures. We have declared more than once that, if it were possible to take this expression by itself, we would have no objection against the implied proposition. We have always emphasized that God's grace is not directed individualistically to a few elect, but to all creatures in organic connection. This, however, is not the case here. This explanation may never be given of the first point. The contrast in the first point is not "elect only or all creatures," but "elect only or also reprobate." It is the teaching of the first point that there is in God a gracious attitude towards all men, among whom also the reprobates are included. Apart from the saving grace of God shown only to the elect, there is also a non-saving grace of God both as an inclination in God and as an operation proceeding upon the creature, in which also the reprobate share. That this is indeed the implication of the first point appears clearly from the discussion which preceded the adoption of this point at synod. This was the issue. This is plain from the texts which the synod quoted to substantiate the teaching of the first point. And this is especially clear from the proof which was quoted from the confession, relative to the preaching of the gospel. Moreover, this also appears from the discussion which later was carried on about the three points. But concerning this there is no difference among us. We cannot accept this gracious inclination of God and operation of grace towards the reprobate wicked. Over against this we maintain that the grace of God goes out to the organic whole of the creatures in mutual affinity, and in connection with the elect in Christ, as the elect kernel. And we declare that at the same time an operation of God's wrath and indignation proceeds upon the reprobate shell.

However, the first point expresses more. Fact is, the synod of Kalamazoo also included the preaching of the gospel in this gracious inclination in God and this operation of grace. Synod, in our modest opinion, did this *nolens volens*. Fact is, it sought proof for common grace in the Reformed Confessions, especially in the Canons. Now those confessions, in the nature of the case, do not speak of common grace in the Kuyperian sense of the word. The synod of Dordrecht busied itself with the question of salvation. A grace, which did not save, simply lay beyond the pale of its views and deliberations....

...And over against this we maintain that the preaching of the gospel is grace only for the elect, and at the same time a savor of death unto death for the reprobates. That the preaching of the gospel is general we understand very well. But we believe that the contents of the preaching is always particular, that is promises salvation only to those who believe, that is to the elect, and that it can never be said that it is an evidence of grace to all who hear the gospel. According to our earnest conviction the synod, with this declaration, passed into the camp of the Remonstrants.

The second point speaks of a general operation of the Holy Spirit, outside of regeneration, whereby sin is restrained in the individual man and in the community. If this means anything at all, it implies that, outside of regeneration, a spiritual-ethical operation of the Holy Spirit proceeds upon sinful man, for his good, with the result that he is not as sinful and corrupt in the reality of life as he would be without that working of the Spirit....

With respect to the third point we can now be brief, inasmuch as it stands or falls with the second. In this third point the synod declares that God, without renewing the heart, so influences man, that he, although incapable of performing any saving good, can perform civil good. It is evident, from the context of the expression, as well as in the light of the discussion which preceded this declaration, that with civil good the doing of good in civil life is meant. Here we meet the "doctrines of spheres" "terreinen-leer." In the "sphere" of the first table of the law man is unable to do any good. This after all is "spiritual" good. But in the "sphere" of the second table of the law he can perform good. And by the "influence" of God, mentioned in this third point, the same is meant, of course, as the "general operations of the Spirit" in the second point.

I would conclude by placing before you certain propositions for discussion:

1. God is God and He always performs all His good pleasure. Therefore He also always proceeds directly to His goal, according to His eternal counsel, while all things, also Satan and sin and the godless world included, serve Him thereunto. At no moment in history whatsoever, from creation to the parousia, can we speak of a frustration of an original plan.

2. God's grace is not directed individualistically particularistically to the elect, but it is directed to the organic whole of the Church in Christ as its Head and that in connection with the organic whole of all creatures of the entire cosmos. However, the godless reprobate is never object of this grace, viewed either as an inclination in God or as an operation of grace.

3. Besides the operation of God's drawing and saving and exalting, glorifying grace, proceeding only upon the elect kernel of the created things, there is also an operation of God's rejecting, repulsing wrath, proceeding upon the reprobate shell.

4. The covenant with Noah is no friendship-covenant of common grace established with the sinful world *qua talis* and outside of Christ, but a revelation of the one covenant of God's friendship in Christ, as it embraces and takes up into itself the entire cosmos....

9. Civil righteousness is an attempt of the sinful man whereby he, inasmuch as he perceives by his natural light the God-instituted relations and laws in the cosmos, and recognizes their usefulness, for his own benefit will adapt his life in connection with the life of his fellow-creatures to those laws of God in an external sense. If he succeeds, God, Who

holds Himself to His own ordinances, grants him success. But success is not blessing. In the way of success he becomes ever greater, becomes ever more responsible, and under the wrath of God increases his own judgment.

10. There is in Holy Writ no essential distinction in meaning between such terms as grace, favor, love, friendship, goodness, mercy. They all concern the relation and operation of God's covenant of friendship towards the elect kernel.

11. The idea of a common grace begins in dogmen-historical sense not with Calvin, neither can it be traced to Augustine, but its beginning must be sought in the age of the Scholastics, particularly with Thomas Aquinas. It cannot be said that this doctrine is preeminently Calvinistic.

12. The Three Forms of Unity know of no common grace. The only place, where the term "common grace" appears, places it upon the lips of the Remonstrants. The "Three Points" are not explanations but additions to the confession of the Reformed Churches.

13. The synod of Kalamazoo, in its "Three Points" has essentially exalted Kuyper's "Gemeene Gratie," Common Grace, to a dogma, and thereby rendered all further study of this question impossible....

14. The Christian does not separate himself in Anabaptistic sense from the world; neither is it his calling to better the "world," but to live, throughout his life in the world, from the principle of regeneration and according to the Word of God, and represent the cause of the Son of God as of the Party of the living God....

RFPA Publications

Behold He Cometh! Herman Hoeksema
Believers and Their Seed Herman Hoeksema
Calvin's Calvinism John Calvin
Come, Ye Children Gertrude Hoeksema
The Doctrine of Scripture Homer C. Hoeksema
Far Above Rubies Ed. Herman Hanko
The Five Points of Calvinism Herman Hanko, Homer C. Hoeksema, Gise VanBaren
God's Covenant Faithfulness Ed. Gertrude Hoeksema (out of print)
God's Eternal Good Pleasure Herman Hoeksema
God's Everlasting Covenant of Grace Herman Hanko
Hyper-Calvinism and the Call of the Gospel David Engelsma (out of print)
In the Beginning God... Homer C. Hoeksema (out of print)
In the Sanctuary Herman Hoeksema
Lori Gertrude Hoeksema
Marriage David Engelsma
The Mysteries of the Kingdom Herman Hanko
The Mystery of Bethlehem Herman Hoeksema
Peaceable Fruit Gertrude Hoeksema
Reformed Dogmatics Herman Hoeksema
Show Me Thy Ways 6 volumes Gertrude Hoeksema*
Studies in Philippians Carl Haak
Suffer Little Children 5 volumes Gertrude Hoeksema*
Therefore Have I Spoken Gertrude Hoeksema
The Triple Knowledge 3 volumes Herman Hoeksema
The Voice of Our Fathers Homer C. Hoeksema
We and Our Children Herman Hanko
When I Survey Herman Hoeksema
"Whosoever Will" Herman Hoeksema
The Wonder of Grace Herman Hoeksema

*Bible curriculum for the Christian school

The Original Titles of the Ten Volumes of
The Triple Knowledge
by Herman Hoeksema

1. *In the Midst of Death*
2. *God's Way Out*
3. *The Death of the Son of God*
4. *The Lord of Glory*
5. *Abundant Mercy*
6. *Baptized Into Christ*
7. *Eating and Drinking Christ*
8. *Love the Lord Thy God*
9. *Love Thy Neighbor for God's Sake*
10. *The Perfect Prayer*

The
STANDARD
BEARER

Volume L, Number 1, October 1, 1973

Cover of
October, 1974, *Standard Bearer*

After Fifty Years
Prof. H.C. Hoeksema

(The text of an address delivered at Calvin Seminary,
December 19, 1974)

Members of the Faculty, Students, and Guests:
First of all, I express my sincere thanks for the invitation
to lecture to you today. I am thankful, too, for the subject
which was suggested to me by Dr. Stob, "After Fifty Years."
I believe it represents something of a milestone in itself that
a Protestant Reformed minister is afforded an opportunity to
speak on this subject at a Christian Reformed Seminary.
Needless to say, I am quite willing and happy to speak to you
on this subject.

That subject is and will be much in the hearts and minds
of us who are Protestant Reformed. In the year 1975 we hope
to celebrate the fiftieth anniversary of our denomination,
which was provisionally organized on March 6, 1925. The
reaching of such a milestone for our denomination, for which
at one time many predicted an early death, gives reason to
pause and to reflect on our origin and our history and to
evaluate our present position in the ecclesiastical world at
large, and especially in the Reformed community. And I
believe that since our denomination had its painful birth
from yours, it should also give reason for reflection and
evaluation on your part. It is my sincere hope that this lecture
will contribute to the achievement of that end.

Although I represent the second generation of the Protestant Reformed Churches and their ministry, I may nevertheless say that I stand before you as a son of the Christian
Reformed Church. This is literally true: for I was born and
baptized a member of the Eastern Avenue Christian Reformed Church one year before the crisis of 1924. I believe,

too, that I am a true son of the Christian Reformed Church — not, of course, as the Christian Reformed Church is today. In that regard I am a son of the Protestant Reformed Churches. But I believe that I am a true son of the Christian Reformed Church according to its true genius prior to 1924. This makes the occasion and the material of my lecture all the more momentous to me — and, I hope, to you.

Finally, by way of introduction, I must point out that my lecture this morning must needs be in the nature of a summary. If I were to review the history in detail, to analyze the doctrinal issues and implications in detail, and to document and prove from Scripture and the Confessions all that I say in summary form this morning, you would have to afford me the opportunity for several lectures of this length. And so I ask you to bear this in mind; and I believe that this was the intention of the invitation that was extended to me. Parenthetically, let me say that if you have questions, I suggest that you write them down. Then, if time does not permit me to answer them here this morning, I offer to answer them in writing in the *Standard Bearer*, in which a transcript of my lecture will also appear.

As I speak to you on the subject, "After Fifty Years," I will arrange my material under the following three questions:

I.   What Happened Fifty Years Ago?
II. What Took Place During the Intervening Fifty Years?
III. What Is the Situation Today?

I.   What Took Place Fifth Years Ago?

Fifty years ago the Protestant Reformed Churches had their origin in the events connected with the common grace controversy, and specifically in the events connected with the adoption of the Three Points of Common Grace by the synod of the Christian Reformed Church of 1924. At that time three pastors, the Rev. Henry Danhof (of Kalamazoo I), the Rev. George M. Ophoff (of Hope, Riverbend — now Walker, Michigan), and the Rev. Herman Hoeksema (of the Eastern Avenue Christian Reformed Church of Grand Rapids) along with their consistories, were deposed from office, following the Synod of 1924, by Classis Grand Rapids East and Classis Grand Rapids West of the Christian Reformed Churches. These consistories and their pastors, along with the greater portions of their respective congregations, felt both for reasons of doctrine and reasons of church government and ecclesiastical justice that they might not recognize this deposition, but considered themselves called of God to continue in the duties and functions of their offices, and therefore, were compelled to organize a self-contained church organization. Pending the disposition of their appeal by the synod of 1926, this organization was at first provisional; and they called themselves Protesting Christian Reformed Churches. After the final disposition of the case in 1926, they organized permanently under the name Protestant Reformed Churches in America. I call attention to this for three reasons. In the first place, because it is a matter of fact that the two Classes mentioned proceeded to do what the Synod of 1924 specifically refused to do, namely, to demand subscription to the Three Points and to discipline the ministers involved, and that, too, in the name of the Formula of Subscription. Besides, it must be kept in mind that the synod had declared Revs. Danhof and Hoeksema to be Reformed in the fundamentals. I mention it, in the second place, because it was in 1924 that the Christian Reformed Churches turned to the hierarchical, or collegialistic view of church government, according to which Classis and Synod are higher (rather than broader) assemblies, and according to which they can assume the power to discipline — something which resides only in the local consistory and the local offices. And I mention it, in the third place, because I must point out that it is a matter of fact that we did not secede, did not leave, did not separate. But we were expelled. Our mother church denied us a place, declared officially that there was no room for us in the denomination, and thus made it necessary for the Protestant Reformed Churches to come into existence. Moreover, these actions received the synodical stamp of approval in 1926 at the Synod of Englewood.

It is a matter of historical fact, therefore, that we are the continuation of the churches which we were before 1924. We are not fundamentally something new. We are not a departure. We are a continuation: in the true sense of the word, a continuing church. And we stand in the line of the church historically.

The second, and by far the most important answer to my first question is: the Three Points of Common Grace were adopted by the Synod of 1924. It is this, from a doctrinal point of view, which led to the origin of the Protestant Reformed Churches. And let me add that although there are related matters which are important, it is this *doctrinal* matter which is by far the most important. If you ask what was the origin of the Protestant Reformed Churches as far as principles were concerned, then the negative answer to that question is: the raising to the status of official church doctrine of the Three Points of Common Grace in 1924.

I cannot take the time this morning to enter into the history of the common grace controversy. Suffice it to say that the Three Points did not drop out of the sky in 1924, but that their adoption was the climax — in some respects, the premature climax — of several years of ferment and debate. And if "common grace" had been left a matter of theological opinion and a subject for free discussion, there would have been no 1924. But that was not to be.

Permit me briefly to summarize the doctrinal issues involved in the Three Points. In this connection, let me emphasize, however, that we do not live as churches by denials. This was and is sometimes alleged. But no church can exist by mere denials. And we certainly do not so exist. Moreover, the very fact that we have been in existence for fifty years should give the lie to that suggestion. And therefore, as I summarize, I will also set forth our positive position.

The First Point speaks of a favorable attitude of God towards all creatures, and not only to the elect. It is the teaching of the First Point that there is in God a gracious attitude toward all men, among whom also the reprobate ungodly are included. Apart from the saving grace of God shown only to the elect, there is also allegedly a non-saving grace of God in which also the reprobate share. This non-saving grace of God is supposedly manifest in the good gifts which God bestows also upon the wicked, such as rain and sunshine, food and gladness, gifts and talents, name and position and might, houses and goods. Over against this idea, we maintain that God's grace is always particular, directed to His elect people alone. Indeed, we do not deny that God bestows good gifts upon men, including the reprobate. But we cannot accept the idea that there is a gracious attitude of God and an operation of grace toward the reprobate wicked. We maintain that the grace of God goes out to the whole creation, the organic whole of His creatures, with His elect in Christ at the center. And we hold that at the same time there is an operation of God's hatred and wrath proceeding toward the reprobate ungodly in and through all things which He bestows on them. "The curse of Jehovah is in the house of the wicked, but he blesseth the habitation of the just" (Prof. 3:33).

But we hold that there is another serious departure from the Reformed truth involved in the First Point. For the preaching was included in this alleged gracious attitude of God and this operation of God's grace toward men in common. The First Point teaches that God is gracious in the preaching of the gospel not only toward the elect, but toward all men, toward all to whom the gospel is proclaimed. This is the error of the general, well-meant offer of grace and salvation to all men — essentially, the error of Arminianism. And that this is, indeed, one of the errors of the First Point is literally plain from a decision of a later Christian Reformed Synod, that of 1926, which spoke of a "goodness or grace of God in causing to go forth a well-meaning offer of salvation to all to whom the preaching of the gospel comes," as well as of a "certain grace or goodness or favorable inclination of God" which "is revealed toward a group of men broader than the group of the elect, and that is, among other things, also evident from the fact that God well-meaningly calls each one to whom the lovely invitation of the Gospel comes." The

Protestant Reformed Churches believe that this presentation of the grace of God and of the preaching of the gospel is contrary to Scripture and the Reformed Confessions. Over against this error of the general, well-meant offer we maintain that the preaching of the gospel is grace only for the elect, and at the same time a savor of death unto death for the reprobate. We maintain, indeed — with our confessions — that the preaching of the gospel is general, or promiscuous, in that it is sent to all, both elect and reprobate, to whom God out of His good pleasure sends the gospel. But we believe — again, with our confessions — that the contents of the preaching is always particular. In the preaching salvation is promised (not offered) only to those who believe and repent, that is, to the elect. It can never be said that the preaching of the gospel is an evidence of grace to all who hear it, including the reprobate. Principally, the position of the well-meant offer of salvation is Arminian. And only too many Reformed churches and church members have, as a result of this view of the preaching been victimized by outright Arminianism and have become enthusiastic supporters of many a wild, God-dishonoring evangelistic movement. We consider it our calling to warn unequivocally against the rampant Arminianism of the day, and to call God's people back to the Reformed truth of the gospel of Christ crucified, Who is "to them which are called, both Jews and Greeks, the power of God and the wisdom of God" (I Cor. 1:24).

The Second Point of Common Grace teaches a restraint of sin. It speaks of a general operation of the Holy Spirit — not saving, and therefore apart from regeneration — whereby sin is restrained in the individual man and in the community. It implies that there is a spiritual, ethical operation of the Holy Spirit upon the natural man which, without renewing his heart, is for his good, with the result that he is not as sinful and corrupt in his actual life as he would be without this working of the Spirit. By this general operation of grace the natural man is improved, except for his heart; his mind and will and all his inclinations can be changed or inclined for good. Now we understand full well and believe, along with our Confession of Faith in Article 13, that God "so restrains the devil and all our enemies that without His will and permission they cannot hurt us." Actually the Confession here speaks of God's "bridling" of the devil and wicked men; that is, God controls and governs them. And He certainly does so unto the realization of His own counsel and the salvation of His own people in Christ. But we deny that there is any operation of grace toward the reprobate ungodly taught here or anywhere in our confessions. And we deny that there is an operation of grace by the Spirit, outside of regeneration, whereby the natural man is improved to any degree whatsoever.

We have many objections against this view. But our chief objection is that it constitutes a denial of the Reformed truth of the total depravity of man. It is Reformed according to our confessions to say that man is by nature so corrupt that he is incapable of doing any good, and inclined to all evil. But in the light of the second point, this totally depraved man is a mere abstraction: due to common grace, there is nowhere in this world a man who actually is totally depraved. As the natural man appears, he is not wholly corrupt, but greatly improved and capable of good. However, Scripture and our Confessions teach the very opposite. Scripture teaches us (Rom. 1:18ff.) that there is an operation of God's wrath revealed from heaven, whereby He so operates upon the wicked who forsakes His way that he is given over more and more to his own sinful lusts and desires, to do things that are unseemly, so that he proceeds from sin to more sin, goes from bad to worse. Hence, while we readily admit that the sinner is restrained and controlled by the all-controlling providence of God and according to His all-wise counsel, we maintain that the process of sin is bound to the development of the human race, so that every man does not commit every possible sin, but each man, according to his own place and time, character and talents, gifts and means, develops the one root-sin of Adam until the completed fruit of sin is wholly revealed and the sinfulness of sin is exposed to the full. This, and not the idea of any improvement of the natural man, is also a realistic view of natural man and of the world in the midst of which we, as the people of God, live today. The Third Point of Common Grace teaches that the natural man, by virtue of the influences of common grace, although incapable of performing any saving good, can perform what is called civil good. By this is meant the doing of good in civil life. In the sphere of the first table of the Law, man is unable to do any good. This, after all, is "spiritual" good. But in the sphere of the second table of the Law, the natural man can perform good. He is able to live a relatively good life in this world. We may point out in this connection that proof from the Confessions was sought for the Third Point in Canons III, IV, Art. 4, where we read: "There remain, however, in man since the fall, the glimmerings of natural light, whereby he retains some knowledge of God, of natural things, and of the differences between good and evil, and discovers some regard for virtue, good order in society, and for maintaining an orderly external deportment." This, however, is only the first part of Article 4. And if we read the rest of this article, we learn that our Canons here maintain the Reformed doctrine of man's total depravity: "But so far is this light of nature from being sufficient to bring him to a saving knowledge of God, and to true conversion, that he is incapable of using it aright even in things natural and civil. Nay, further, this light, such as it is, man in various ways renders wholly polluted, and holds it in unrighteousness, by doing which he becomes inexcusable before God." This quotation very succinctly expresses our Protestant Reformed position. In all his nature, the natural man is totally depraved; and in all his existence he always sins, and does so in every area of his life. Good works, according to our confessions, are those works which are in harmony with the Law of God, are performed to the glory of God, and proceed from a true faith. Good works, therefore, are performed only by the Christian. And the natural man, the man outside of Christ, being by nature totally depraved, always sins.

It will be readily seen, whether you agree with our Protestant Reformed position or not, that the matters touched on in the preceding go to the very heart of the Reformed position. They are not insignificant, but crucial. They are vital. And the differences of position which we have set forth above are fundamental. And let me add: they are issues which must needs affect not only the doctrinal stance of a church, but the very heartbeat of the church's life — the preaching — as well as the actual walk of God's people in the midst of the world. And I believe that fifty years of history will bear this out.

There are two more items which I deem important to mention in this connection.

The first goes back more than fifty years, namely, the so-called Janssen Case. I mention this because that case, which concerned, if you will, what is today referred to as the nature and extent of the authority of Scripture, was connected with 1924. Not only was there a historical relationship, but there was an intrinsic relationship. I believe that Dr. Janssen's erroneous position with respect to Scripture was rooted in the principle of common grace. And I believe that in the light of recent developments in your denomination as well as in The Netherlands, the importance of that intrinsic relationship between common grace and the errors of Dr. Janssen looms ever larger, even as the importance of the relation between a correct view of Scripture and the maintenance of sovereign, particular grace looms ever larger.

The second item which I must mention is that of the doctrine of the covenant. In a way, that also goes back more than fifty years. For the view which was for many years taught and maintained in your denomination with respect to the covenant of grace was that of Prof. W. Heyns. Without going into detail, let me point out that his view was principally that of a general, conditional promise and common covenantal grace to all the children of believers head for head. Principally, that is the First Point of 1924 applied to the doctrine of the covenant. I mention this, because it was that view which became the occasion for the development of our position with respect to the covenant of grace. And I mention this because I believe that here is an area of rich positive development in our Protestant Reformed theology, preaching, and world and life view. Again, I cannot go into detail. But let me briefly characterize that view as the organic conception of God's covenant, understood as the relation of friendship between God and His elect people in Christ, which is realized organically with believers and their seed, in the line of generations, and which embraces the entire cosmos.

That brings us to the second main question.

II. What Has Taken Place in the Intervening Fifty Years?

Our Protestant Reformed Churches are about to reach a milestone. Fifty years of history have been made by us — full and busy and eventful years. No one, you see, stands still. Individuals and also churches develop. And they develop in the fundamental direction which they have chosen. That is true for us of the Protestant Reformed Churches; it is also true for you of the Christian Reformed Church.

And let me insert one thing right here. We are not perfect, and have not claimed and do not claim perfection as a church. We have been characterized by many weaknesses, faults, sins, shortcomings — as is always the case with the church in the world. But of one fact we are convinced: we began on a fundamentally Reformed basis, and all our history and development has proceeded from that basis in a Reformed direction. We started out Reformed; we very definitely want to be recognizably Reformed; and we are Reformed today. I believe that no one can successfully deny that.

Let me very briefly recount something of our historical and ecclesiastical development.

1. From the outset we engaged in mission activity. That mission activity has been chiefly at home: we considered it our calling specifically to proclaim and to develop the Reformed truth in opposition to the evident departure in the direction of Arminianism and liberalism here in our home land. And we engaged and still engage in that home missions activity always in response to Macedonian calls to "come over and help us." We have also engaged in mission

activity beyond our national borders — notably, in Jamaica and in Indonesia.

2. We have a radio broadcast, the Reformed Witness Hour, which is almost as old as your Back To God Hour.

3. From the outset we have maintained our own theological school, something without which no communion of churches can successfully exist. From that school all our ministers have graduated. In our school we have provided training for the ministry in harmony with the stand of our churches. And in that training we use as much as possible our own instructional materials, in the form of textbooks and syllabi.

4. Over the years we have developed a distinct Protestant Reformed literature: our periodicals, our *Standard Bearer,* our *Beacon Lights* (for young people), our Sunday School *Guide,* our catechism books. But also many books of a theological and expository nature have been published and have emanated from the circle of our churches.

5. As a matter of our Reformed principles, we have developed as far as possible, and wherever possible, our own educational system — parental schools in which we strive to apply Reformed principles to education.

6. By 1940 we had also attained a full-orbed ecclesiastical organization, with consistories, two classes, and a synod; an organization under the Church Order of Dordrecht and in which we are averse to every form of ecclesiastical hierarchy.

And so we grew slowly numerically also; we have never enjoyed a rapid growth. This growth continued until at one point about 22 years ago we numbered 24 churches, had 28 active ministers, and numbered about 1,400 families from Ontario, Canada to the West Coast.

And then came a crisis in our denomination, a crisis precipitated in part by our contact with the so-called Liberated Churches of The Netherlands and with immigrants in Canada from those churches. I cannot take the time to recount that history this morning. I only want to point out, first of all, that fundamentally the issue was principally the same as in 1924; only this time it involved the matter of the covenant of grace. The issue was whether the promise of the covenant is a general, conditional promise for all who are baptized. In other words, the issue was whether, in the sphere of the covenant, grace is general or particular. The DeWolf group held the former. And that the issue *was* indeed the same as in 1924 is, I believe, confirmed by history: the DeWolf group could not and did not maintain a separate existence, but readily found their way back into your denomination, without any essential change being made on your part as to the Three Points. That is a fact of record.

The second aspect of that crisis which I would mention is the fact that numerically we were decimated, of course. But the Lord preserved us as a denomination. He also strengthened us through this struggle. And also outwardly we have revived. Today we are 20 congregations, from New Jersey to the West Coast. We number some 800 families. We are active in home missions. We have some 20 active ministers. We have a vibrant theological school. We have a press which receives world-wide attention. Our original leaders, Revs. Hoeksema and Ophoff, have gone to glory. Most of our corps of ministers is of the second and third generation, though there are still among us several of our veterans, active since our early years. And from all our pulpits are sounded the same clear notes of the pure and lively preaching of the Word, Reformed according to the confessions.

But there is another question concerning those fifty years. How have our two denominations stood in relation to one another during that period? Was there any contact? Were there any efforts to heal the breach? In answer to this question, I call your attention to the following facts:

1. Officially, there were two approaches made by our synods to the synod of the Christian Reformed Church. One was by our synod of 1940. The second was by our synods of 1957-1959. Both times we called attention to the wrongs of 1924, and we urged that steps be taken to remove what separated us as churches, and declared ourselves ready for full discussion of our differences. Both times our overtures for reconciliation were rejected.

2. Unofficially, in 1939 there was an abortive conference at the Pantlind Hotel between our ministers and several ministers of the Christian Reformed Church, Dr. K. Schilder of The Netherlands being present. Conspicuous by the absence were the Christian Reformed leaders who had played a leading part in 1924. The Rev. Herman Hoeksema came prepared with a position paper at that conference. Thereafter, however, there was no progress because of a refusal on the part of the Christian Reformed participants to engage in discussion. Nothing further developed.

3. At various times throughout these years our *Standard Bearer* has called for steps to be taken to remove whatever obstacles exist by way of thorough and open discussion. None of these calls has ever been heeded.

That brings me to my final question, which I must needs answer very briefly.

III. What Is Our Stance Today?

Where do we stand as Protestant Reformed Churches?

In the first place, it should be evident from the preceding that we have not changed fundamentally since 1924. We have developed. Our theology has been refined and enriched. We have matured. But we stand *fundamentally* where we stood 50 years ago, and our development has been in that line. We stand unabashedly and unequivocally on the basis of the infallible Word of God and our Reformed Confessions.

In the second place, I call your attention to the fact that our denomination is unique in this respect, that we are not internally troubled by any of the numerous heresies and other departures and innovations which are troubling churches throughout the world and throughout the Reformed community today. Why? Not because we live in isolation; that is impossible. Not because we pay no attention to these developments: for we follow them closely, in your denomination and in others, at home and abroad. We are theologically aware. But because the Lord preserves His church in the way of faithfulness, love of, and adherence to the truth of His Word. I say that not in pride, but in utmost humility. As churches we have nothing to boast of in ourselves; what we are, we are by the grace of God only.

But there is a second aspect to this question. That is this: where do we stand as Protestant Reformed Churches with respect to the Christian Reformed Church today?

To answer that question, I must briefly call attention to the fact that the Christian Reformed Church has also passed through fifty years of history since 1924. *Fundamentally*, you have not changed. Your stance with respect to the crucial issues involved in the Three Points is basically the same. But you have developed. And you have developed, I am convinced, in the fundamental line of 1924.

For the most part, I believe, that development has taken place in the past 20 years, roughly since the time when the generation of 1924 passed from the scene. They did not develop much along the common grace line. Partly, I believe, this was due to the fact that they were too traditionally Reformed to accept all the consequences involved in '24. But as James Daane put it, the winds of change began to blow through your denomination. And although there were other influences at work also, chiefly those winds of change blew from the direction of 1924. In some cases, the changes were directly related to the Three Points; in other instances, the relationship is less direct.

Permit me to mention a few items.

First of all, with respect to world-and-life-view, I mention:

1. Your tolerance of membership in worldly labor unions.

2. Your change of stance with regard to the Film Arts, the decision on which appealed directly to the Second Point of 1924.

3. The increasing marriage of Jerusalem and Athens in the area of education.

Secondly, with respect to doctrine, I mention:

1. The general atonement theory put forth by Prof. Dekker in the 1960s. This was directly related to the First Point of 1924 — so much so, that no one on either side could

discuss the matter without reference to 1924 and the well-meant offer.

2. In close connection therewith was also Dr. Stob's claim at that time that God hates no one.

3. There is the open denial of sovereign reprobation, and, in fact, of all "decretal theology" by Dr. James Daane in *The Freedom of God*.

4. There is the as yet uncondemned universalism put forth by Dr. J. Harold Ellens.

5. There are the various departures in the area of Scripture, including Report 36-44, the increasing incidence of some form of evolutionism, the denial of the literal and historical character of the events recorded in Genesis 1-3, etc. These we see as the ultimate development of 1924 in connection with the views put forth by Dr. Janssen prior to 1922.

There are more items which can be mentioned. I have not mentioned such things as Key '73 and Evangelism Thrust, nor the effort to relax the Formula of Subscription and the admitted signing of that Formula with mental reservations, nor the movement for liturgical revisionism.

Now admittedly you are seeing your denomination through the eyes of another. And I want you to know that I mention these things not with pride and boasting and joy, but with sadness and pain of heart. But I will defend the proposition that your present ills are all related — doctrinally, practically, church politically, and ethically — to 1924. I have stated this publicly many times.

And therefore, in conclusion, my answer to the question concerning our stance in relation to your denomination is: it is basically the same now as in 1924. We call you to return from those errors to the old paths of the Reformed faith and to stand where we stand. Only, today that call is more urgent than ever before. If you look back only about 20 years, you yourselves can observe that you no longer stand where you stood then as a denomination. You are fast losing your Reformed character. Return!

Thank you for your attention.

Congregations in the Denomination

In the Area of Classis East

1. Byron Center, MI
2. Chatham, Ontario, Canada (disbanded)
3. Covenant, Wyckoff, NJ
4. Creston, Grand Rapids, MI (disbanded)
5. Faith, Jenison, MI
6. First, Grand Rapids, MI
7. Fourth (now Southeast), Grand Rapids, MI
8. Hamilton, Ontario, Canada (disbanded)
9. Grand Haven, MI (disbanded)
10. Grandville, MI
11. Holland, MI
12. Hope, Walker, MI
13. Hudsonville, MI
14. Kalamazoo, MI
15. Norristown, PA
16. Oaklawn, IL (disbanded)
17. Randolph, WI
18. Roosevelt Park (now Southwest), Grandville, MI
19. South Holland, IL
20. Waupon, WI (disbanded)

In the Area of Classis West

21. Bellflower, CA (disbanded)
22. Bethel, Elk Grove Village, IL
23. Doon, IA
24. Edgerton, MN
25. First, Edmonton, Alberta, Canada
26. Forbes, ND (disbanded)
27. Hope, Isabel, SD
28. Hope, Redlands, CA
29. Hull, IA
30. Immanuel, Lacombe, Alberta, Canada
31. Los Angeles, CA (disbanded)

32. Loveland, CO
33. Lynden, WA
34. Manhattan, MT (disbanded)
35 Orange City, IA (disbanded)
36. Oskaloosa, IA (disbanded)
37. Peace, Lynwood, IL
38. Pella, IA
39. Rock Valley, IA (disbanded)
40. Sioux Center, IA (disbanded)
41. Trinity, Houston, TX

Pastors

who have served in the Protestant Reformed denomination

These names are divided into three groups, according to the approximate times these men have served.

Group 1

1. Andrew Cammenga
2. Henry Danhof
3. John DeJong
4. Cornelius Hanko
5. Herman Hoeksema
6. Bernard Kok
7. George Lubbers
8. George Ophoff
9. Richard Veldman
10. William Verhill
11. Leonard Vermeer
12. Gerrit Vos

Group 2

13. John Blankespoor
14. Sebastian Cammenga
15. Peter DeBoer
16. Hubert DeWolf
17. Lambert Doezema
18. Emanuel Emanuel
19. Martin Gritters
20. Robert Harbach
21. John Heys
22. Homer Hoeksema
23. Walter Hofman
24. James Howerzyl
25. Edward Knott
26. J.G. Kooistra
27. Henry Kuiper
28. James McCollam
29. Alvin Mulder
30. Andrew Petter
31. Marinus Schipper
32. Gerald VandenBerg
33. John VanderBreggen
34. James VanWeelden
35. Herman Veldman
36. Peter Vis

Group 3

37. Wayne Bekkering
38. Wilbur Bruinsma
39. Ronald Cammenga
40. Robert Decker
41. Arie denHartog
42. Michael DeVries
43. Russell Dykstra
44. David Engelsma
45. Richard Flikkema
46. Barrett Gritters
47. Carl Haak
48. Herman Hanko
49. Kenneth Hanko
50. Ronald Hanko
51. Mark Hoeksema
52. Steven Houck
53. Meindert Joostens
54. Marvin Kamps
55. Steven Key
56. Kenneth Koole
57. Jason Kortering
58. Dale Kuiper
59. George Lanting
60. Rodney Miersma
61. Thomas Miersma
62. Richard Moore
63. James Slopsema
64. Jon Smith
65. Charles Terpstra
66. Gise VanBaren
67. Ronald VanOverloop
68. Bernard Woudenberg

Byron Center PRC Michigan 1983*

Covenant PRC Wyckoff, New Jersey 1973

Faith PRC Jenison, Michigan 1973

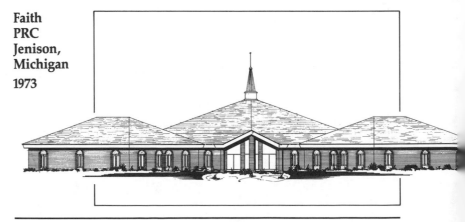

Classis East   *Signifies date of organization.

**First
PRC
Grand
Rapids,
Michigan
1879**

**First
PRC
Holland,
Michigan
1929**

**Grandville
PRC
Michigan
1984**

Hope
PRC
Walker,
Michigan
1916

Hudsonville
PRC
Michigan
1926

Kalamazoo
PRC
Michigan
1927

Classis East

Norristown
PRC
Pennsylvania
1989

Southeast
PRC
Grand
Rapids,
Michigan
1944

Southwest
PRC
Grandville,
Michigan
1927

Classis East

**Bethel
PRC
Elk Grove
Village,
Illinois
1989**

**Doon
PRC
Iowa
1926**

**Edgerton
PRC
Minnesota
1938**

Classis West

First
PRC
Edmonton,
Alberta,
Canada
1975

Hope
PRC
Isabel,
South
Dakota
1915

Hope
PRC
Redlands,
California
1932

Hull
PRC
Iowa
1925

Immanuel
PRC
Lacombe,
Alberta,
Canada
1987

Loveland
PRC
Colorado
1958

Classis West

**Lynden
PRC
Washington
1951**

**Peace
PRC
Lansing,
Illinois
1988**

**Pella
PRC
Iowa
1928**

Classis West

Randolph
PRC
Wisconsin

1943

South
Holland
PRC
Illinois

1926

Trinity
PRC
Houston,
Texas

1977

Classis West

Rev.
George M.
Ophoff

PR
Seminary
Grandville,
Michigan

Rev.
Herman
Hoeksema

**Covenant
ERC
Singapore**

Sister Churches

First ERC Singapore

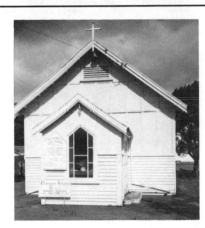

New Zealand

Sister Churches